What Is Veiling?

Islamic Civilization and Muslim Networks

CARL W. ERNST AND BRUCE B. LAWRENCE, EDITORS

*A complete list of titles published in this series
appears at the end of the book.*

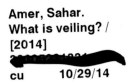
WHAT IS
Veiling?

Sahar Amer

The University of North Carolina Press CHAPEL HILL

Publication of this work was assisted by a generous gift from
Florence and James Peacock.

Designed by Kimberly Bryant
Set in Charis and Myriad types by Tseng Information Systems, Inc.
Manufactured in the United States of America
The paper in this book meets the guidelines for permanence and durability of the
Committee on Production Guidelines for Book Longevity of the Council on Library
Resources. The University of North Carolina Press has been a member of the
Green Press Initiative since 2003.

Library of Congress Cataloging-in-Publication Data
Amer, Sahar.
What is veiling? / Sahar Amer.
pages cm. — (Islamic civilization and Muslim networks)
Includes bibliographical references and index.
ISBN 978-1-4696-1775-6 (cloth : alk. paper) — ISBN 978-1-4696-1776-3 (ebook)
1. Hijab (Islamic clothing) 2. Veils—Religious aspects—Islam.
3. Muslim women—Clothing. I. Title.
BP190.5.H44A535 2014
297.5′76—dc23
2014007168

Mohja Kahf's "Hijab Scene No. 2" and "Hijab Scene No. 7," from her book *E-mails from
Scheherazad*, are reprinted with permission of the University Press of Florida.

18 17 16 15 14   5 4 3 2 1

For Ruth Mitchell Pitts,
who first encouraged me to research this book,
and who did not live to see it completed.

For my dad (1928–2014), whose progressive forward thinking
allowed me to write in the first place.

Contents

Illustrations

Acknowledgments

I could not have completed this book without the unfailing support of family, friends, and colleagues, and I wish to express my most sincere gratitude to them. I am mentioning only some people here; others are not named for reasons of privacy, even though their support and help has been equally instrumental to my writing over the last two years. They will no doubt recognize themselves in some of the stories recounted in the following pages. To them also goes my deepest appreciation.

First of all, I would like to thank the two anonymous reviewers of the University of North Carolina Press whose close reading and countless suggestions have helped me strengthen, clarify, and deepen some of the points I was making in earlier chapter drafts. I also thank my wonderful editor, Elaine Maisner, whose vision, unswerving encouragement, cheerfulness, and invigorating conversations over lunches and coffees helped me stay the course and keep to the schedule of publication. Her assistant editors, Caitlin Bell-Butterfield and Alison Shay, have both been models of organization, patience, and punctuality. My project manager, Paul Betz, and copyeditor, Petra Dreiser, have helped with all details, big and small, of editing and production.

At the University of North Carolina at Chapel Hill, I would like to gratefully acknowledge the support of the College of Arts and Science, the Heloise Catherine Merrill Faculty Excellence Fund, the Center for European Studies, the Carolina Center for the Study of the Middle East and Muslim Civilizations, and the Department of Global Studies for research leaves, funds, and assistantships that supported the completion of this book. My research assistant, Jessica Tobin, has been a true gem in helping me organize and obtain illustrations and copyright permissions. Her IT skills, persistence, and laughter have facilitated immensely the entire process.

I would like to thank the many colleagues across the country and abroad who have invited me to speak about veiling practices on their campuses or at conferences, as well as the engaged audiences I had at each one of these events. I also thank my students, especially those who enrolled in my "Muslim Women and Veiling" class at the University of

North Carolina at Chapel Hill, and the K–12 teachers I worked with at numerous outreach events. Their interest in my work, the questions they asked, and their genuine desire to learn about Islam and Muslim women have always been motivating and a veritable source of inspiration.

My family, friends, and colleagues have all sustained and nourished me intellectually, mentally, and physically throughout the process. My late father, Mohamed Amer; my mother, Hoda Mostafa; my sisters, Noha, Ghada, and Nadia; and my nephews and nieces, Magued, Walid, Inès, and Norah, have always been my most solid cheerleaders throughout my academic career. They have sent me countless articles, images, cartoons, jokes, and stories to ensure I had seen all sorts of possible resources related to veiling. My father, until his last breath, and my sister Noha, like my good friend Muriel Davis, tirelessly read and commented on multiple versions of earlier chapters. My friends and colleagues (listed here in alphabetical order) encouraged me through all the ups and downs of my research and writing: Carolyn Allmendinger, Isabella Archer, Rose Aslan, Liz Bucar, Karen Carroll, Chris Currie, Eglal Doss-Quinby, Todd Drake, Nahed Eltantawy, Carl Ernst, Sandrine Gil, Banu Gökariksel, Colette and Michel Guggenheim, Regina Higgins, Carla Jones, Kenny Levine, Christilla Marteau d'Autry, Tariq, Laura, and Nadia Nasir, Oana Panaite, Lisa Pollard, Cara Robertson, Sarah Shields, Nour Soufi, Candy Walter, and Ali Yedes.

Last, but not least, my dearest friend, Martine, has helped me stay sane when things have become chaotic, has cheered me on when the writing has been slow, and has read and reread every chapter in its new execution. I could not have begun or finished this book without her ceaseless support and endless affection.

What Is Veiling?

Muslim Women—we just can't seem to catch a break. We're oppressed, submissive, and forced into arranged marriages by big-bearded men.

Oh, and let's not forget—we're also all hiding explosives under our clothes.

The truth is—like most women—we're independent and opinionated. And the only things hiding under our clothes are hearts yearning for love.

Everyone seems to have an opinion about Muslim women, even those—*especially* those—who have never met one.

—Ayesha Mattu and Nura Maznavi, introduction to *Love Inshallah: The Secret Love Lives of American Muslim Women*

INTRODUCTION

What *Is* Veiling?

Islam did not invent veiling, nor is veiling a practice specific to Muslims. Rather, veiling is a tradition that has existed for thousands of years, both in and far beyond the Middle East, and well before Islam came into being in the early seventh century. Throughout history and around the world, veiling has been a custom associated with "women, men, and sacred places, and objects."[1]

Few Muslims and non-Muslims realize that Islam took on veiling practices already in place at the dawn of the seventh century around the Mediterranean Basin. Islam inherited them from the major empires and societies of the time along with many other customs and patriarchal traditions related to the status of women. To understand the meaning of veiling in Islam today, one must recognize the important yet neglected history of veiling practices in the pre-Islamic period and appreciate the continuities and similarities among cultures and religious traditions.

Given that veiling has been practiced during the past two millennia by Christian, Jewish, and Muslim women, why does the veil continue to be associated primarily with Muslims, and how did it become one of the most visible signs of Islam as a religion? Why is it that when Mus-

1

lim women wear a veil, many non-Muslims and some secular Muslims tend to assume that someone coerced these women to dress in that way? Why do many people believe that veiled Muslim women are oppressed, ignorant, extremely pious, or politically militant? Why not view Muslim women in neutral terms, as women who choose or just happen to wear a headscarf? How did this piece of clothing become so emotionally and politically charged for both Muslims and non-Muslims?

My goal in *What Is Veiling?* is to offer an overview and an appreciation of the complex history and meanings of Muslim veiling. Addressing the questions posed above from the multiple perspectives necessary for understanding veiling will lead us to see that the practice has never had a singular meaning for all Muslims.

Throughout this book, I also aim to give voice to veiled Muslim women and to illuminate the variety of Muslim veiling practices in both Muslim-majority and Muslim-minority societies. I examine the main reasons why so many Muslim women choose to veil today and why others, in a handful of nations and only recently, have been forced to adopt a particular style of dress. Above all, my goal in *What Is Veiling?* is to show that, even though veiling is one of the most visible signs of Islam, it is also its most debated and least understood practice.

VEILING AND ISLAM

"Veiling" today is not simply a descriptive or neutral term. It is also a judgmental term, especially when associated with Islam. Muslim veiling is a notion that often evokes fear, anxiety, and a rising sense of threat, particularly in the aftermath of 9/11, the onset of the war in Afghanistan, and the 2003 U.S. invasion of Iraq. Veiling is a practice that foments heated debates among ordinary citizens and policy makers in North America and in Europe, as well as in many Muslim-majority societies around the world. It has become a surprisingly powerful symbol.

The veil may symbolize any number of perceived threats. For some, the veil represents the rise of fundamentalist Islam worldwide, a constant reminder of the Iranian Revolution, and the plight of women in Afghanistan. For others, it demonstrates Muslim women's subordination to Muslim men and the impossibility of assimilating Muslim immigrants into Euro-American secular societies. Others still view the veil as a threat to national security, a potential cover-up for suicide bombers, and a troublesome reminder that the world is not safe at the turn of the new millennium. The veil's appearance in most public spaces has been taken as proof that Islam is quintessentially opposed to women's rights. The veil has even come to stand in for the ultimate otherness and inferiority of Islam.

Considering the intensity of the emotions that arise in discussions of veiling, however, the obsession with Muslim women's veiling practices is a relatively recent phenomenon. Only since the nineteenth century has it been an integral part of Euro-American discourses on Islam and the Middle East.

VEILING SINCE THE NINETEENTH CENTURY

Euro-American fascination with the Muslim veil coincided with European military incursions into Muslim-majority societies and with colonial expansions. It was then that the veil first became viewed as a symbol of Muslim women's alleged subordination to Muslim men and as a justification, at least in part, for the Western civilizing mission.[2]

Yet while today many perceive the Muslim veil as a sign of possible militancy and religious extremism, in the nineteenth-century it carried an exotic, erotic connotation.[3] In colonial literature, arts, music, and films of the period, veiled Muslim women were consistently depicted as available, eager, and acquiescent sexual partners in Western sexual fantasies. They were imagined to be locked up in harems, where they eagerly awaited their rescue from brown men by white men. Rather than protect women's modesty, the veil in effect heightened white men's sexual desire, and thus became more of an erotic accessory than a piece of material culture with a history of its own (see chapter 4).

Liberating veiled Muslim women became a leitmotif of nineteenth-century European discussions about Muslim societies, and a key component of what has come to be known as the White Man's Burden. Some of the same ideas were perpetuated in paintings. Art museums around the world, large and small, boast collections of what has been dubbed "orientalist art," that is, nineteenth-century paintings depicting the way Europeans and Americans imagined Middle Eastern Muslim women. The Louvre in Paris, the Metropolitan Museum of Art in New York City, the more specialized Dahesh Museum of Art in Greenwich, Connecticut, and many university art museums hold important orientalist art collections. In most of these works, Muslim women are seen lounging in luxurious harems, wearing titillating clothes (by nineteenth-century

Victorian standards), and looking invitingly toward the viewer. These Muslim women were understood as sexually available, having purposefully cast their veils beside them. They were ready to fulfill men's sexual fantasies while also awaiting their rescue by these same European and American men.

During the twentieth century, the Hollywood film industry played a crucial role in perpetuating the image of the harem beauty saved by a Western hero in the image of Rudolph Valentino and in films such as *The Sheik* (1921) or *The Thief of Bagdad* (1924). In these movies, women seem to exist only as part of a harem and are consistently portrayed wearing transparent clothes and veils. They also always appear prepared for a sexual encounter or their rescue.

The desire to "save" Muslim women, veiled ones in particular, remains a recurring motif in many of today's popular and political debates both in the United States and in Europe. Contemporary Muslim women continue to be viewed as subservient objects to male authority and subject to manipulation by fathers, brothers, and fundamentalist regimes. In this view, contemporary veiled Muslim women too await their liberation by Western forces, who are known today as the spreaders of democracy. Laura Bush famously called for the "liberation" of Afghan women as part of the Bush administration's justification of the American war in Afghanistan.

An obsession with the Muslim veil is not just a Euro-American phenomenon. Muslims themselves, especially in Muslim-majority societies, have also focused on the significance and symbolism of veiled women. At least since the nineteenth century, the sight of unveiled European women had impressed both male and female upper-class Muslims, who were fascinated by European women's status in society, in particular by their good education and by their less pronounced segregation from men. Such elite Muslims came to view the veil as the key symbol of Muslim women's oppression and as the principal stumbling block to their quest for modernity. They thus adopted European views of the veil as they sought to modernize and reform their own societies. By the early twentieth century, unveiling Muslim women and uncovering their heads became the single clearest indicator of modernity in Muslim-majority societies and one of the earliest mandates of Arab feminists (see chapter 7).

In the nineteenth century, and in some secular and liberal circles still today, the Muslim veil is inextricably associated with discussions of development, reform, and progress, and women's garb is the key measure by which to judge a society's modernity. In the first quarter of the twentieth century, modernizing a Muslim-majority society became equivalent to unveiling its women; keeping women veiled was the quintessential sign of a society's backwardness and oppressive mores.

Because the very notions and measures of modernity and progress had been first introduced by European colonialists, some Muslims have viewed them with suspicion at times. These Muslims condemned early Arab and Middle Eastern feminists and secularists who had readily assimilated to Western ideas of civilizational worth and progress and called for the unveiling of Muslim women. So while for some Muslims, unveiling Muslim women meant liberation and progress, for others, it meant the exact opposite—the loss of cultural identity and surrender to Western domination. For the latter group, fighting against colonial and neocolonial impositions meant holding onto the veil as a symbol of cultural authenticity, pride, and political resistance.

Of course, veiling is not solely a reaction to Euro-American views. It is also a sign of piety, of obedience to God's mandates, and at times of adherence to a political form of Islam. The new Islamic revival movements that have characterized Middle Eastern societies since the 1980s are also partly responsible for the increase in veiling practices we see today.[4]

The more research I do on veiling, the more I realize that veiling is not and has never been a neutral phenomenon. It has never been simply a personal, religious, or cultural practice. Veiling has always had a multiplicity of competing meanings and motivations at different times and in different places. To fully understand Muslim veiling practices, it is important to take a step back and learn about the larger history of veiling in the world before the establishment of Islam.

VEILING BEFORE ISLAM (1200 BCE TO 610 CE)

Scholars have dated the first reference to veiling to a thirteenth-century BCE Assyrian legal text. The Assyrians were one of the earliest urban civilizations in Mesopotamia—the region roughly corresponding to today's Iraq, Iran, Syria, and Southeastern Turkey—that traced their ancestry back to the Sumerians and Akkadians. In Assyrian society, veiling (and female segregation) were well-established practices codified in law.

Clause 40 of the Assyrian laws linked women's social status and

Brief Historical Timeline

Ancient Mesopotamia	3000 BCE
Canaanites	late Bronze Age, 1500–1200 BCE
Assyrian Empire	1200 BCE
Persian-Achaemenid dynasty	ca. 500–350 BCE
Ancient Greece	500–323 BCE
Roman Empire	30 BCE–393 CE
Persian-Sassanid dynasty	224 BCE–651 CE
Byzantine Empire	306–1453 CE
Prophet Muhammad	570–632 CE
First Qur'anic Revelations	610 CE

sexual availability to their dress, and it set specific penal regulations for infractions. Married women and concubines accompanying their mistresses were required to veil their heads when going out in public. On the other hand, slaves and prostitutes (except married hierodules, former sacred prostitutes) were prohibited from veiling and could incur punishment if they did.[5]

Clause 41 in the Assyrian laws also addressed the question of veiling. If a man wanted to marry his concubine, he needed to summon five or six witnesses, veil her in front of them, and say "she is my wife." Veiling in this case meant to become legally married.[6]

Heir to the Assyrians, the Persian Empire—from the Achaemenid through the Sassanid dynasties—upheld the social meaning of the veil. As during Assyrian rule, veiling under the Sassanids distinguished upper-class women. A veiled woman signaled an aristocratic lady who did not need to go out to work, unlike peasant women or slaves.

In addition to requiring the veiling of aristocratic women, the Iranian Sassanids introduced further restrictions on women, which led to a general decline in their social position. Under the Sassanids, women could no longer serve as witnesses; they could engage only in limited legal transactions, and their numbers rose significantly in harems. The harem of Khusrau, the Sassanid king who ruled on the eve of the Muslim conquest (640 CE), is estimated to have included some twelve thousand women. The Iranian King's harem thus was three hundred times the size of an Assyrian harem in the twelfth century BCE, which numbered approximately forty women. While some may contest the authenticity of these numbers, they still give us a sense of greater control over women throughout history.

Similarly, in all ancient Mesopotamian Mediterranean cultures around 3000 BCE—among them the Canaanites, ancient Greeks, and Romans—upper-class women were secluded, wore a shawl that could be drawn over their heads as a hood, and covered their hair in public. Veiling distinguished aristocratic women from prostitutes, slaves, and women of ill repute more generally. This is likely why on ancient statuettes, vases, and other vessels, we often see upper-class women wearing ornate head covers.

The political and cultural dominance of Greece and then Rome in the Mediterranean meant that the entire region inherited the Hellenic traditions of veiling and androcentric hierarchies. Eventually, these patriarchal mores and sartorial practices were assimilated by peoples converting to Judaism, Christianity, and later to Islam.

Early Jewish societies placed a variety of restrictions on women, and Judaism, as it spread, perpetuated those restrictions. Jewish laws limited women's access to divorce, their right to inherit property, and permitted polygamy. Jewish women were also required to dress modestly, covering their bodies from the neck to the knee, exposing only the face and hands.[7] Married Jewish women were expected to cover their hair, considered a sign of beauty and a private asset that could not be shown in public.

The tradition of modest dress and of covering the hair continues to be practiced by conservative, and especially Hasidic, Jewish women. The ultraorthodox (from Hungary, Ukraine, and Galicia) shave their heads, and wear wigs with or without a scarf (called a *tikhl* in Hebrew). Haredi women in Israel today cover their heads and bodies with veils, sometimes referred to as *burqa*.[8] In fact, it is impossible to tell from pictures alone a Haredi Jewish woman from a Muslim woman wearing a black *burqa*.

Church Fathers went further in their restrictive attitudes toward women. Like the Jews, early Christians, both in the eastern and western Roman Empire, considered a woman's hair an intrusion of materiality into the holy space of the church and hence banned its appearance in churches.[9] Saint Paul's first letter to the Corinthians advises women to

Funerary Relief (Noʻom, wife of Haira, son of Maliku): Roman woman from
Syria wearing a head cover c. 150 CE (Ackland Art Museum, University of North Carolina
at Chapel Hill, The William A. Whitaker Foundation Art Fund)

enter the church and pray with their head covered (1 Cor. 11:5) and prohibits them from shaving their hair or cutting it. If for whatever reason
a woman's hair cannot be covered, it should be kept long, so that it may
itself serve as a covering (1 Cor. 11:15).

Even today, particularly in conservative Catholic communities and
in some Protestant denominations around the world, women wear hats
when going to church; others keep their hair long to serve as a head

The Virgin of the Annunciation, c. 1450–1460
(Ackland Art Museum, University of North
Carolina at Chapel Hill, Ackland Fund)

cover. Moreover, most of the Catholic and Orthodox nuns throughout
the Middle East wear the habit, though many nuns in the West dispensed
with the practice in the 1960s. We should also not forget that early sculp-
tures and paintings of the Virgin Mary regularly portray her with a veil
covering her head and body.

When Islam arrived on the scene in early seventh-century Arabia, it
came into a region with a long tradition of patriarchal authority, misogyny, and restrictions toward women in the public sphere. Islam developed in a world region in which Jewish and Christian women, like
those who belonged to some of the polytheistic religions of the Mediterranean, were veiled, secluded, and in which few played important
public roles.

As peoples from the various regions east and west of Arabia converted to Islam, and as new economic and political alliances were forged
among them, some Islamic mores became similar to those of Judaism

and Christianity. Rather than completely reject the traditions and practices of the societies that came under their rule, Muslims assimilated and adapted them. In this regard, veiling was not a radical Muslim innovation in the seventh century, but a legacy of Byzantine, Persian, Jewish, and Christian traditions.

This is not to say that Muslims adopted wholesale prevailing seventh-century attitudes toward women or that they did not challenge some of the period's misogyny. They did, and at times significantly.

For example, Islam banned female infanticide and gave women the right to inherit half of a man's share. Both were extraordinary propositions at the time. In addition, Islam sought to combat the well-established androcentrism of other religions by promulgating the spiritual equality of the sexes. Women are not inherently sinful in Islam, nor do they require an intermediary to relate to God. Muslim women and Muslim men are equal in terms of faith and in their relation to God.

Islam did not, however, bring about a radical change in women's sartorial practices. In terms of women's dress, Islam borrowed, adopted, and adapted existing social practices. In other words, Islam did not invent the veil and therefore cannot claim ownership of the tradition of the full-body and head covering. The Muslim veil is just one of the surviving legacies of earlier Hellenic and Abrahamic cultures.

WHAT IS A VEIL?

In English, the word "veil" refers to an item of clothing, made of cloth, that covers a woman's hair, and at times most of her face. The online *Merriam-Webster* English dictionary lists the first meaning of the term "veil" as "a length of cloth worn by women as a covering for the head and shoulders and often, especially in Eastern countries, for the face." While the dictionary definition goes on to mention specifically the nun's headdress and the bride's ornamental head cover as examples of veiling, do not most Euro-Americans typically think of veiling as an almost exclusively Islamic practice?

In reference to Islam, the veil takes on a particular connotation in the contemporary Euro-American popular imaginary. Veiling for non-Muslims in Europe and America is not often equated with the black or white liturgical or monastic headdress, or with the sheer bridal veil. Rather, it is fused with images of the black cloak (*chador*) covering Muslim women from head to toe in Iran—an image popularized in films such

Most Common Types of Muslim Dress and Veils

Burqa Face veil worn by some conservative Muslim women that usually covers the eyes. In Taliban-controlled areas of Afghanistan and Pakistan, *burqa* is the term used for a garment worn by women covering the entire body and having a crocheted section for the eyes.

Chador Iranian cloak, often black, that covers both the head and entire body and is held in place with one's hands.

Hijab Umbrella term for what is considered appropriate Muslim dress. It refers both to the body cover and to all types of hair covers.

Niqab Another term for the face veil that leaves the eyes uncovered.

Shalwar Qamis While this is strictly not a veil, this outfit is often worn in lieu of *hijab* among many South Asians. The term refers to the traditional outfit of South Asian men and women, regardless of religious affiliation. It consists of a knee-length tunic and pants. Women often accompany their attire with a long transparent matching scarf (*dupatta*).

See the glossary for an expanded list of Muslim veils.

as *Not without My Daughter* or *Persepolis*. The Muslim veil often also evokes the blue or white *burqa* that conceals the head, face, and body of Afghan women, an image that has circulated repeatedly on television and on the Internet, on the front pages of newspapers, and in magazines and books since the attacks of 9/11.

But there are many different kinds of Muslim veils. Walking down the streets of any metropolitan city in either a Muslim-majority or a Muslim-minority society, or wandering through the aisles of any large neighborhood mall, one commonly sees Muslim women wearing a variety of head covers and veiling styles. We see women clad in black from head to toe, sometimes including a face veil, who are working, shopping, or enjoying an afternoon with family and friends. We also see women dressed in Westernized clothing who would not look any different from non-Muslim women if it were not for a carefully wrapped and color-matched scarf concealing the hair more or less fully. We of course also often see non-veiled Muslim women whom we tend to overlook because they look exactly like non-Muslims.

The only kind of Muslim attire that one almost never sees in Euro-American societies, or even in most Muslim-majority countries, is the full-body *burqa* with crocheted eyeholes—the type of veil worn by Afghan women living under the Taliban. All other styles of Muslim attires and veils have today become an increasingly common part of life in our interconnected, global world.

Despite the variety of veiling styles, popular Western discourse barely differentiates among them. In conversation, all head coverings are generally referred to by a small number of terms, most commonly *chador* or *burqa*, especially when speaking about the oppression of women in Iran or Afghanistan, and the generic "veil" or *hijab* in all other contexts. We also hear representatives of broadcast and print media in Euro-American societies using the singular "veil" indiscriminately to encompass styles from the least covering (a simple scarf) to the most covering (full-body and head dress).

Use of the singular word (veil) instead of the plural (veils) fosters the false sense of a uniform dress code, of one unique way of thinking about and donning the veil. The truth, as we will see, is that Muslim veiling practices range widely, as do other types of dress and fashion customs. The English word "veil" is, therefore, best thought of as an umbrella term that refers to all kinds of Muslim women's veiling practices.

Precisely because of such variation in Muslim veiling practices, no one Arabic word exists for "veil." Nor is there a direct equivalent for "veil" in the non-Arabic languages spoken in Muslim-majority societies. While the Arabic word *hijab* (or in Indo-Persian languages, *purdah*) is not a direct translation of the English word "veil," it may be the closest equivalent.

Hijab, however, does not mean veil as in a piece of cloth, a scarf, or a specific kind of female attire. The term *hijab* comes from the Arabic root *h-j-b*, which means to screen, to separate, to hide from sight, to make invisible. It does not mean veiling as a female sartorial practice, and it certainly did not mean that in the early seventh century when Islam was established.

In fact, as we will see in chapter 1, the use of the word *hijab* in the Qur'an never refers to Muslim women's clothing, nor is it ever used in the holy book of Muslims to prescribe a particular dress code for women. Over time, however, among Muslims, the word *hijab* has come to refer to the principle of women's proper dress. Moreover, and unlike in English usage, the word *hijab* never refers to a face covering. Muslims commonly distinguish between *hijab* and *niqab* (face veil), and the distinction will be maintained throughout this book.

Just as the words for any given female item of clothing are numerous in the West, so are the names for *hijab*. The diversity of veiling practices among Muslims is indeed reflected in the multiplicity of terms in Arabic and in the various languages spoken in Muslim-majority societies used to describe the different styles of modest dress, the variety of head coverings, and the various types of face covering that some Muslim women wear. The glossary at the end of the book gives a sense of the tremendous linguistic variation of the vocabulary related to veiling.

Just as there are many different types of veils, there are many different types of *hijab*. As we will see in the following chapters, each type of *hijab* is the result of a complex interplay between factors such as religious interpretation, customs, fashion, race, ethnicity, geographic location, and the political system in place at a given time. Within each society, within each subgroup within that society, the term *hijab* refers to a different set of clothing.

I myself had never realized there were so many different types of *hijab* until I was an undergraduate at Bryn Mawr College in the early 1980s. Born in Egypt and having grown up in France, I had always thought that all Muslim women veiled in the same way. I thought that if they veiled, they would wear a *hijab* that looked like the one I had seen on my grandmothers and aunts (at that time, very few women wore *hijab* in Egypt or in France, except when praying): an opaque scarf covering every strand of hair, accompanied by clothing with long sleeves and hemlines.

That was my understanding until I met fellow Muslim students from South Asia, from India and Pakistan especially. I was shocked to see that, when praying, Indian and Pakistani students simply loosely pulled their *dupattas* (long scarves, often transparent) over their hair, letting their bangs hang on their foreheads, and they did not seek to cover up their arms protruding from the short-sleeved tunic of their *shalwar qamis*. "That is not *hijab*," I remember thinking. I was not sure what it was, but I knew it could not be *hijab*, not the *hijab* I was familiar with. First, the scarf was transparent; second, some hair was showing, and third, they wore short sleeves. *For me, that was definitely not* hijab!

After many lively conversations about whether my new friends were wearing *hijab* or not, and about what exactly *hijab* meant, I began to acknowledge that *hijab* was not one thing, but that it could take many different forms depending on more factors than I had ever considered.

I also began to recognize that *hijab* was not just a religious prescription but was also shaped by culture and geography and had no universal meaning. I realized then that it was essential to acknowledge the variety of veiling practices across the Muslim world. Part of my education, therefore, has been to learn to look more closely and openly at human cultures. Doing otherwise leads one to dangerously misleading conclusions about great varieties of peoples and to a biased approach to understanding our world.

My experience is not unique. The heterogeneity of Muslim veiling practices is a phenomenon that remains insufficiently acknowledged by Muslims and non-Muslims alike. Many Muslims living in, for example, North Africa, often know very little about veiling practices in other parts of the world, such as in China, or in the remote villages of Senegal or Mali. They often assume that all Muslims dress similarly and that concepts of female modesty are universal.

Similarly, many Muslims and non-Muslims are familiar with *a few* of the many veiling practices—those they see in the media, or those that their neighbors wear. Many assume that the more conservative types of veils in the darkest colors are the more "authentic" kinds, thereby blending and reducing the range of meanings that the veil has for Muslim women.

Many non-Muslims (and some Muslims) also assume that all Muslims are Arabs and that Arabs therefore have a more authentic understanding of Islam and follow more accurate practices of veiling. These assumptions are not borne out by the facts. Only one quarter of all Muslims in the world are Arabs. The majority of Muslims live in Indonesia and in South Asia. Muslim-majority countries span the world from northern Nigeria to Uzbekistan, from Great Britain to Indonesia, and from North America to China. There are Muslims on every continent except Antarctica.

It should be emphasized that Arabs are no better Muslims than other ethnic groups, and that their dress is no more authentic than that adopted by other Muslims. In reality, Muslim women veil differently depending on their particular situations, on whether they are at home, at work, in the neighborhood, or attending a party. Vast variation in Muslim dress truly is the norm.

What Is Veiling? explains variations in veiling practices among Muslims and demonstrates that Muslim veiling practice—or, in Arabic, *hijab*—has no fixed or predetermined meaning and certainly no singular

World Distribution of Muslim Population

This 'weighted' map of the world shows each country's relative size based on its Muslim population. Figures are rounded to the nearest million.

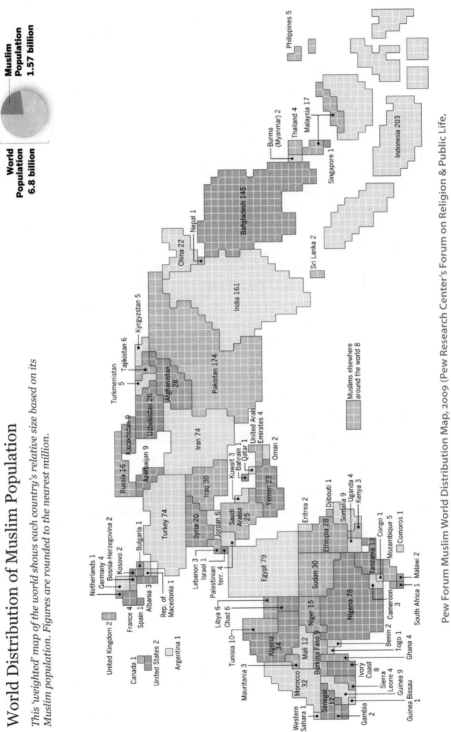

Pew Forum Muslim World Distribution Map, 2009 (Pew Research Center's Forum on Religion & Public Life, "Mapping the Global Muslim Population," © 2009, Pew Research Center, http://pewforum.org/)

patterns, colors, or characteristics. Veiling means and has always meant differently at different times for different people in different locations.

GOALS OF *WHAT IS VEILING?*

My primary goal in the following chapters is to give an overview of the multiplicity of meanings and the complex history of veiling practices in Muslim-majority and Muslim-minority societies, and to provide a richer and more balanced understanding of veiling practices among Muslims in the world today. Most studies of veiling focus on only one element of the topic, or are highly specialized. They do not provide the bird's eye view of veiling throughout history that *What Is Veiling?* offers.

I aim to show that the meaning of the veil extends well beyond the religious and political accounts often considered the totality of any discussion of veiling. While religion and politics certainly help explain why some Muslim women veil, they are insufficient by themselves to elucidate the ebb and flow of veiling practices over time, or the role that fashion, the economy, or individual circumstances play in determining whether a woman will veil or not. They also fail to account for the much more complicated meaning of veiling in Muslim-majority and Euro-American societies today. And they even deafen us to Muslim women's own voices of resistance and to their struggles both to combat stereotypes of the "veiled Muslim woman" and to resist the forces of political manipulation by conservative Islamist regimes in Muslim-majority societies.

To be an informed "reader of the Muslim veil," it is necessary to take into consideration the multiple facets of veiling—yes, the religious and political discourses, but also, and as important, the changing contexts of its appearance, its socioeconomic ramifications, and the multiple challenges brought by progressive religious scholars and artists to conservative readings of Islam and to women's proper attire. In the following chapters, I will explore veiling practices among Muslims around the world from this multiplicity of perspectives.

What Is Veiling? is organized around three main topics. First, it lays out the historical and geographical background of the institution of veiling and examines the core Islamic discourses that conservative Muslims believe dictate a dress code for Muslim women. A summary of the debates about the interpretation of these texts and attention to the numerous regional variations in veiling practices across Muslim-majority societies will give a sense of the tenuous relationship between the religious discourse of Islam and the contemporary Islamist political injunctions about veiling.

Second, *What Is Veiling?* reviews the contemporary debates about the veil in Euro-American societies, debates best understood, I believe, when contextualized within their nineteenth-century colonial lineage. I will assess the recent intensification of anxieties surrounding veiling and Islam in Europe and in the United States, as well as the legislative actions that bear on what Muslim women are allowed to wear in public.

Third, *What Is Veiling?* considers the various meanings that the veil has had for Muslim women during the past century and recounts female resistance to stereotypical images of the veil disseminated by both Euro-American media and fundamentalist Islamist discourses. The reasons for wearing the veil are extremely diverse and, we will see, Muslim women cannot be reduced to the common stereotypes depicted in Euro-American popular and political discourses or in extremist Islamist clerical pronouncements.

Each of the chapters in *What Is Veiling?* focuses on an aspect of Muslim veiling: history, religion, conservative and progressive interpretations, politics and regionality, society and economics, feminism, fashion, and art. As a whole, the book offers a deeper understanding of veiling and a more complex appreciation of the range of perspectives on the veil.

What Is Veiling? intends to show the complexity of elements that must be taken into account when examining the topic of veiling. I want to demonstrate that Muslim sartorial traditions cannot be homogenized or oversimplified, as they often tend to be. As I hope will become clear, I am neither defending nor criticizing the Muslim practice of veiling, nor Muslim women themselves and their decisions about how to dress. My aim is to listen to and amplify the diverse voices of Muslim women who struggle to be heard and who, veiled or not, demand their right to live spiritual, personal, and public lives in dignity and peace.

The exploration of the meaning of veiling that I invite you to undertake with me in this book is enriched by my personal experiences as a Muslim woman who wore the veil for one year from 1983 to 1984 while living in Egypt and in the United States. My firsthand knowledge of the religious, social, and political stakes involved in what often appears to be simply a personal decision complements the multiple interviews I have conducted with Muslim women, veiled and unveiled, during the past twenty years, as well as my friendships with Muslim women of all ages and from around the world. I wish to thank all of them for sharing with me their stories, their challenges, and their hopes for the future.

PART ONE

Islam, Politics, and Veiling

This section focuses on why veiling has become associated with Islam, and with Muslim women in particular. It also examines how the governments of some Muslim-majority societies have at times emphasized and implemented particular interpretations of core Islamic texts.

In chapter 1, I investigate what the three sacred Islamic traditions (the Qur'an, *hadith*, and Islamic law) say about veiling and how these traditions have been interpreted by orthodox Sunni Muslim scholars and schools of Islamic law from the ninth to the thirteenth century.

In chapter 2, I explore how these same core Islamic texts are being reinterpreted by contemporary progressive Muslim scholars and how these new interpretations differ from those maintained by classical and medieval Muslim theologians.

In chapter 3, I discuss why the governments in some Muslim-majority societies have followed particular interpretations of Islamic texts and the legislations they have enacted to enforce what they believe sacred Islamic traditions prescribe to women.

The goal of this first section is to give the reader a richer sense of the complexity and ambiguity of Islamic discourses on veiling and of the tenuous relation between conservative discourses on veiling and contemporary Islamist and pious injunctions that Muslim women veil.

[Headscarves] create a tent of tranquility. The serene spirit sent from God is called by a feminine name, "*sakinah*," in the Qur'an, and I understand why some Muslim women like to wear their prayer clothes for more than prayer, to take that *sakinah* into the world with them.
—Mohja Kahf, "Spare Me the Sermon on Muslim Women" (2008)

CHAPTER ONE

Understanding Veiling in Islamic Sacred Texts

Muslims and non-Muslims alike commonly believe that Muslim women are required to veil and that Islam prescribes veiling in no uncertain terms to its female adherents. Indeed, most veiled Muslim women I have met report that they cover primarily because the Qur'an prescribes it. And when asked whether they feel hot with their entire body and head covered, many reply with a smile that they do indeed feel hot, but that "the heat of Hell is even hotter." This observation is echoed by many Muslim men who consider veiled women more pious than those who do not veil. Similarly, many non-Muslims attribute veiling to strict religious observance, and at times to familial or political pressure.

It thus makes sense that we should begin our exploration of the meaning of Muslim veiling by looking at how and what Islamic sacred texts tell us about Muslim women's clothing.

Three main textual sources can help us investigate this. The central source for answers to anything to do with Islam is of course the Qur'an, the holy book of Islam that observant Muslims consider the direct word of God revealed to the Prophet Muhammad beginning in 610 CE. Muslims believe that the Qur'an has been preserved in an unaltered form since it was standardized in the Arabic Quraysh dialect by order of the third caliph, Uthman, in the middle of the seventh century.

Even though the Qur'an is indeed Islam's sacred text, its poetic language often makes it difficult to understand even for educated native speakers of Arabic. It is thus accompanied by a lengthy tradition of commentary (*tafsir*) that has for centuries provided dominant modes of interpretation. These commentaries have today circumscribed the meaning of the Qur'an and given rise to a community of practice that delimits all possible interpretations. In other words, it is not just what the Qur'an *itself* says about veiling that must be taken into account to understand Muslim women's veiling but also how some of the Qur'an's key commentators have interpreted the text.

The second main textual source that can shed some light on the general rules of Muslim women's dress is the multivolume collection known as *hadith*. The Islamic scholar Barbara Freyer Stowasser has defined *hadith* as "both a record of what Muhammad actually said and did and also a record of what his community in the first two centuries of Islamic history believed that he said and did."[1] In other words, *hadith* provides brief eyewitness reports of some of the sayings and doings of the Prophet Muhammad and his companions. It represents a major source of information about Islam, and it is the place where the idea that pubescent Muslim women must start veiling is most clearly articulated.

The third source of information about Muslim veiling is Islamic jurisprudence. Since its formal establishment more than one thousand years ago, the goal of Islamic jurisprudence has been to translate the Law of God (*sharia*) contained in the Qur'an and *hadith* into a practical legal system for the Muslim community. It is thus another important tradition in which to search for clues on Muslim veiling practices.

Taken together, the Qur'an with its exegesis, *hadith*, and Islamic jurisprudence are the three sacred Islamic traditions establishing the rules and ethical principles that Muslims consider fundamental to their religious identity, to their ritual and spiritual practice. It is these three traditions that I invite you to explore with me to understand why Muslims invoke religion first to explain veiling practices.

LOOKING FOR VEILING IN THE QUR'AN

Because the English term "veil" has no simple or direct Arabic equivalent (see introduction), a discussion of discourses on veiling in the Qur'an must focus instead on a variety of other Arabic terms. It is worth beginning with an investigation of the Arabic word *hijab*, which today is perhaps the most widely and commonly used one to refer to veiling and appropriate Muslim dress. How is the term *hijab* used in the Qur'an?

The term *hijab* occurs a total of seven times in the Qur'an (Q 7:46; Q 17:45; Q 19:16–17; Q 33:53; Q 38:32; Q 41:5; Q 42:51). Surprisingly, in five of these occurrences, the term *hijab* describes situations that have nothing to do with women and that do not treat the subject of a dress code.

Rather, the primary meaning of *hijab* in these five Qur'anic verses is a separation between people, a division or a distinction between groups or categories. The word *hijab* in Q 7:46, for instance, designates a separation between the inhabitants of Hell and those of Paradise; in Q 17:45, it separates the believers from the unbelievers; in Q 38:32, it refers to the sunset, thus the separation of day and night; in Q 41:5, the term *hijab* refers to the veil that the polytheists have on their heart, which prevents them from hearing and understanding the preaching of the Prophet; and in Q 42:51, *hijab* describes the shield that God uses to speak to humans to protect them from His divine light.

Only on two occasions (Q 19:16–17 and Q 33:53) is the term *hijab* used in relation to women, though it refers to women's clothing in neither case. In Q 19:16–17, *hijab* refers to the space of seclusion and silence that the Virgin Mary seeks when she learns of her virginal pregnancy. In Q 33:53, *hijab* again points to a spatial separation: this time, it describes a screen between the Prophet's wives and other men.

Veiling to protect the privacy of the Prophet's wives (Qur'an 33:53)

Q 33:53 is a very important *sura* often cited by scholars and Muslims to assert veiling as an Islamic duty. In fact, it is sometimes referred to as "the verse of the *hijab*" and is considered as the earliest revelation on the subject of Islamic veiling.

I provide two English translations of this Qur'anic verse because each translation comes with its own biases and set of exegetical assumptions. The first translation is by M. A. S. Abdel Haleem and the second one by Arthur Arberry, both of which are well-respected renditions assigned in introductory Islamic studies courses. The word *hijab* is highlighted in each translation below:

> Q 33:53: Believers, do not enter the Prophet's apartments for a meal unless you are given permission to do so; do not linger until [a meal] is ready. When you are invited, go in; then when you have taken your meal, leave. Do not stay on and talk, for that would offend the Prophet, though he would shrink from asking you to leave. God does not shrink from the truth. When you ask his wives for something, do so from behind *a screen* (*hijab*): this is purer both for your hearts and for theirs.

> Q 33:53: O believers, enter not the houses of the Prophet, except leave is given you for a meal, without watching for its hour. But when you are invited, then enter; and when you have had the meal, disperse, neither lingering for idle talk; that is hurtful to the Prophet, and he is ashamed before you; but God is not ashamed before the truth. And when you ask his wives for any object, ask them from behind *a curtain* (*hijab*); that is cleaner for your hearts and theirs.

Contrary to what we might have expected, the word *hijab* is not used here to describe or prescribe a particular dress code for Muslim women. In this verse, *hijab* refers to a physical partition or a dividing curtain between men and the wives of the Prophet—a separation between people or groups, as when the word appears elsewhere in the Qur'an.

The context of this Qur'anic passage sheds further light on the specific meaning of *hijab* in this case. According to a *hadith* compiled by al-Bukhari (d. 870) and Muslim (d. 875), Q 33:53 was revealed to the Prophet Muhammad while he was in Medina, about to celebrate his marriage to Zaynab bint Jahsh. The wedding guests overstayed their visit, delaying the long-awaited moment of the couple's privacy. To aid the Prophet, who was unsure how to encourage his guests to leave, this Qur'anic passage addressing the value of household privacy was revealed to him.

Hijab in Q 33:53 is therefore above all a physical, spatial marker (equivalent to the Indo-Persian notion of *purdah*) intended to safeguard the Prophet's privacy and that of his wives. It is important to note that the responsibility of observing *hijab* as a spatial curtain is placed here on men, not on women. They are the ones who must speak to the Prophet's wives from behind a curtain, (presumably) to maintain the wives' privacy and to preclude any type of inappropriate sexual desire. This passage thus stands in contrast to contemporary practices in some Muslim communities that place such responsibility on women.

Because this Qurʾanic revelation refers specifically to the Prophet's wives, considered exceptional among humankind, Muslims continue to debate whether this physical *hijab* or the *hijab* as a spatial divider between men and women is also required of other Muslims. The Qurʾan, in fact, never specifically addresses this question. It thus remains subject to discussion and interpretation.

Some conservative interpreters of the Qurʾan invoke this verse to assert that *all* believers, not just the Prophet's wives, are expected to avoid mixed-gender interactions. According to this view, Muslim men and women must keep separate quarters, or a spatial visual partition must be installed to ensure the separation of the sexes, thus emulating the model of the Prophet and his wives.

The same *sura* has also been invoked to justify the separation of Muslim men and women during ritual prayers in mosques. This partition, which always places the men's prayer quarters in front of women's, sometimes takes the form of opaque curtains that divide the prayer hall; at other times, women are relegated to a basement or a different floor or section of the building. In some countries, and in some mosques in the United States and around the world, no space is allotted to women, in effect banning them from ritual prayers at the mosque.

Although the Qurʾan never uses the word *hijab* to refer to women's clothing, some passages do treat the attire of women using other terms. The verses below continue to be regularly cited by Muslims to justify their veiling practices; they are also some of the passages that have generated the most controversy concerning their exact meaning. Every word of these excerpts matters, since they influence the style of veiling some Muslim women adopt.

The first passage uses the Arabic word *jilbab* to speak of women's clothing.

Veiling to distinguish and protect free women (Qurʾan 33:59)

Q 33:59: Prophet, tell your wives, your daughters, and women believers to make their *outer garments* [*jalabib*, sg. *jilbab*] hang low over them so as to be recognized and not insulted: God is most forgiving, most merciful.

Q 33:59: O Prophet, say to thy wives and daughters and the believing women, that they draw their *veils* [*jalabib*, sg. *jilbab*] close to them; so it is likelier they will be known, and not hurt. God is all-forgiving, all-compassionate.

This passage encourages all Muslim women, not just the Prophet's wives and daughters, to draw their *jilbab* around them to be recognized as Muslim women and not be harassed. Once again, the context of the *sura* helps us understand the historical setting of this passage, sometimes referred to as "the mantle verse."

In his *al-Tabaqat al-Kubra*, ibn Sa'd (d. 845), an early biographer of the Prophet Muhammad, reports the following: "When the wives of the Prophet of Allah, Allah bless him and grant him salvation, had gone out at night by necessity, some of the hypocrites used to prevent them and molest them. They [the people] complained about it. But the hypocrites said, 'We do it to the slave-girls only.' Then this Qur'anic verse [33:59] was revealed."[2]

Q 33:59 thus addresses a particular situation at a particular historical moment: the prevalence of shameless men at a time of moral decay in Medina, the molestation of women, and the confusion between slave girls and free women. The solution to this situation was to have Muslim women draw their *jilbab* around them so that they would become visually marked as free, and therefore as sexually unavailable.

If the historical context of this *sura* is relayed consistently from the ninth to the fifteenth century, the exact meaning of *jilbab* and what body parts it covered continue to be debated. In contemporary English translations, the word is usually rendered as veils, outer garments, mantle, or cloak.

Research conducted on the Qur'anic exegetical tradition by Soraya Hajjaji-Jarrah and Emi Goto indicates that before the advent of Islam, *jilbab* referred to an outer garment that both women and men loosely wrapped around their bodies and that formed an integral part of women's attire on the Arabian Peninsula. At times, this pre-Islamic *jilbab* covered a woman's face and showed one eye, or it was worn above the eyebrows covering the head.

We can thus conclude that the Qur'anic passage cited here is likely not instructing Muslim women to wear new articles of clothing or advocating a new dress code that differed from what women had been wearing on the Arabian Peninsula for centuries. Instead, the Qur'an recommends to adapt clothing already in use to changing circumstances to distinguish Muslim women from slaves and to protect them from harassment in public.

The third passage in the Qur'an that is regularly cited to justify a religious basis for Muslim veiling occurs in Q 24:31 and uses the Arabic term *khimar*, as well as the much debated words *juyub*, *zīna*, and *ʿawra* to speak of women's dress.

Veiling to cover women's beauty and ensure their modesty
(Qur'an 24:31)

Q 24:30–31: [Prophet], tell believing men to lower their glances and guard their private parts [*furujahum*]: that is purer for them. God is well aware of everything they do. And tell believing women that they should lower their glances, guard their private parts [*furujahunna*], and not display their *charms* [*zīna*] beyond what [it is acceptable] to reveal; they should let their *headscarves* [*khumur*, sg. *khimar*] fall to cover their *necklines* [*juyub*] and not reveal their *charms* [*zīna*] except to their husbands, their fathers, their husbands' fathers, their sons, their husbands' sons, their brothers, their brothers' sons, their sisters' sons, their womenfolk, their slaves, such men as attend them who have no sexual desire, or children who are not yet aware of women's *nakedness* [*ʿawra*]; they should not stamp their feet so as to draw attention to any hidden *charms* [*zīna*]. Believers, all of you, turn to God so that you may prosper.

Q 24:30–31: Say to the believers, that they cast down their eyes and guard their private parts [*furujahum*]; that is purer for them. God is aware of the things they work. And say to the believing women, that they cast down their eyes and guard their private parts [*furujahunna*], and reveal not their *adornment* [*zīna*] save such as is outward; and let them cast their *veils* [*khumur*, sg. *khimar*] over their *bosoms* [*juyub*], and not reveal their *adornment* [*zīna*] save to their husbands, or their fathers, or their husband's fathers, or their sons, or their husbands' sons, or their brothers, or their brothers' sons, their sisters' sons, or their women, or what their right hands own, or such men as attend them, not having sexual desire, or children who have not yet attained knowledge of women's *private parts* [*ʿawra*]; not let them stamp their feet, so that their *hidden ornament* [*zīna*] may be known. And turn all together to God, O you believers; haply so you will prosper.

This passage clearly advocates general rules of modesty for both men (Q 24:30) and women (Q 24:31), though the rules for women are more detailed and extensive than those for men. Both men and women are instructed to lower their gazes and to control their private parts (masc. *furujahum*; fem. *furujahunna*), but women are also enjoined to cover their necklines (*juyub*), not stamp their feet, and to conceal some of their adornments (*zīna*) and private parts (*ʿawra*) unless they are in the company of a number of specific blood relations.

The main question that continues to perplex scholars is which adornments (*zīna*) women are allowed to show and which ones they are expected to hide with their *khimar*. What part of the female body is private and shameful (*ʿawra*) and thus must be covered? The meaning of the words *khimar, zīna,* and *ʿawra* continue until today to be hotly debated.

Considering how often Muslims refer to this verse to argue that the Qurʾan requires Muslim women to veil, the *lack of specificity in the actual Qurʾanic text* seems striking. My students, including many of my veiled Muslim students, are consistently puzzled by this ambiguity, which is not a problem of translation. In fact, the Arabic text is perhaps even vaguer, because it is more multilayered than is possible to render in English.

Like the *jilbab*, the *khimar* was also an item of clothing (in this case, a veil or a scarf) commonly worn by women of all religions in the pre-Islamic era. *Juyub* is usually translated as bosom or neckline, but Liz Bucar has recently reminded us that the root of this word is an opening or a space in between. She thus offers that it meant "technically, a woman's cleavage."[3] In this *sura*, therefore, Muslim women were enjoined to cover their cleavage with the scarf that they already wore.

It is a lot more difficult to interpret the words *zīna* (adornment) and *ʿawra* (shameful, private parts), however, and there is no consensus as to their exact meaning. To understand what was considered an adornment in seventh-century Arabia, and therefore to interpret what adornment had to be covered and which ones could be left unconcealed, let's review how religious exegetes from the ninth to the fourteenth century glossed these words.

ZĪNA AND ʿAWRA

An example of an important Qurʾanic commentary is that by al-Tabari (d. 923). This fully extant piece of interpretative work has today become the standard, authoritative, and orthodox view of Islam. At times, it takes precedence over the Qur'an itself when it comes to understanding the holy book's metaphorical language or to applying its words of moral guidance to the everyday situations faced by Muslims in contemporary society.

In his exegesis completed three hundred years *after* the Prophet's death, al-Tabari follows the complex methodology developed by earlier commentators to elucidate the meaning of Qur'anic words that were no longer familiar to his generation. He writes that the women's adornments (*zīna*) to be concealed included the "anklets, bracelets, earrings, and necklaces." He adds that women's adornments that could be left uncovered were the face and the hands.[4]

Al-Zamakhshari (d. 1144), another theologian, glosses the word *zīna* as jewelry, kohl (natural eyeliner), and hand dye. Al-Zamakhshari allows, however, a woman's face, hands, and feet to remain uncovered, because he writes, "she needs to use her hands when she works, and to show her face when she testifies or gets married."[5]

Three hundred years later, this Qur'anic reading became not only normative but led to even more restrictive interpretations. Under the pen of later exegetes, additional limitations were placed on what Muslim women were allowed to reveal. Fakhr al-Din al-Razi (d. 1209/10), another important Muslim exegete, echoes and builds on some of al-Tabari's conclusions.

According to al-Razi, modesty lies at the core of Q 24:31.[6] His exegesis focuses largely on the definition of the term *ʿawra*, the shameful, private body parts that had to be covered. Because his definition of the term is necessarily based in the practices of his own time, al-Razi distinguishes the *ʿawra* of the sexually available woman (to an owner or purchaser) and that of the sexually unavailable one.

He posits the slave woman at the very bottom of the social ladder. As such, the slave woman is not only *not* modest but she is also not expected to be. Her *ʿawra* (those private parts and adornments she had to conceal) are similar to a man's, namely, the parts between her navel and the knees. He justifies his interpretation by pointing out that since slave women are property, they must be evaluated by the buyer, including an investigation of the head, arms, chest, and legs.

In contrast, the legally marriageable, free Muslim woman exists at the top of al-Razi's social ladder. Being of the highest social status, her entire body is *ʿawra*, or what al-Razi dubs "shameful nakedness." This means that it ought to be concealed entirely. Al-Razi does, however, ultimately also rehearse al-Zamakhshari's more cautious position and grudgingly concedes that upper-class women's hands and faces may remain visible as they are essential to their business activities.

One last example will serve to show the same tendency toward increasingly greater restrictions on Muslim women's dress stemming from Qur'anic commentators over time. Abd al-Rahman ibn al-Jawzi (d. 1200), a contemporary of al-Razi, echoed and built on al-Razi's already strict interpretation of women's clothing. For him, concealing a woman's entire body is no longer a sufficient observance of the Qur'anic injunction that a woman's adornments be covered. Ibn al-Jawzi submits that to observe complete modesty, Muslim women must be "imprisoned" in their homes, concealed behind a solid veil made of stone: "Imprison them in the homes . . . [for] like female snakes, women are expected to burrow themselves in their homes."[7]

The same strict view of women's bodies has led some theologians to argue that the entire female body and voice are 'awra, and therefore that women ought not to speak in the presence of men. Others, such as medieval theologians ibn Taymiyya (d. 1328) and al-Baydawi (d. 1282) believed that women's faces and hands could be uncovered only during prayer, while others still have advocated face veils, gloves, and socks.

This brief overview of Qur'anic exegesis on Q 24:31 indicates that contrary to what we may have expected or perhaps wished for (and in contrast to what many Muslims genuinely believe), the Qur'an does not describe the type or color of dress that Muslim women are supposed to wear. The Qur'an does not mandate clearly the covering of any particular part of the female body either. And the Qur'an does not state explicitly that Muslim women are required to wear a headscarf, a full-body cloak, a face veil, or indeed any of the other pieces of clothing often seen covering many Muslim women today.

Rather, male Muslim theologians are the ones who have defined women's adornments and therefore proper clothing, and they have done so in increasingly restrictive terms over time. While in the early tenth century the Qur'anic injunction for women to cover some of their adornments was interpreted as a call to conceal their bodies except for the hands and face, three centuries later, this same passage was interpreted as a mandate to avoid jewelry and makeup, to cover the neck, ears, and arms, and ultimately for women to disappear entirely from the public sphere. By the early thirteenth century, appropriate Muslim women's dress had already been firmly defined as one that covered the entire body and hair. The only points of debate remained over the face and the hands and whether they too ought to be covered.

During the same period, any discussion of Muslim women's clothing entailed a preoccupation with social class. Clothing as dictated by social class became fused with clothing allegedly dictated by religion. Today, the intimate link between veiling and social class has largely been forgotten, except by some scholars. The commonly held view today that Islam requires women to veil constitutes a selective memory, as veiling was, in fact, borrowed from the older and more established Assyrian tradition of veiling for upper-class women.

Over time and throughout Muslim-majority societies, interpretations that defined with greater and greater specificity those female body parts considered shameful (*'awra*) or those adornments considered immodest (*zīna*) became accepted orthodox Islamic views. These conservative exegeses have today become the source for those who wish to enforce a strict dress code on women, displacing the Qur'an's own flexible and open-ended message.

Once one is familiar with the conservative, restrictive voices of early Qur'anic commentaries, one readily recognizes them in popularized form behind the sermons of many *imams* in contemporary Muslim-majority and Muslim-minority societies. Once these sermons are propagated on satellite channels and their message is printed in self-help Islamic books or leaflets, we witness stricter and stricter views of Islamic veiling followed by more conservative veiling practices around the world.

The same views of women's *'awra* and the same restrictions on women's adornments (*zīna*) are repeated on orthodox Islamist websites, conservative blogs, and columns; they restate views of Muslim women's clothing formed in the thirteenth century. They perpetuate the principle that Muslim women must be modest, a notion interpreted as the necessary concealment of their bodies underneath a veil made of cloth, if not one made of stone.

LOOKING FOR VEILING IN *HADITH*

Muslims are guided in their daily practice not only by norms established in the Qur'an and its exegesis but also by the tradition of *hadith*.

Sunni Muslims consider *hadith* the second scriptural source after the

Qur'an, one that sheds light on some Qur'anic passages and provides practical guidance for Muslims' everyday actions. In fact, Qur'anic commentators themselves have relied on the sayings of the Prophet to buttress their interpretations of various Qur'anic verses, and *hadith* collections have been a key source of practical information for the formulation of legal rulings on Muslim women's attire.

The reports that make up *hadith* are said to have been memorized and passed down orally shortly after the death of the Prophet, before being compiled in multivolume collections in the ninth century CE. There are six *hadith* collections that Sunnis consider canonical and that contain the most authentic reports of the Prophet's sayings and doings: those by al-Bukhari (d. 870), Muslim (d. 875), Abu Dawud (d. 888), al-Tirmidhi (d. 892), ibn Majah (d. 889), and the *Musnad* by ibn Hanbal (d. 855). There are also important *shii hadith* collections that include the sayings and doings of the *imams*. They would certainly merit examination, but they have thus far received little scholarly attention in English and fall outside the scope of this discussion.

In Sunni *hadith* collections, each report is preceded by a chain of reporters generally going back all the way to the Prophet Muhammad or to one of his companions to ensure its authenticity. An essential aspect of the work of *hadith* compilers was therefore not only to assemble reports and organize them but also to carefully evaluate each individual oral report to establish its reliability and omit any that may have been falsely attributed to the Prophet Muhammad. Each report is graded on a complex scale of reliability from the most trustworthy to the unacceptable and false.

Linda Clarke's study of veiling in *hadith* has revealed that no discrete bundle of authoritative reports addresses the topic of women and veiling.[8] Even as clothing and adornment (*zīna*) in general are important topics in *hadith* collections, occupying at times entire chapters that review approved or unapproved clothing for believers, *most of them focus on modesty for men, not for women.*

Moreover, despite today's popular tendency to associate the notion of shameful parts (*ʿawra*) with women, nearly all the references to the term in *hadith* collections refer to the private or shameful parts of men. Among the extensive material, reference to women's covering is incidental at best, and much of it occurs in texts whose main subject is not clothing, but rather the distribution of booty, or the injunction to both men and women to avoid ostentatious long dresses and decorations worn out of pride.

There is a surprising absence of authoritative reports explicitly addressing the question of women's hair or the requirement to cover the head. Clarke points out that the many references in *hadith* are to both men's and women's hair—including appropriate length, color, washing, binding, and braiding styles—but that there is no clear statement that women ought to cover either the head or their hair and no warning that women who expose their hair will be punished. One would expect that if women's covering were of the importance accorded to them by Qur'anic exegesis or contemporary Muslims, it would have merited at least a mention in the *hadith* tradition.

Of the thousands of reports included in the six canonical Sunni *hadith* collections, Clarke identifies only one that addresses the requirement for women's covering. She points out that this *hadith* is included *only* in Abu Dawud's late ninth-century compilation and is reported by Abu Dawud himself *without* the requisite chain of reporters. It is also the only *hadith* listed under a chapter heading that echoes the language of Q 24:31 "That of a woman's adornment that may [be allowed to] appear." Even though this *hadith* exhibits all the traits of a report that ought to have been discarded immediately for being unreliable, it has actually become a central one in the Islamic justification of veiling.

This particular *hadith* tells of an incident in which Asma (the daughter of Abu Bakr, the Prophet's closest friend and the first caliph at Muhammad's death) came to the Prophet wearing see-through clothes. He is said to have turned away, stating: "Asma, if a woman reaches the age of menstruation, it is not fit that anything be seen of her except this and this." According to Abu Dawud, the Prophet pointed to his face and hands.

It is interesting to note here that the specification of body parts is made in gestural language by the Prophet and is only spoken by the *hadith* reporter himself (Abu Dawud). Put differently, even though the Prophet's statement does not actually name the body parts that he thought could remain visible, Abu Dawud, as official reporter of the *hadith*, identifies the woman's body parts in need of concealment. The body parts that had been left unspoken and vague in the Prophet's own words became definite and immutable under the pen of the *hadith* reporter.

The obligation to conceal the entire body of the post-pubescent Muslim woman of course recalls the Qur'anic commentaries by al-Tabari, al-Razi, and others who had interpreted the reference to adornments in Q 24:31 to mean everything other than the hands and face. One must wonder whether the agreement on this dress code for Muslim women in *hadith* and *tafsir* was reached independently, or if one tradition does not always rely on the other in the process of arriving at a particular interpretation of the source text (be it the Qur'an or the Prophet's words).

Even though Muslims consider the Qur'an and *hadith* two separate sources, the two texts actually echo, inform, and reinforce each other. They ultimately proclaim the same viewpoint on women's dress, and this viewpoint has gained absolute authority by virtue of its repetition. Not surprisingly, the *hadith* of Asma and the Prophet's reaction, much like the passage of Q 24:31, is regularly cited today to justify the adoption or the requirement of a particular way of veiling, one that conceals the woman's entire body except for the hands and face.

Despite the limited information on veiling contained in the Qur'an and in *hadith*, some contemporary Muslim clerics have not shied away from making that material seem more significant than it actually is by choosing whichever *hadith* or *tafsir* best suits their own conservative ideological bent. They have thus advanced new interpretations that place greater restrictions on women's dress. Such is the case, for instance, with one of today's most conservative Pakistani Islamist scholars, Shaykh Hindawi.

Contesting what he considered a liberal reading of Abu Dawud's *hadith*, Shaykh Hindawi has recently argued that it actually requires what he dubs "total *hijab*," that is, the covering of a woman's entire body, *including* the face and hands. He refutes the interpretation of Muslim scholars and clerics who consider the face and the hands licit and not shameful, and who maintain that they ought to be left uncovered.

Shaykh Hindawi cites an additional *hadith* report in support of his restrictive reading, one that prohibits women from concealing their faces and hands during pilgrimage to Mecca. He submits that if such a *hadith* had to be reported at all, it was most likely because women during the time of the Prophet typically covered their faces and hands. In his view, therefore, the only acceptable form of Islamic dress for women is complete covering.

Although neither the words of the Qur'an nor those of the Prophet specify the exact kind of dress Muslim women ought to wear, many Muslims (scholars and lay people) believe in the existence of a normative dress code dictated by religion. They do not disagree about whether women should veil, but rather about which female body parts *hijab* is supposed to cover.

LOOKING FOR VEILING IN ISLAMIC LAW

Exploring the meaning of veiling in Islam would be incomplete without looking at Islamic jurisprudence or Islamic law. Oftentimes, the notion of Islamic jurisprudence (*fiqh*) is confused with the term *sharia*, even though these are different, albeit interrelated, concepts.

Sharia is a loaded term in Euro-American societies and in the print and broadcast media. It is often assumed to be synonymous with "Islamic law" and placed in simplistic opposition to Christian, democratic values. When I ask my students what comes to mind when they hear the word *sharia*, they always invoke the specter of a violent, radical, and political Islam bent on the oppression of women and regularly carrying out horrific punishments such as stoning and mutilation.

Yet this is a completely erroneous view that stems from sensationalistic media attention to some of the most violent and ideologically motivated actions of some Muslim-majority governments and individuals today. It is important, therefore, to begin by clarifying the actual meaning of the word *sharia*. *Sharia* literally means "path." In the Qur'an, *sharia* is defined as the body of rules established by God Himself, one that humans must follow to be saved: "We have set you [Muhammad] on a *clear religious path*, so follow it. Do not follow the desires of those who lack [true] knowledge" (Q 45:18, translated by M. A. S. Abdel Haleem; emphasis added).

However, because God's law/*sharia* was not as specific as one may have wished, and once the Prophet was no longer alive to interpret the divine laws for the Muslim community, highly educated scholars and jurists began elucidating God's law. It is the body of laws that jurists extracted from the Qur'an that came to be known as Islamic jurisprudence (*fiqh*), and which stands in contrast to *sharia*, which is God's Law.

Fiqh deals with matters of personal morality, marital and family obligations, social etiquette, hygiene, property rights, business agreements, and inheritance much more than with state organization and policy. Contrary to what many Muslims and non-Muslims believe, it is not a homogeneous or monolithic legal code that has remained unchanged since the seventh century. Rather, it has always varied greatly depending on geography, history, and local cultures.

The diverse character of the Islamic legal tradition is evident in the fact that by the end of the eleventh century, four schools of Sunni Islamic jurisprudence had emerged: Maliki, Shafiʿi, Hanafi, and Hanbali. There also developed a number of Shii legal schools, the most prominent of which is the Jaʿfari. These schools trained and licensed jurists (functioning in this regard similarly to guilds) and their jurists elucidated God's law for the rest of the Muslim community.

Even as they disagreed over questions of methodology and interpretations, the four schools of Sunni Islamic jurisprudence embraced the diversity of opinions generated. They believed that all Islamic interpretations of divine law were equally valid, if only because they were imperfect by definition, having been formulated by human beings, in contrast to divine law, which alone was infallible, though also often unknowable. To provide stability in what could have easily become a chaotic normative pluralism, jurists from all schools of jurisprudence agreed that Muslims could follow any one of the main schools.

Muslim jurists developed a five-part moral scale to evaluate every conceivable human act: it ranged from mandatory, to recommended, to morally neutral or permissible, to reprehensible, to prohibited. This scale guided Muslims in obeying God's law.

From the perspective of Islamic jurisprudence, the subject of veiling was part of Islamic etiquette, not a required Islamic behavior. In other words, the whole debate over clothing was not considered part of *mandatory* religious practices (*fard*) such as praying, fasting during Ramadan, or giving alms to the poor. Rather, veiling was considered *wajib*, a customary, ethical practice.

The juridical discussion of women's attire therefore did not treat the specific question of *hijab*, or of appropriate Islamic dress to be worn by women in public. It focused rather on the topic of ʿ*awra* (private, shameful parts). In contrast to what is often assumed, *there is no Islamic law on hijab, only laws on ʿawra*. The two central questions that Muslim jurists debated were: In a historical context in which clothing was as scarce as in seventh-century Arabia, what parts of the body had to be covered during prayer? What female body parts was a man permitted to see before marrying a woman?

Muslim jurists disagreed on all of these elements. Like Qur'an commentators of the thirteenth century, such as al-Razi, many jurists distinguished the *ʿawra* of slave women from that of free women and claimed that slave women's *ʿawra* was the same as men's. Only the section from the navel to the knee had to be covered, while the rest of the slave woman's body could be (in fact, *had to be*) left unconcealed.

The *ʿawra* of a free woman, on the other hand, was her entire body except for the hands (understood at the time to be the hands and arms up to the elbows) and the face. Debates continued as to whether a woman's feet and neck also constituted *ʿawra* or not.

Over time, the four Sunni schools of Islamic jurisprudence came to agree that *all* Muslim women were required to cover their hair and to wear pants or long dresses that covered their ankles. Yet like Qurʾanic exegetes and *hadith* reporters and compilers, they continued to disagree about the covering of the hands and face.

Most Maliki and Hanafi jurists believed that the entire body of a woman, except for the face and hands, had to be covered. The Hanbali and Shafiʿi schools of jurisprudence, being the most conservative of the four on this issue, thought that the face and hands were parts of a woman's *ʿawra* and thus had to be concealed.

The medieval tradition of Islamic jurisprudence with its multiplicity of voices and interpretations, its pluralistic rulings, and the mutual respect among its different legal schools did not survive the encounter with colonialism. As early as the eighteenth century, European judges began treating Islamic law as an absolute legal code with rulings that were immutable and universal.[9] This perspective had significant, long-term consequences for the way Muslim women's veiling became viewed by both Muslims and non-Muslims.

■ Even though veiling is regularly explained away as an Islamic requirement, this requirement cannot be found in explicit or definitive terms in core Islamic texts. Attributing veiling practices to religion alone is clearly a gross oversimplification that fails to take into account the multiple factors that go into any Muslim woman's decision to veil. The following chapters will each explore some of the other facets essential to a more nuanced understanding of veiling among Muslim women today.

Speak the truth even if it hurts you. — Prophet Muhammad

Today, we have reduced Islam to a veil (*niqab*), a scarf (*hijab*), and a beard.
— Dr. Suad Saleh, Professor of Islamic jurisprudence, Cairo (2009)

If you think that the difference between heaven and hell is 45 inches of material,
boy will you be surprised. — Amina Wadud, *Inside the Gender Jihad* (2006)

CHAPTER TWO

What Do Progressive Muslims Say about Veiling?

The mainstream and restrictive interpretations of Qur'anic verses on female dress and the *hadith* tradition regularly cited in support of women's veiling, like the imposition of *hijab* on women by some Muslim-majority governments, have all been challenged by a contemporary group of Muslims, many of whom self-identify as "progressive." Many Muslims and non-Muslims know little about these modern progressive movements within Islam, and little also about Islamic reform movements and their challenge to conservative readings of Islamic texts.

The first time I learned that Muslims were actually encouraged to engage in critical thinking and invited to engage personally with the Qur'an was in the mid-1980s, when I was a senior at Bryn Mawr College, taking a class on Sufism. I still remember my shock when I heard the professor explain to the class that the first word of the Qur'anic revelation to the Prophet Muhammad was to "read" (Q 96) and that this was a call to Muslim adherents to participate in the creation of knowledge, rather than be passive recipients of it. I had never considered this possibility. I had grown up believing that I was supposed to follow the Islamic teachings handed down to me and that I was in no position to challenge, question, let alone reject any part of them.

I heard about "progressive Muslims" much later, in the late 1990s when I first began my research into Muslim veiling. By then, progressive Muslims had already been actively publishing books, articles, and online materials. While this production is widely distributed, it still remains better known within scholarly circles than among non-specialists. The reader may thus well wonder who these progressive Muslims are and on what basis they question centuries-old interpretations proffered by the most esteemed religious authorities, thereby challenging practices intimately associated with Islam.

WHO ARE PROGRESSIVE MUSLIMS?

Progressive Muslims are male and female Muslim academics, activists, theologians, lawyers, and intellectuals. Diverse in background and occupations, progressive Muslims are living around the globe and are actively striving to create a just and pluralistic society through a critical engagement with Islam and modernity. What unites progressive Muslims is that they challenge received notions about Islam, question the assumption that Islam is incompatible with progressive humanist ideals, confront Euro-American stereotypes and escalating Islamophobia, and dispute the restrictive interpretations of Islamic texts produced by conservative Islamic authorities over time.[1]

Progressive Muslims live on every continent and are part of every society. Progressive Muslims living under more restrictive Islamist regimes (e.g., in Iran, Saudi Arabia, or Afghanistan) face many more challenges and tend to be more isolated than those living in Euro-American societies, who usually enjoy some degree of freedom of expression. Those living in the diaspora believe they have a responsibility to provide new paradigms of leadership, interpretation, and activism to Muslims worldwide precisely because of where they live. Today, they are part of an ongoing global movement to transform Islam and to reinterpret Islamic religious texts outside of sexism and homophobia.

The central goal of progressive Muslims has been to recover Islam's basic teachings and reconnect Muslims with the egalitarian spirit of the faith clearly expressed in Q 33:35:

For men and women who are devoted to God—believing men and women, obedient men and women, truthful men and women, steadfast men and women, fasting men and women, chaste men and women, men and women who remember God often—God has prepared forgiveness and a rich reward.

This Qur'anic passage describes explicitly the absolute equality of male and female Muslims as believers in front of God. For progressive Muslims, this equality of the sexes, their rights and responsibilities as individuals endowed with free will, and the elevation of women as persons in their own right represent Islam's core teaching and the foundation of the new community that the Prophet Muhammad sought to establish in the seventh century.

According to progressive Muslims, the liberating and egalitarian message of the Qur'an, and the role the Prophet played in exemplifying it throughout his life, has long been lost to tribal and aristocratic customs. According to them, the Qur'an's egalitarian message has also been lost to culturally based patriarchal traditions and to politically manipulated interpretations of Islamic texts. Progressive Muslims point out that the basic egalitarian principles stated in the Qur'an have been replaced by traditional and restrictive interpretations passed down by conservative patriarchal religious communities (see chapter 1). For most Muslims who have received any kind of formal or informal religious education, reading the Qur'an almost always means assimilating or internalizing the interpretations given by those in authority—parents, the *imam*, or the community—and heard on the radio, on television, and in the sermons preceding Friday prayers, or read on the Internet.

Seeing how my younger cousins and the children of neighbors are educated in Egypt today, I am always astonished that the Qur'an continues to be taught as having a single interpretation, as being a source of absolute truths applicable to all times and for all peoples. For many, questioning the meaning of the Qur'anic text is tantamount to heresy.

Orthodox readings of sacred Islamic texts sustain their authority because Muslims are often not taught some of the basic disciplines necessary to develop a critical mind and are strongly discouraged from personally engaging and interpreting sacred texts. Many Muslim religious figures and teachers, secure in their undisputed expertise and fully aware that their interlocutors (women especially) lack the scholarly or theological background to challenge their interpretations and rulings, easily reduce the general community around them to silence.

Progressive Muslims refuse to be silenced, however. They want to be part of the debate and voice their own interpretations. They thus seek to acquire knowledge in those very same fields of Islamic theology that have thus far been the almost exclusive province of traditionally trained and conservative scholars. Today, progressive Muslims are gaining expertise in disciplines such as linguistics, the history of the Arabic language, Islamic history, Qur'anic commentaries, the *hadith* tradition, the elaboration of Islamic jurisprudence, biographical accounts of early Muslims, pre-Islamic poetry, and the literature of the early centuries of Islam. This is a monumental undertaking, and progressive Muslims are not shying away from it.

In addition, progressive Muslims are learning to read core Islamic texts free from others' interpretations, approaching them as they are written and not as they have been taught. In other words, progressive Muslims strive to be continuously aware of the reading grids that have been imposed on texts, to hold them at bay, and to fend them off carefully to engage directly with Islamic texts.

Progressive Muslims are becoming scholars of those religious texts that every Muslim knows but that few beyond the most conservative and traditionally trained scholars probe. While some prefer to consider only the Qur'an without its accompanying exegetical tradition (*tafsir* and *hadith*), others opt to re-examine that tradition and ground their new interpretations firmly in Islamic history. They thus cite the most respected and esteemed historical sources and commentators, the same ones that created the restrictive Islamist perspectives in the first place. Ultimately, it is this personal engagement, rigorous study, and vast background knowledge that can give progressive Muslims the legitimacy and authority they need to challenge conservative interpretations of Islamic texts and that will allow their voices to move from the margins to the center.

Progressive Muslims are often dismissed by Muslim critics and deemed "insufficiently Muslim" precisely because they confront orthodox and authoritarian interpretations. In addition, because many progressives live in Euro-American societies, they are looked upon with mistrust, suspected of sympathies with American foreign policy, and accused of being "too Westernized."

Nevertheless, progressive Muslims remain committed to a comprehensive and systematic rereading of core Islamic religious texts and to challenging many traditional interpretations of Islam as they relate to the modern world. In addition, they are working to produce a new body of Islamic laws (a new jurisprudence) consistent with the spirit of gender equality present in the Qur'an. It is in this context and in an effort to reconnect with the egalitarian spirit of Islam and to produce change on the sociopolitical scene that they have addressed the highly controversial topic of modesty and appropriate Muslim women's attire.

PROGRESSIVE MUSLIMS AND VEILING

Progressive Muslims' careful analysis and individual engagement (*ijtihad*) with Islamic texts have led them to vastly different conclusions than those inherited from medieval commentaries. In particular, progressive Muslims have pointed out that Qur'anic verses on veiling are open to multiple interpretations and have questioned the persistent assumption that Muslim women are clearly or specifically required to veil in the Qur'an.

In their in-depth research on women's modesty and attire, progressive Muslims have pursued four main lines of investigation: (1) a systematic study of the language and vocabulary of Qur'anic verses on women's clothing; (2) a contextualization of Qur'anic verses and *hadith* reports within specific historical and cultural moments; (3) an excavation of the early history of Muslims, and of Muslim women in particular; and (4) a systematic study of *hadith* and a closer look at the validity of those reports allegedly mandating the veiling of women.

Reexamining the Language and Vocabulary of the Qur'an on Veiling

Progressive Muslims have been rereading and offering new interpretations of the few Qur'anic verses on women's attire (Q 24:31, Q 33:53, and Q 33:59). Since the ninth century, the traditional interpretation of these verses has been that the Qur'an mandates the veiling of a woman's entire body, except her hands and face (see chapter 1).

Progressive Muslims, on the other hand, have argued that the terms used in these Qur'anic verses to refer to body parts and clothing, most specifically *zīna* (adornment); *khimar* (headscarf), *juyub* (bosoms, necklines), *jilbab* (cloak), and even verbs such as *yadribna* (they should throw/cover), are a lot less specific than Qur'anic commentators rendered them between the tenth and the fourteenth century.

For progressive Muslims, medieval and contemporary Qur'anic commentators erred because they failed to take into account the meaning of these particular sartorial terms in seventh-century Arabia and the historical and cultural context of the Qur'anic revelations in question. Progressive Muslims' ongoing research reveals that all the words mentioned in the Qur'an allegedly addressing women's proper attire are attested in the pre-Islamic period and refer to clothing worn by *all women of the Arabian peninsula at the time, regardless of religious, tribal, and ethnic background.*

They have pointed to the social customs of pre-Islamic Arabia, where women in both Mecca and Medina used to wear a *khimar* or a transparent veil that fell behind their back. Women from the pre-Islamic period also traditionally wore a *jilbab*, which was a type of vest or shirt open in the front that left the chest entirely exposed.

In a society where poverty was prevalent and clothing scarce, the Qur'anic verses mandating women to cover their bosoms with their *khimars* (Q 24:31) and to draw their *jalabib* closer to their bodies (Q 33:59) did not mean, as early commentators asserted, that women were expected to cover completely. Rather, for progressive Muslims, these Qur'anic verses are best interpreted as *general guidelines about modesty and morality*, as a recommendation to Muslim women to cover their chests with the same pieces of cloth they were already wearing.

For progressive Muslims, *hijab* in Islam is much less about clothing, much less about an injunction to wear specific attire, than it is about adopting a modest demeanor, remaining humble, and avoiding pride and conceit.

Contextualizing Qur'anic Verses and Hadith *Reports on Veiling*

Progressive Muslims believe that the historical and cultural contexts of Qur'anic verses cited in support of veiling (Q 33:59 in particular) are crucial to a deeper understanding of why seventh-century Muslim women were encouraged to draw cloaks closer to themselves when venturing into public spaces. I am quoting Q 33:59 and again providing two translations, the first one by M. A. S. Abdel Haleem and the second one by Arthur Arberry:

Q 33:59: Prophet, tell your wives, your daughters, and women believers to make their *outer garments* [*jalabib, sg. jilbab*] hang low over them so as to be recognized and not insulted: God is most forgiving, most merciful.

Q 33:59: O Prophet, say to thy wives and daughters and the believing women, that they draw their *veils* [*jalabib, sg. jilbab*] close to them; so it is likelier they will be known, and not hurt. God is all-forgiving, All-compassionate.

Progressive Muslims have pointed out that this passage was revealed to the Prophet Muhammad in 627 AD, five years after he had migrated to Medina to escape his enemies in Mecca. Although the Prophet had initially succeeded militarily against those who did not believe in his revelations, he was at that time recovering from serious military losses, while being threatened by enemies from outside and inside Medina. His adversaries were mostly aristocrats who felt menaced by the new ethics of gender equality that Islam preached. For these aristocrats, the rights of women to inherit and the principle that children born to slave women were free threatened the basis of the pre-Islamic economy and placed the power that men had held in Arab societies for centuries in serious jeopardy.

In these circumstances, Medina had become the site of a veritable civil war and it had become dangerous for anyone, particularly for women, to circulate freely on the streets. Muslim women, including the wives of the Prophet, were harassed regularly and required protection. When the Prophet inquired about the reasons for this increased harassment, he was informed that men believed the women on the streets to be slaves. In the culture of the time, this meant that they could be purchased, were sexually available, and toward whom sexual aggression was permitted.

For progressive Muslims, Q 33:59 has to be interpreted in the context of this civil war and the resulting aggressions against women. If this verse directs women to draw their cloaks (*jalabib*) closer over themselves, it was to ensure that they would be recognized as wives of the Prophet, as daughters of Muhammad, or as Muslim women, and thus would be protected.[2] In contrast to official Islamic teachings, wearing a *jilbab* was a response to a specific historical situation, a practical solution to a whole web of military conflicts and social tensions. It was not an injunction to dress in a particular way, valid for all women at all times and in all places, regardless of the safety of their environs.

In addition, some progressive and feminist scholars, beginning at least with Fatima Mernissi's 1987 *The Veil and the Male Elite*, have argued that Qur'anic prescriptions on clothing (like those enunciated in *hadith*) are addressed specifically to the Prophet's wives who are often heralded as unique among women. For example, we read:

Q 33:32–33: *Wives of the Prophet, you are not like any other woman.* If you are truly mindful of God, do not speak too softly in case the sick at heart should lust after you, but speak in an appropriate manner; stay at home, and do not flaunt your finery as they used to in the pagan past; keep up the prayer, give the prescribed alms, and obey God and His Messenger. (emphasis added)

Q 33:32–33: *Wives of the Prophet, you are not as other woman.* If you are godfearing, be not abject in your speech, so that he in whose heart is sickness may be lustful; but speak honourable words. Remain in your houses; and display not your finery, as did the pagans of old. And perform the prayer, and pay the alms, and obey God and his Messenger. (emphasis added)

This passage explicitly singles out the wives of the Prophet and instructs them to avoid flaunting their finery. *Only they* were expected to behave in a particular way, in contrast to Muslim women in general. Moreover, the injunction to not flaunt their finery and to behave in a certain way is not made using any of the terms discussed in chapter 1 (*hijab* or *zīna*). The passage here uses a different word, *tabarruj*, which means to avoid drawing attention or making a spectacle of oneself. There is no specific mention of clothing or of veiling even in this verse addressed to the Prophet's wives.

Moreover, an analysis of a *hadith* reported by al-Bukhari on the Prophet's marriage to Safiyya Bint Huyayy has led several progressive Muslim scholars to point out that in seventh-century Arabic, the verb "to take the veil" was used as an equivalent to "to become the Prophet Muhammad's wife."[3] This linguistic and cultural information clearly marks veiling as a practice specific to the privilege of being one of the Prophet's wives. It thus recalls one of the Assyrian laws on veiling discussed in chapter 1.

On this basis, some progressive Muslims have asserted that veiling was primarily a mark of social and spiritual status (being married to Muhammad) and was never supposed to become an obligation for all women. Generalizing that original context and turning these early pronouncements into prescriptions for all Muslims is to do violence to the Qur'an and to the early history of Islam. Yet this is precisely what the majority of Muslims believe and what most legal Islamic schools of jurisprudence maintain.

EXCAVATING THE EARLY HISTORY OF MUSLIM WOMEN

As they endeavor to free the Qur'an from conservative interpretations, and to offer more culturally and linguistically sensitive interpretations compatible with the central Qur'anic principle of gender equality, progressive Muslim scholars have conducted extensive archival research into the early history of Islam. They have been involved in excavating Islam's cultural memory, in recalling events, facts, individuals, situations, and contexts that have been forgotten or disguised to advance a patriarchal or conservative interpretation of Islam.

Progressive Muslims are in the process of perusing the numerous extant early Islamic biographical collections to unearth what they teach us about the early Muslim community and the involvement of women therein.[4] They have started to reconstruct the extraordinary public, economic, and political role played by Muslim women in the early Islamic period, their involvement in military expeditions alongside men, their active participation in mosques side by side with men, their partaking in ritual prayers, and their role as teachers (especially after the Prophet's death), including for male students. The wide-ranging public roles that early Muslim women regularly played contrast sharply with the stereotype of the subservient, veiled Muslim woman often portrayed in the media whose only legitimate space is the private, the home, or behind an austere and oftentimes imposed *hijab*.[5]

There is also evidence that in Medina (in contrast to Mecca), during the time of the Prophet, women were not secluded but were outspoken members of their community who consulted the Prophet on various matters of personal and social nature and asked questions related to religious practice. The Prophet himself regularly received delegations from around Arabia and beyond who came to inquire about Islam or to establish political and economic ties with the fast-growing religious community. He received these delegations either in the mosque or in private, but often in the presence of one of his wives who did not simply sit quietly in the background, but who intervened to express her opinion on the matters discussed.

Moreover, according to Mernissi, the Prophet Muhammad is said to have frequently taken two of his wives along on all military campaigns, a practice criticized by many of his companions and used as fodder for attacks from his enemies over the loyalty of women and of his wives in particular. Clearly, the Prophet was opposed to an absolute separation between his private and public life. He sought to uphold the message of gender equality preached in some key realms by the Qur'an, had faith in women's intellectual capacity, and believed that they could play a significant role in society. In fact, early historians speak about some of the women from the early Islamic period as *sahabiyyat,* a feminine form of the masculine *sahabi,* which refers to the Prophet's male companions. That the Prophet had female companions shows that misogyny was not the dominant practice of seventh-century Arabia.

In other words, women in early Islam, fleeing the tribal restrictions of the pre-Islamic period, became full participants in the establishment of the new Muslim community, partook in council meetings, spoke directly and freely to the Prophet, disputed with men, and contributed to military and political affairs. After the Prophet's death, his youngest wife, Ayesha, along with other women, became our main source of information about the Prophet's private and public life. It was women who became teachers of men and who instructed them in the ways of the Prophet. It is safe to say that women in the early Islamic period were not victims of the now familiar public-private division, but were in fact the first voices of *hadith* reports (they were, after all, the most familiar with the Prophet's ways) and thus active agents in the public space.

This new research that has unearthed the extraordinary political and social role played by Muslim women in the early history of Islam makes clear that some commonly held views about Islam and women are nothing but an imposed construction. Notions now prevalent in Islam, such that women are shameful ('awra), that they introduce social disorder (*fitna*) into society and hence ought to be secluded, covered underneath a veil (*hijab*), and confined to the private arena, contradict everything progressive Muslims have discovered about early Islamic history.

Just as they methodically study the Qur'an and early Islamic history, progressive Muslims have also been actively rereading *hadith* and revisiting the validity of those reports allegedly mandating the veiling of all Muslim women. Not surprisingly, they have focused on the single *hadith* reporting the Prophet's reaction when Asma, the daughter of Abu Bakr, came to him wearing see-through clothes (see chapter 1). They have urged caution in interpreting this *hadith* as irrefutable proof that the Prophet Muhammad instructs all Muslim women who have reached the age of puberty to veil.

Linda Clarke has pointed out this report's questionable reliability despite its inclusion in Abu Dawud's canonical late ninth-century *hadith* collection. For one, it is cited only in his collection and is not attested anywhere else. It thus exhibits a feature marking possible fraudulent reporting according to the complex evaluation system of authentification developed by classical *hadith* scholars.

Moreover, this report is cited by Abu Dawud, who lived in the ninth century, two hundred years after the Prophet's death, and is not supported by an unbroken chain of reporters going all the way back to the Prophet or to one of his companions to guarantee its authenticity.

Finally, it is the only *hadith* cited in Abu Dawud's chapter "That of a woman's adornment that may [be allowed to] appear," as though he was desperately trying to find a report to support his interpretation of Q 24:31, or perhaps, his own views on women's proper attire. For these three important reasons, Clarke has concluded that Abu Dawud's report cannot be considered an indisputable proof of Muslim women's requirement to veil their entire bodies except the face and hands.

PROGRESSIVE MUSLIMS AND THE DIVERSITY OF VEILING PRACTICES

Progressive Muslims' personal engagement with sacred Islamic texts and early Islamic history does not mean that they all reach the same conclusions about the requirement of veiling in Islam. In other words, just as there are gradations of conservative Muslims, there are also shades of progressive Muslims. Even after delving into the meaning of Qur'anic verses, uncovering their historical contexts, recovering the abundant legacy of female leaders since the time of the Prophet, investigating the validity of *hadith* reports, and challenging conservative interpretations of Islamic texts, they still hold a variety of opinions about veiling.

Contrary to what some might believe, being a progressive Muslim (just like being a secular Muslim) does not automatically mean opposition to veiling, or that one goes about unveiled, or even that one veils consistently. In her *Inside the Gender Jihad*, the Islamic scholar Amina Wadud has written in detail about when, where, and how she wears or does not wear her *hijab*, demonstrating the complexity and fluidity of such practices in the life of one person.

Some progressive Muslims embrace veiling because they consider it a cultural practice specific to the Muslim-majority nation to which they (or their ancestors) belong and which they want to maintain. This applies, for instance, to many African Muslims, for whom covering the hair in some fashion is part of their cultural tradition. For them, veiling represents a way of reconnecting deeply with their cultural and religious heritage, their faith and spirituality.

Some progressive African American Muslims adopt *hijab* as a sign of self-affirmation and symbolic healing from the trauma their ancestors experienced during their forced unveiling and exposure on the slavery auction block.[6] Others choose veiling because they want to be readily and unmistakably acknowledged as Muslims, hence heeding the second part of Q 33:59, which instructs Muslim women to veil to be recognized. Some progressive Muslim women report feeling a greater sense of empowerment and safety as a result of veiling by choice and personal engagement with the Islamic textual tradition.

Other Muslim women describe a sense of freedom when veiled, and liberation from the practical aspects of daily life (having a bad hair day, making decisions about clothing). And for some, wearing the veil allows them to be constantly attuned to their beliefs, to their spirituality, and the sanctity of their soul. For them, their veil and outward appearance serve as a reflection and permanent reminder of their faith.

Of course, some progressive Muslims also reach the opposite conclusion based on the same personal engagement with and interpretation of Islamic sacred texts. They thus decide not to veil, or to de-veil after having veiled for some time once they discover that neither the Qur'an nor *hadith* prescribe specific female attire.

Some choose not to veil because they want to follow the spirit of the Qur'anic verses on modesty, which enjoins women (and men) to not draw attention to themselves. Oftentimes, this is a reason invoked by Muslim women living in Muslim-minority societies who argue that veiling while living in the diaspora only serves to draw more attention to them and thus contradicts the principle set forth in Q 33:59. This is certainly the main reason why I stopped wearing the veil when I was in my twenties.

Others do not veil because they believe that modesty is more about humility in general attire, speech, and actions rather than about a head or body covering. They reason that they can be modest without *hijab*, and that their focus on spirituality is unrelated to their outer appearance. Their goal is, as Wadud described it, to "achieve modest integrity over formulas and symbols."[7]

Whether they decide to veil or not, progressive Muslims maintain that veiling has no singular meaning, though it has been overloaded with symbolic significance. They urge everyone to move beyond the obsession with veiling that divides the Muslim community and serves as a lightning rod for debates in Muslim-majority and Euro-American societies. Such fixation ultimately deflects attention from other more pressing issues facing both Muslim and non-Muslim women.

In the introduction to *Living Islam Out Loud: American Muslim Women Speak*, Saleemah Abdul-Ghafur, a progressive Muslim who serves on the board of the Progressive Muslim Union, speaks for many Muslim women when she asserts, "most of us are exhausted with the *hijab* debate and envision a future where we move beyond the judgments of women with and sans *hijab*."[8] Like the progressive Muslims whose voices we read in the present book, Abdul-Ghafur urges us to shift attention instead on a serious discussion of issues such as poverty, family violence, education, government oppression, patriarchy, and other topics of global significance. Ultimately, addressing these very real problems will go a much longer way toward achieving a future focused decidedly on women's rights and gender equality.

VEILING, AUTHORITY, VOICE, AND SPACE: LEADING GENDER-MIXED CONGREGATIONS

The legitimacy many progressive Muslims are still striving to gain is pressing, since their ultimate objective is not just to produce new scholarship that reinterprets Qur'anic verses or *hadith* in more gender-equitable and humanistic ways but to instigate change at the level of individuals, society, and governmental policy. In fact, in her essay entitled "On the Edges of Belonging," Khalida Saed defines progressive

Islam as "the belief that working toward social justice is an integral part of religion."[9] In other words, progressive Muslims engage equally with Islam on an intellectual level and on the practical level of social activism. Being a progressive Muslim means that one works toward social change and strives to take the intellectual, scholarly discussions and discoveries to the local, grassroots level to generate far-reaching sociopolitical change.

While there may be some exceptions, one of the changes that many progressive Muslims are striving to institute is the application of the principle of gender equality to the space of the mosque. This means that they are working to challenge the conventional separation of Muslim men and women during ritual prayer, the male leadership of the prayers themselves within the mosque, and the delivery of the Friday sermon by men.

These questions about space, leadership, and voice relate to our discussion of veiling because the concept of *hijab*, we will recall, also refers to the curtain separating men and women (Q 33:53). In this Qur'anic verse, the term *hijab* signified the physical partition between the private and the public to screen the Prophet Muhammad and his new bride from his lingering guests (see chapter 1). Conservative interpreters of the Qur'an have taken this passage to mean both that Islam mandates women's veiling *and* that it forbids mixed-gender interactions.

In practical terms, such interpretations of Q 33:53 have led to gender segregation in mosques and prayer halls. It has now indeed become commonly accepted in Muslim communities that women represent a potential sexual distraction to the spiritual concentration of men, and thus, if they are at all allowed inside a mosque, they must be relegated to a space unheard and unseen to ensure men's undisturbed prayer.

Both in Euro-American societies and throughout Muslim-majority nations, some mosque officials continue to refuse to allow women to participate in ritual prayers in their buildings, while others consign women to a cramped basement, to the back section of the mosque, or to a different floor behind walls or heavy curtains. The front entry of most mosques around the world, and in North America in particular, continues to be treated as a male-only access to the main prayer hall.

In her 2005 documentary film *Me and the Mosque*, which charts Muslim women's presence and participation in Canadian mosques, Zarqa Nawaz describes her own experience in such gender-segregated spiritual spaces: "I pray in a room where there is a one-way mirror, so the men cannot see me. I am told we are a distraction. I look out and I see them but they just see a mirror. The presence of women in my mosque has been erased."[10]

Nawaz is not alone in her experience of erasure in the mosque. Many other Muslim women report a sense of exclusion, alienation, and disenfranchisement when physically relegated elsewhere. Some protest that they can barely hear or see the male prayer leader (*imam*) who always stands in front of the men in the main prayer hall. African American Muslims especially resent this practice, which for many summons the race segregation they and their families encountered until the late 1960s.

Despite their frustration with what some have dubbed "gender apartheid" in mosques, most Muslim women do not dare to question the status quo for fear of being further marginalized or alienated. The separation of men and women in mosques and during ritual prayers, as well as the unquestioned belief that the *imam* must necessarily be male, are conventional practices that proceed from the interpretation of *hijab* as a curtain or separation, and they are some of the discriminatory practices that progressive Muslims are actively challenging.

Some denounce these exclusionary practices along with male authority and leadership in mosques through stand-up comedy. Such is the case with the American Muslim comedian Azhar Usman who bitingly denounces these practices with his well-known humor and logic: "You know, there is this hot issue: women in the mosques. What exactly is the issue here? I just don't get it, I mean, women, they need to pray, this is a mosque, a house of worship. Maybe, the women should be in the mosque."[11]

Others have taken daring steps to reinscribe Muslim women's presence, participation, and leadership in mosques. Amina Wadud came to prominence when she led a mixed-gender congregational prayer on Friday, March 18, 2005, at the Synod House, owned by and adjoining the Episcopal Cathedral of Saint John the Divine, in Manhattan's Upper West Side. She acted as *imam* in front of a mixed congregation of about sixty Muslim women and forty men who prayed together without the traditional gender separation of prayer quarters.

In doing so, and as Juliane Hammer has detailed at length, Wadud openly challenged several principle characteristics of Islamic ritual practices: She acted as *imam* when most believe that *imams* can only be men; she delivered the Friday sermon (*khutba*), which is also always given by a man; she stood in front of the Muslim followers, when it is expected that, as a woman, she should never place herself ahead of the other members; and she allowed men and women to pray side by side behind her.

As might be expected, this symbolic event, while not the first Muslim woman–prayer initiative to occur,[12] was met with protest and stern condemnation by the majority of scholars who spoke out and by Muslim religious authorities around the world. They concurred that while a woman may lead a woman-only congregation, or possibly her own family in prayer, she was not permitted by any school of jurisprudence and under any circumstances to act as *imam* to a mixed-gender congregation.

In contrast, and in support of Wadud and of others who followed suit and led Friday prayers around the world, Khaled Abou El Fadl, a progressive Muslim and a male religious scholar at the UCLA School of Law, issued a religious ruling (a *fatwa*) permitting a woman to lead the ritual prayer of a mixed-gender congregation, as long as she is the most learned one in terms of Qur'anic recitation and ability to teach the community about Islam.

According to Abou El Fadl, however, when a woman leads other men and women in prayer, she ought to stand side by side with, and not in front of them. He bases his ruling on the fact that the Qur'an does not dictate that only men can be *imams*, that *hadith* is indecisive on this topic, and that the exclusion of women from leading prayer is more a matter of customary practice and male consensus than of theological textual evidence. However, he did not explain the reasons why a woman *imam* ought to stand side by side with other congregants, and not in front of them, as a male *imam* would.

Wadud's action was not meant to be defiant. Rather, her goal, consistent with that of progressive Muslims, was to stimulate debate, challenge male privilege, and bring about much-needed transformations in Islamic practices, especially as far as the role and status of women are concerned. Before she led the congregation in prayer, Wadud had stated: "I don't want to change Muslim mosques. I want to encourage the hearts of Muslims, both in their public, private, and ritual affairs, to believe they are one and equal." Her act was above all symbolic, enacting the primary goal of progressive Muslims, that of affirming the equality of the sexes before God.

Wadud's model proved a watershed event that prompted some mosques

Hui Chinese female Muslims praying in a dedicated female mosque in
Pingliang, Gansu Province, China, 2008 (Courtesy of Sharron Lovell)

to become more woman-friendly, to adopt the "Islamic Bill of Rights for Women in Mosques" developed by the progressive Muslim Asra Nomani, and to include women on their boards and in their decision-making processes. Equally important, Wadud's courageous initiative spurred many other women to lead prayers and question various conventional interpretations and alleged Islamic practices.

Inspired by the Wadud-led prayer event in 2005, and encouraged by Abou El Fadl's *fatwa*, other Muslim women have indeed since then led mixed-congregation prayers, offered the *khutba*, and made the official call to prayer (*adhan*) that precedes the actual ritual worship. Such initiatives have taken place around the world, including in some mosques, notably in South Africa, Canada, Spain, and the United Kingdom.

Also since the Wadud event, more attention has been devoted to China's women-only mosques (*nüsi*), which have existed since the late eighteenth century, and to the unique tradition there of having officially trained and sanctioned women *imams*.[13] It is worth noting that Beijing's tight control over religious practice has meant that Chinese Hui Muslims have been isolated and therefore somewhat protected from the more conservative trends sweeping across Muslim-majority and Muslim-minority societies worldwide.

Ironically, and because of the communist stance on the equality of the sexes, some Islamic traditions that have disappeared elsewhere continue to be practiced in China, including the existence of women prayer leaders. Currently, there are efforts to establish similar women-only mosques and to appoint women *imams* in India and Iran. Nevertheless, it remains unclear whether the creation and proliferation of such women-only mosques would support or hinder progressive Muslims' efforts to break down the gender division in Islam and promote the equality of men and women as believers in front of God, all praying side by side in one row, without any separation.

■ The scholarship carried out by progressive Muslims represents radically innovative ways of rethinking Muslim veiling, Islam as a religion, and its increasing appeal to women worldwide. Progressive Muslims are truly at the forefront of new humanistic and feminist interpretations of Islam and of the Qur'an, offering visions of an empowering, gender-equitable faith that has space for a divine feminine energy and a lineage of female spiritual masters and role models.

Armed with this fresh understanding of Islam, progressive Muslim women are reclaiming and reconnecting with the faith and actively participating in its spiritual and intellectual development. While embracing fully the notion that the words of the Qur'an are eternal, they challenge the view that their interpretations are etched in stone.

Progressive Muslims highlight the notion that the Qur'an provides guidance for humans in all times and emphasize its open-ended ability to speak in different ways to different peoples living in different periods and contexts. It is this flexible voice of Islam and of the Qur'an especially that progressive Muslims are striving to recover for the twenty-first century as a first step toward the elaboration of a new jurisprudence respectful of human and women's rights and cognizant of the spirit of equality that traverses the Qur'an. In that new reading of Islam, veiling or not veiling is a personal decision, individually embraced, and incompatible with any externally imposed requirement or injunction.

It has been proven that the hair of a woman radiates a kind of ray
that affects a man, exciting him out of the normal state.
—Abolhassan Bani-Sadr, Iran's first post-revolutionary president

It is not that we wear burqa because it is shameful to go without it,
but because it's beautiful to go with it.
—Woman from Oman

My scarf covers my head, not my brain.
—Hayrunisa Gül (wife of Turkey's president Abdullah Gül)

CHAPTER THREE

Politics and Sociocultural Practices of Veiling

Religion and piety are not the only factors that determine whether a Muslim woman will veil, or even how she will veil. In a handful of Muslim-majority societies, the government mandates *hijab* and legislates the particular form that veiling must take.

The Euro-American print and broadcast media reports disproportionately on these conservative Muslim-majority countries and their restrictive veiling practices. As one student interviewed by the anthropologist John Bowen astutely pointed out, "on the television, it is as if there are only two Muslim countries in the world, Afghanistan and Iran."[1]

Covered far less are the specific historical context of governmental veiling legislation and the voices of resistance from Muslims to such veiling regulations. The coverage of government-mandated veiling practices also fails to mention that in most Muslim-majority societies, veiling is adopted voluntarily because it is a common cultural practice and often out of deep piety.

POLITICS, HISTORY, AND VEILING REGULATIONS

Until 1979, Saudi Arabia was the *only* Muslim-majority society that required the veiling of women (both native and foreign) when going out in public. Today, veiling is imposed on women in four countries in the world: Saudi Arabia, Iran, the Sudan, and the Aceh Province of Indonesia.[2] This means that the requirement to veil in Muslim-majority societies is a rare and very recent phenomenon, one tied to specific historical and political conditions.

In Iran, for instance, *hijab* was imposed on women after the 1979 Islamic Revolution that established the Islamic Republic of Iran under the leadership of the Ayatollah Khomeini. At the time, a great number of Iranian women had demonstrated on the streets in support of the revolution and demanding their right to wear the *chador*.

Euro-American broadcast and print media at the time marveled at Iranian women's enthusiastic adoption of a conservative form of Muslim dress during the revolution. What was not generally understood, however, was that the adoption of the *chador* did not indicate a sudden rise of piety among the population or a wholehearted embrace of conservative forms of Islam. Rather, wearing the *chador* largely symbolized resistance against Shah Mohammad Reza Pahlavi who had banned the veil in 1936 and imposed Western dress.

Many of the secular and modern Iranian women who appeared in the newsreels of Iran's 1979 Islamic Revolution had adopted veiling not always because of their own religious beliefs but in support of the thousands of pious Iranians who had been oppressed and excluded from education and government jobs simply as a result of the Shah's forced sartorial policies. Their veiling symbolized solidarity especially with the working-class Iranian women who had been subjected to mandatory *un*veiling under the Shah.

After the 1979 revolution, however, Iranian women who had demonstrated for their right *to choose* to wear the *chador* unexpectedly found themselves *forced* to wear it. According to today's Iranian Islamic Penal Code, women who are caught unveiled or improperly veiled (wearing long boots over their pants, hats instead of scarves, or the wrong color — anything but black, blue, or brown) are fined or face penalties ranging from seventy-four lashes to a two-year prison term.

Chief Brigadier General Morteza Talaie of the Tehran police reports that 30 percent of all complaints made to the Iranian police today concern inappropriately attired women. The business proceeds of such mandatory veiling are enormous: the sale of black veils has become a $40 million industry in Iran, profiting conservative bazaar merchants who have become staunch supporters of the current Iranian government.

Just as the Shah used physical force to implement his compulsory unveiling policies in the late 1930s, today's Iranian government employs a special morality police (referred to as *Kommiteh*) to enforce compulsory veiling. Similar policies hold true in Saudi Arabia,[3] the Sudan, and the Aceh Province of Indonesia. Moreover, in Iran, theater, restaurant, and hotel owners are instructed not to serve unveiled women, just as they had been ordered to refuse to cater to veiled women under the Shah. Violators risk hefty fines for their noncompliance.

While Iran imposes *hijab* on all women, Muslims and non-Muslims alike, Turkey lies at the other end of the spectrum, with a strict ban on Muslim veils (*tesettür*) in all government spaces. And yet, Iran and Turkey used to have similar legislation in the early twentieth century when both countries mandated the unveiling of women. They have differed in their approach to Muslim women's dress only since the 1979 Iranian Revolution.

A decade before the Shah banned the *chador*, Mustafa Kemal Atatürk, the first president of the Republic of Turkey, had undertaken wideranging Westernizing and modernizing reforms throughout the country (1924–38). For Atatürk, *hijab* was a sign of backwardness and a major obstacle to the progress of the Turkish Republic and its secularization. While he never banned the Muslim veil outright, he undertook various initiatives to strongly discourage its adoption (see chapter 7).

Turkey began to officially regulate the wearing of *hijab* in the 1970s and has prohibited civil servants from wearing religious attire at work ever since. In 1982, a headscarf ban was formally instituted in Turkish universities, requiring female students to wear "modern" dress. The ban soon spread to other public spaces, including the military, the courts, and the parliament. One of the unexpected consequences of this ban has been a drop in the total number of female students attending Turkish universities. This became especially noticeable in the 1990s, when middle- and upper-class students wishing to wear *hijab* emigrated to other countries (often in Europe but also the United States) to gain an education.[4]

While the ban on headscarves remains in place since the 2011 reelection of the Islamically oriented Adalet and Kalkınma Partisi (AKP, Justice and Development Party), it is no longer implemented in most Turkish universities. Efforts to introduce legislation that would actually permit elected officials and civil employees to wear some type of *hijab* are still being considered.

The examples of Iran and Turkey provide clear evidence that veiling has never been uniformly, strictly, or fully enforced in any Muslim-majority society since the birth of Islam in the seventh century (except perhaps Saudi Arabia). They also indicate that veiling has never been adopted solely for religious or spiritual reasons, but that politics and history play an equally significant role in the imposition or banning of veiling in different societies.

LOCAL MEANINGS AND SOCIOCULTURAL PRACTICES OF VEILING

Veiling has local and sociocultural meanings as well. At times, such meanings are more significant than religion or politics, and they are the ones that determine if and how some Muslim women veil. This is the case in the majority of Muslim-majority societies today.

In countries such as Bangladesh, Egypt, Indonesia, Jordan, Lebanon, Malaysia, Mali, Morocco, and Senegal, for example, no legislation prescribes veiling practices. Women have the freedom to choose whether and how to veil. Because of the prevalence of Islam and the lack of governmental regulations on veiling, these countries offer the greatest diversity in Muslim attire. Many of the variations are due to local customs, age, education, social class, familial and group background, profession, and, at times, peer pressure.

While Muslims generally agree that they ought to dress modestly and that the purpose of *hijab* is to reflect this modesty in both men and women, they disagree widely about the meaning, exact form, shape, or color of that *hijab*. Each society, each community, and each individual interprets the Qur'anic injunction to be modest, to hide one's charms, differently, and thus carries out the goal of not drawing attention to the self differently. What is considered appropriately modest clothing in one region, community, or even family may be wholly unacceptable in others.

We should also remember that veiling in some Muslim-majority societies is not exclusively a female practice. At times, men are the ones who traditionally cover their bodies and faces. Such is the case with some North African Tuareg tribes where men are dressed in a light blue dress and their heads and faces are entirely covered, revealing only the eyes. This veil, called *tagelmust*, marks men's fertility, masculinity, and modesty.[5] Tuareg women, on the other hand, do not cover their faces and usually wrap only a loose scarf around their heads.

As far as women's veiling is concerned, in most societies, veiling is practiced by adapting indigenous clothing traditions. Many customs of dress evolved independently of Islam, but have, over time, become fused with Islamic teachings. In countries where women are permitted to wear whatever they choose, many continue to wear what their foremothers have worn for centuries.

For example, the Pakistani *shalwar qamis* and the Indian *sari* are traditions from South Asia that have become, in some areas and with time, normative Muslim attires. The *shalwar qamis* is worn by both men and women and consists of pants, the *shalwar* (baggy or straight legged), worn with a matching knee-long tunic (*qamis*); women add a matching long scarf (*dupatta*) over one shoulder. The *sari* has been the traditional costume of India for thousands of years. Its form has evolved over time, but in its present variety, it is made of a cloth measuring 5.5 yards by 1 yard, worn over a long petticoat and blouse.

Both the Pakistani *shalwar qamis* and the Indian *sari* have traditionally been worn by *all* South Asians, be they Parsis (South Asian Zoroastrians), Hindus, Christians, or Muslims. South Asian Muslims from rural areas in Gujarat and South India often pull the tail end of their *saris* over the head, in lieu of a headscarf, as a sign of modesty and during ritual prayers. Other Muslims from India tend to add a headscarf that matches their *saris*.

Similarly, some Senegalese women have started assigning a religious (Islamic) meaning to their traditional clothing. The *boubou* and *grand boubou* are large, baggy garments with elongated armholes made of imported cotton batik and a matching headscarf, known as *moussor*. The *boubou* is worn by both men and women, by Muslims and Christians, and by adherents of local African religions. The *moussor* is traditionally a required item for married women of all religions. Because the *boubou* covers the entire body and does not show a woman's shape, and because the *moussor* covers the woman's hair, these clothing items have been taken by some to fulfill the basic requirements of *hijab*. In this way, a cultural style of dress has become a religious type of attire.

Afghan women at Mazzar-i-Sharif's Blue Mosque, 2004 (Courtesy of Sharron Lovell)

In Afghanistan, the *burqa* that covers the woman's entire body and head, with a mesh screening the eyes, is a regional style of female clothing characteristic of the Pashtun ethnic group. The *burqa* had existed in that region well before the advent of Islam and was the mode of dress worn by respectable women of any social class. After the Taliban took over Afghanistan in the 1990s, its use became more widespread and was imposed on women as the most, if not the only, religiously appropriate

Politics and Sociocultural Practices **61**

attire. In other words, the *burqa* represents a cultural practice more than "authentic" Islamic attire. If it were otherwise, it would not make sense that many Afghan women continued to wear the *burqa* even after the Taliban's departure and Afghanistan's "liberation" by the United States in 2001. They were simply continuing to wear what they had always worn.

The diversity of societies and cultures in which Islam is practiced means that there is no universal agreement as to what *hijab* is or how to observe modesty. If in some areas the *burqa* indeed represents the conventional style of veiling, in other communities, *hijab* is understood to be a simple scarf (at times sheer) either tied underneath the chin or wrapped back around the neck. For some Muslims, a veil needs simply to cover the hair, while for others, it must also cover the neck and ears. At times, the veil is a long scarf that covers the hair, ears, and drapes over the neck and shoulders. In some regions and for more traditional women, *hijab* refers to the head cover and loose overcoat (*abaya*) worn over home or street clothes and covering the woman's entire head and body. The most conservative believe that to observe *hijab*, women must also wear gloves to cover their hands and thick socks to cover their ankles.

Many veiled women choose to wear a bandana or a bonnet underneath their headscarves to ensure full coverage of their hair and that the scarf will not slip during the day. Others may (purposefully or not) let a few strands of hair or full bangs show. The addition of a face veil in countries where women have the freedom of choice with regard to veiling is a much less common phenomenon, though its adoption is certainly on the rise (see chapters 7 and 8).

There is no universal agreement among Muslims as to whether *hijab* should be worn only outside when venturing into public space or when interacting with men, or whether it should be donned at all times, including inside one's home. There is also no agreement about whether more veiling is always commensurate with deeper piety, and no consensus on the most appropriate color or shape of a *hijab*, or the age at which veiling ought to commence.

In many countries, older and more conservative women prefer dark *hijabs* and thus opt for black, dark blue, brown, or gray *abayas*. In some African societies, girls start wearing their *hijab* at a very young age, while in others, girls veil only after puberty. In other countries still, such as in Oman, Yemen, and the United Arab Emirates, only married women

Women from Oman wearing metal *burgu* (face veil) (Photo by author)

Leather *lithma* (face veil) from the Gulf region (Photo by author)

commonly veil, and older women wear a metal or leather mask (*burgu* or *batula, lithma*) in lieu of a face veil.

Besides the sober colors of *hijab* that some pious women prefer, many choose the full range of color schemes, including bright, patterned, embroidered, or sheer fabrics. In many societies, women take off the head cover once they reach menopause, or after their child-bearing age, while others continue to wear it throughout their lives.

In our globalized world, sartorial traditions, concepts of female modesty, and even attitudes toward gender are also increasingly imported from one culture into another, often transforming local clothing traditions. Female migrant workers from Southeast Asia, Indonesia, and Sri Lanka who are employed in the Arabian Peninsula and the Gulf States, for example, increasingly return home dressed in recognizably Arab-style *abayas*, *niqabs*, and conservative headgear.

Similarly, the families of a large number of Egyptians who worked and lived in Saudi Arabia and the Gulf in the 1970s and 1980s, following the open-door economic policy introduced by President Anwar el-Sadat, brought back new clothing customs. Today, it is not uncommon to see Egyptian women wearing black Saudi or Saudi-like *abayas* on the streets of Cairo or other metropolitan cities. Such attire, now increasingly adopted because of its convenience and availability in lower-cost versions, often serves to visually mark veiled women as pious or as part of Egypt's growing class of nouveaux riches.

Abayas are also increasingly adopted in Sanaa (Yemen), though with a different meaning than in Saudi Arabia. Whereas Saudi women wear *abayas* because it is government-mandated attire, Yemeni women in the capital have adopted it as a modern, freely chosen form of dress that offers them much more practicality and ease of movement than their more elaborate traditional clothing. Likewise, Senegalese urban women are increasingly replacing their customary scarves (*moussor*) with Saudi-type *abayas* and wrap-around head veils.

Since the late 1990s, Iranian-style *chadors* have also been introduced into the Sudan as a result of the newly imposed governmental clothing regulations. These *chadors* are increasingly replacing the Sudanese traditional dress, the *tobe*, an eleven-yard-long, loose, wrap-around cotton dress for centuries worn by Sudanese women.

These imported clothing traditions, access to international media, the Internet, and long-distance travel, as well as a greater awareness about Muslim practices throughout the world have worked together to stimulate local fashion industries and transform home cultures. They have established the more conservative types of head and full-body veils in other Muslim-majority countries where women's clothing had traditionally been less conservative.

The cross-fertilization of cultures has had the effect of homogenizing Muslim dress and of erasing some of the diverse histories and identities of Muslims. Often Muslims themselves forget or become unaware of the erasure of their cultural specificities, thus unwittingly contributing to the construction of an imagined unified Muslimness in terms of dress, identity, and culture.

Nevertheless, and despite the rise of more conservative styles of Muslim dress throughout the world, it is important to remember that veiling is not a monolithic practice. Rather, it runs the gamut from the most conservatively dressed women in black to the most glamorously clothed women "Islamifying" the latest European fashion with a matched scarf barely covering the hair.

All these different types of veiling practices fall under the umbrella of *hijab*, and each vies to assert itself as a valid, if not the most "authentic," expression of religious identity. Yet despite some conservative groups' insistence, none of these veils is more authentically Islamic than another. They all simply represent sociocultural traditions, each reflecting different conceptions about female modesty that often stem from a regionally specific history of sartorial practice.

SOCIAL PRESSURES OR CHOICE TO VEIL?

Even in those countries without legislation either imposing or banning the veil, some Muslim women face social and cultural pressures to adopt *hijab*. This is not to say that Muslim women never adopt *hijab* of their own volition; of course, many of them do (see chapters 2 and 7). To understand this, we must first examine and redefine the concept of choice.

Choice is often associated with an American style of individualism that stems from the tradition of political liberalism. But choice is not universally just about individual desires. It can also imply allegiance to a larger community. In societies that emphasize group allegiance over individualism (and this is the case in many Muslim-majority societies), choice is not about doing what one wants, independently of the group, but about adopting what is best for the group. Affiliating oneself with the community is not considered a coercive imposition but rather a rational, voluntarily chosen act of morality.

Therefore, when I say that some Muslim women adopt veiling by choice, I mean two things simultaneously. On the one hand, I mean that some women choose modest clothing after much deliberation and soul searching. Their decision, independently reached, resembles the meaning of choice in Euro-American societies. But I also mean choice in the sense that some Muslim women choose to follow what their family, friends, or community do and that they would feel out of place if they acted differently. These women do not experience the adoption of their family's traditions or wishes as coercion or compulsion, but rather as their way of asserting their sense of belonging and of claiming their place within the community.

This explains why some young Muslim women report that they started wearing *hijab* voluntarily in their mid- to late teens because it made them feel "grown-up" and taken seriously by their families and neighbors. Others say they adopted *hijab* voluntarily after a life-changing event (usually a death, marriage, or pilgrimage to Mecca), because they felt they had to conform henceforth to social expectations of a later stage of life.

While some may consider such reasoning indirect forms of pressure, this is not how many Muslims experience or describe their decision to veil. This is not to say that there are no pressures to veil among Muslims. There are. In fact, evidence of direct pressures to veil is omnipresent in Muslim-majority societies. It is visible on the advertisements, posters, or bumper stickers seen on store windows, at bus and metro stops, or in the graffiti painted on street walls that display well-known Qurʾanic verses or *hadith* mandating the veiling of women. At times, such ads proffer popular proverbs on women's modesty or offer lessons on "correct" *hijab* styles. Some warn women of eternal hell fire and damnation if they do not heed their teachings.

A friend of mine shared with me a poster she saw displayed everywhere in Beirut in 2007, titled "Campaign to correct *hijab*."[6] The top part of the poster portrays a woman covered in a long and ample dress with a head cover that comes down to her wrists. Next to it is a caption in Arabic that asserts that this is the "right" type of *hijab*, one that is not transparent and does not show a woman's body form.

Underneath this image are three other sketches, each showing "wrong" types of *hijab*: a woman wearing tight jeans, a woman wearing a long skirt with a shape-revealing long-sleeved shirt, and a woman wearing a headscarf wrapped around the head and the neck. The caption this time is given in both Arabic and English, stating "this is not *hijab*." Perhaps the creator of this poster assumed that women who wear Westernized clothes (tight jeans, shape-revealing shirts, or small headscarves) are more likely to understand English, the language of improper clothing culture.

Because this poster (like the bumper stickers or ads on the windows of buses and trains) is anonymous, it is unclear who sponsored it and from whom stemmed the social pressure to veil. Yet the power of such advertisements cannot be underestimated. Like ads in any country, the veiling ads work surreptitiously to change people's minds and make them turn to veiling, seemingly entirely out of personal choice.

VOICES OF RESISTANCE: BAD *HIJAB* AND ALTERNATE *HIJAB*

Whenever Muslim women have been forced to either adopt or shed their *hijab*, they have not remained passively submissive to governmental legislation or indirect social pressures. Rather, they have found ways to resist and assert their individuality and voices.

In Iran, for instance, and at least since the government of President Mohammad Khatami (1997–2005), there has been increased resistance to veiling laws particularly among the younger generation. This resistance to forced veiling practices and to the clerical obsession with female hair is known as "bad *hijab*." It is *bad* because it is a style of dress or *hijab* that conservative Muslims view as inappropriate and immodest. Younger Iranians, however, are reclaiming this bad *hijab* and elevating it to a new, fashionable style of covering.

Bad *hijab* consists of a shape-concealing coat (*manteau*) or of a shorter, colorful, and shape-revealing overcoat (*maghnaé*). Bad *hijab* also includes brightly colored, patterned, and at times transparent scarves that let a few strands of highlighted hair stray out. These new styles of *hijab*, commonly seen on the streets of every major city in Iran and openly defying the morality police, obey the letter but not always the spirit of covering a woman's body modestly.

In addition, the rise of the Muslim fashion industry and the proliferation of Muslim haute couture shows can be considered a form of bad *hijab* (see chapter 8). Similarly, the number of cosmetic surgeries and the consumption rate of cosmetics in Iran are all part of this social movement of resistance to the imposed black Iranian *chador*. Muslim women are far from passively submitting to governmental impositions and legislation.

Since the late 1990s, a similar movement of resistance has cropped up in Turkey, where female students are increasingly affirming their right to religious expression. They are no longer letting the governmental ban on *hijab* deter them from observing what some view as their religious duty

Turkish students "accessorizing" their *hijabs* by wearing
a hat over the scarf, 2009 (Photo by author)

and their human right to observe the mandates of their faith. This move-ment of resistance has taken different forms in different places. Some of the best-publicized examples have included completely shaved heads and the covering of hair with blonde, 1960s-style wigs. Both acts were intended to challenge the ban on veiling by bypassing or transcending it altogether.

When I was conducting research in Turkey in the summer of 2009, I witnessed another fascinating manifestation of Turkish students' resis-tance to the veiling ban. At the University of Marmara's School of The-ology (located on the eastern side of Istanbul), I saw female students wearing headscarves with woolen caps over them. I was told that the uni-versity's administration had adopted this measure to address the great drop in the enrollment of female students. University administrators had introduced a policy that allowed female students to attend school wearing a veil as long as it was "accessorized" (the administration's own term) with a hat. When worn in this fashion, the school administration argued, the cap cancelled the religious meaning of the headscarf and rendered it technically a modern, secular accessory. Police agents are posted at the university entrance gates to enforce this policy of accessorized veiling. Such negotiations show the flexibility and imagination that form part of veiling practices in contemporary societies.

ANXIETY ABOUT THE *NIQAB* AND *BURQA*

While most Muslims acknowledge covering one's hair as a religious duty, many have strong, often negative, feelings about the face veil, whether it is a *niqab* or *burqa*. They believe that the face veil is not an Islamic prescription, but rather a cultural tradition from certain geographical areas (notably, from Pashtun areas in Pakistan and Afghanistan, and from the Gulf region) that has been superimposed on Islam and fused with its teachings. To substantiate their condemnation, they point to the fact that wearing a face veil is forbidden during the pilgrimage to Mecca (*hajj*). They also assert that the face veil signals an extremist, radical interpretation of Islam, and they tend to be wary of those who cover their face in the name of Islam.

There are many jokes that circulate in Egypt about women who wear the *niqab* or *burqa*. Many are published in daily newspapers with or without cartoons and relished by younger and older people alike. One such joke comments on people's reactions when seeing a woman wearing a black *burqa*: "Which part of her is the front and which is her back?" Another one that surfaced as I was completing this book was made in the context of the removal of Mohamed Morsi from Egypt's presidency in July 2013 and the flight of key members of the Muslim Brotherhood. This joke comments on Mohammad Badie, the brotherhood's spiritual leader, who had disappeared for fear of arrest and who was rumored to have escaped wearing a *burqa*: Badie suddenly hears another woman calling him by his name. Shocked at being discovered, he asks her how she recognized him. She responds, "that is because I am al-Shater." (Khairat al-Shater is the Muslim Brotherhood's second in command.) While such jokes may offend some and shock others, they voice the anxiety some Muslims feel around women whose entire bodies and eyes are covered.

In an illustrated book now translated into several European languages and titled *Burqa!*, Simona Bassano di Tuffilo, an Italian artist, drew twenty-four illustrations to accompany a short piece written by Jamila Mujahed, an Afghan journalist. The text describes Mujahed's experience as a woman before and after the takeover of Afghanistan by the Taliban. The story tells of her difficulties at the news that she had to stop work and wear a *burqa*, her challenges learning to wear it and walk around covered from head to toe, and the violence against women perpetrated by the Taliban that she witnessed on the streets.

The illustrations in the book depict some of the ironic social consequences of all women wearing the *burqa*. In one of the illustrations, for instance, a small terrorized boy searches for his mother in a room full of women all dressed alike, screaming, "Mommy!" In another, two women in *burqas* speak to each other, one of them asking, "Who are you?," and the other responding, "Your sister." And in a third one, one woman in a *burqa* says to another, "Sorry to be late, I did not know what to wear."

Other illustrations focus on men's hypocrisy when they force women to wear the *burqa*, on the one hand, and then, on the other, take advantage of women's anonymity to flirt with them with impunity. My favorite is the one in which two men attend an event full of women in *burqas*. They look around with concern and say, "You never know if your wife is observing you."

I enjoy these cartoons because they humanize both men and women who act in recognizable ways, whether in a Muslim-majority society or in a Muslim-minority one. I also enjoy them because they voice genuine questions and thoughts that many people have when faced with a woman whose face is covered.

I am not unfamiliar with such questions. I have often had mixed feelings about women who wear a *niqab* or *burqa*. I even admit to having felt some anxiety when I encountered women who wore ultra-conservative styles of veiling. I understand why many non-Muslims (and some Muslims) are afraid of women in *niqabs* and *burqas*, or why they perceive them as passive and oppressed.

I have, however, been powerfully challenged in my own thinking since the news coverage of the Arab Spring, or the 2011 revolutions that rocked the Arab world. I have been struck by the way some Arab and Muslim women have been portrayed during the various Arab revolutions and until today. Many of the women who appeared on newscasts and who expressed strong political views against Arab dictators and offered sophisticated analyses were veiled. Some of them wore the *niqab*.

Such images have made me question some of my own presuppositions about women who chose to cover their faces. These women could not be labeled as ultra-conservative or cast away as brainwashed. And they were certainly not silent or submissive. In fact, these women surprised

Cartoon of *burqa* 1: child calling for his "Mommy," 2007
(from Jamila Mujahed and Simona Bassano di Tuffilo, *Burqa!*, Rome:
Donzelli editore, 2007; courtesy of Carmine Donzelli)

me and the world. These were revolutionary women who did not let men speak for them and who were not shy to speak their minds in front of national and international cameras. It did not matter how they were dressed and what their faith was. What mattered were their staunch beliefs and political actions.

So today, when I see a woman wearing the *burqa*, I recall news coverage of women during the Arab Spring and remind myself that a woman who wears the most conservative style of *niqab* or *burqa* still has a mind, a political perspective, and a voice. The *niqab*, like the *burqa*, may cover her face and head, but it does not cover her mind.

Cartoon of *burqa* 2: two anxious men, 2007 (from Jamila Mujahed and Simona Bassano di Tuffilo, *Burqa!*, Rome: Donzelli editore, 2007; courtesy of Carmine Donzelli)

■ The various examples described above show that contrary to what many people assume, no single type of Muslim veil has ever been embraced by all Muslims at any time in history. There is no such thing as an "authentic" *hijab* and no such thing as a singular proper way of veiling.

Instead, there is great diversity in Muslim women's veiling practices, a diversity of styles of clothing all referred to by the same term, *hijab*: this is a product of transnational trends, the Arabization of Islamic terminology, the development of fashion, and socioeconomic changes among Muslims in the world. At times, these veiling styles closely resemble one another; at other times, they significantly differ from one another. There is also much shading in veiling practices depending on factors such as politics, history, geography, and sociocultural traditions.

These elements play a central role and often explain more fully some reasons behind the practice of veiling. They also clarify why Muslim women veil in such divergent ways around the globe. In the next chapters, I will explore many other historical, political, social, and economic reasons that are equally important for an even deeper and richer understanding of Muslim veiling practices.

PART TWO

Veiling in Euro-American Societies

This section focuses on current debates about the veil in Euro-American societies. These discussions can best be understood when contextualized in their long historical and political lineages. For this reason, I begin this section with a chapter on veiling during the nineteenth century, a period marked by European imperial incursions into and control over much of the Middle East. European views of Muslim-majority societies and of veiled Muslim women of this time period have a profound impact on the way these topics are understood today.

As we will see, the period of colonialism introduced and popularized a set of stereotypes and leitmotifs associated with Islamic veiling. It was then that the veil first became viewed as a symbol for Muslim women's subordination to and imprisonment by Muslim male tyrants. It was then also that veiled Muslim women became depicted as available, eager, and acquiescing sexual partners in European and American male sexual fantasies. The veiling of Muslim women quickly became one of the central justifications for the European civilizing mission, as well as for continued military incursions in the Middle East.

The goal of this section is to highlight the continuities between past imperialist visions and contemporary controversies. Chapter 4 on veils, harems, and the civilizing mission will thus serve as an introduction to the following two chapters, which examine veiling in Europe (chapter 5) and veiling in the United States (chapter 6).

Whilst he was thus swallowed up with grief, an object presented itself to his view, which quickly turned his thoughts another way. A secret gate of the sultan's palace opened all of a sudden, and there came out at it twenty women, in the midst of whom marched the sultaness, who was easily distinguished from the rest, by her majestic air. This princess, thinking that the king of Tartary was gone a-hunting with his brother the sultan, came up with her retinue near the windows of his apartment, for the prince had placed himself so, that he could see all that passed in the garden, without being perceived himself. He observed, that the persons who accompanied the sultaness threw off their veils and long robes, that they might be at more freedom; but he was wonderfully surprised when he saw ten of them blacks and that each of them took his mistress . . .

Modesty will not allow, nor is it necessary, to relate what passed betwixt the blacks and the ladies. . . . This amorous company continued together till midnight, and having bathed altogether in a great pond . . . , they dressed themselves, and re-entered the palace by the secret door. —*Arabian Nights*, prologue

CHAPTER FOUR

Veils, Harems, and the
Mission to Civilize

This scene, excerpted from the prologue of *Arabian Nights*,[1] has contributed much to the way Muslim women, veiled ones especially, have been perceived in Euro-American societies since at least the early eighteenth century. This fictional tale, like many others from the same collection, was received as truth by its European audiences and considered a factual representation of what veiled Muslim women are like and what veiling means for Muslims.

The scene reproduced here tells the story of Shahzenan, Shahrayar's younger brother, spying on his sister-in-law, the sultaness, while she is in her private garden with her retinue. The reader assumes this group to be entirely composed of women, since they are all veiled.

Contrary to our expectation, however, the twenty fully veiled figures who appear in this scene turn out not to be all women. In fact, only half of them are. The other half are men dressed as veiled women so as to be safely allowed inside the women's private quarters. In Middle Eastern culture, such female-only private space inside the home is what the term "harem" denotes.

Looking into this harem, Shahzenan is positioned as a voyeur, a peeping Tom who relishes watching a forbidden scene. His experience partly teaches him, as well as the reader, that a harem is not just a private women's space but also, especially, a space of liberal sexual encounter. From this scene, he learns that veiling conceals erotic possibilities, that a veiled woman is never what she appears to be, and that underneath her full-body covering lies the fulfillment of his male fantasies. The veils that Shahzenan sees are remarkable because they can be so easily removed. The harem to which he is privy is what Europeans and Americans will come to assume it is: a titillating sexual orgy.

Since the translation and publication of *Arabian Nights* in the early eighteenth century by the French diplomat Antoine Galland until today, the erotic and sexual dimensions of veiling have formed an integral part of the Euro-American popular imaginary. This text popularized the idea that veiled Muslim women were available, eager, and acquiescing sexual partners in Western male sexual fantasies.

Veiled Muslim women were imagined to be, like the sultaness and her retinue in this scene, locked up in harems where they passed their time with forbidden pleasures while awaiting their liberation from brown men by white men. Their veils, rather than protecting their modesty, had the sole purpose of heightening men's sexual desire and were thus only too willingly cast off.

These Euro-American fantasies were not just based on *Arabian Nights*. They became an integral part of all cultural productions of the nineteenth century in Europe and increasingly in the United States. They were reaffirmed in political documents and diplomatic missives, as well as in travel narratives, paintings, photographs, posters, operas, belly dancing choreographies, and early Hollywood films. Under European and American pens and paint brushes, on postcards and in front of Hollywood cameras, the meaning of Muslim veiling was voided of spirituality and faith and instead made replete with sexual fantasies, erotic fulfillment, and prospects of penetration and possession.

NINETEENTH-CENTURY PAINTINGS
OF VEILED MUSLIM WOMEN

Middle Eastern women with veils and the imagined interiors of harems were undoubtedly European and American artists' favorite scenes of the Middle East throughout the nineteenth century. This artistic output is part of a huge canon of works called "orientalist," a concept made especially famous by Edward Said's 1978 book *Orientalism*. By this term, Said referred to the system of knowledge, the scientific discourses that Europe created to speak, learn about, and ultimately to control its Middle Eastern ("oriental") territories.

Painting served as one of these pseudo-scientific discourses, along with anthropology, ethnography, linguistics, and biology. It was art, of course, but it also supported the hegemonic project of the developing European empire and helped sustain its military interests in the Middle East and in Muslim-majority societies.

Art was often sponsored by European monarchs (Napoleon being a prime example) as a means of illustrating their military successes overseas and to depict, for those who did not travel, what imperial possessions and colonial subjects looked like. Art justified imperial military incursions and established the moral superiority of Europe over its colonies.

In the orientalist painting tradition, veiling became a recurring metaphor, a visual shorthand for invoking the Middle East, for signaling its ultimate otherness, and for speaking about Muslim women, all the while enhancing the overall exoticism and seductiveness of any imaginative work. Unveiling Oriental Muslim women became the obsession of visual artists, most of them male.

No orientalist painting of the nineteenth century has had as much influence on Euro-American views of veiled Muslim women as Eugène Delacroix's *Femmes d'Alger dans leur appartement* (*Algerian Women in Their Apartment*), which established certain motifs and themes that quickly became canonical. This painting, completed in 1834, a mere four years after France colonized Algeria, is housed today in the Louvre Museum in Paris.

Delacroix's painting represents an Algerian harem. In nineteenth-century Europe, the harem was understood as a private space where many women were available for the sexual gratification of one man. In this case, we see three women sitting passively in the luxurious private

Delacroix, *Algerian Women in Their Apartment*, 1834
(© RMN–Grand Palais / Art Resource, NY)

setting of their home while a black slave draws back a curtain. The door left ajar in the background, like the slave's drawing back the curtain and revealing the three harem women, emphasizes the overall sensuality and exoticism of the scene. Such a representation echoes the fantasies established at least since Galland's translation of *Arabian Nights*.

Delacroix's allegedly authentic representation of an Algerian harem is based on the contentious claim that during his five-month travels in Morocco and Algeria in 1832, when he was accompanying the Comte de Mornay's diplomatic mission, he received privileged, if not secret, access to a real harem. The artist is considered to be the first male painter to have ever had such access, and the first one to represent a harem based on a supposed eyewitness experience.

The harem functions here as a metaphorical veil that hides Oriental women from view and that Delacroix successfully uncovers for the aesthetic and sensual pleasure of his European audience. This metaphorical veil, while titillating European men's forbidden fantasies and inviting them to partake in its pleasures, also stands as a reminder that Oriental women are oppressed behind the walls of the harem. It thus serves to inspire European men to save Oriental women from the alleged despotism of their imagined Oriental husbands. Such a goal was often invoked to justify France's colonizing expeditions and the country's purported civilizing missions.

At first glance, we do not see any veil covering the women's heads or faces. But for a nineteenth-century European audience, with its puritan Victorian sensibilities, the unlaced tops of the women's dresses revealing their necks and bosoms, the pulled-up sleeves of the blouses, and their short pants connoted naked female bodies. The Algerian women painted here may thus appear distant and mysterious to us, but they were in fact decidedly available and accessible to the penetrating gaze of the contemporary European artist and viewer.

As was the case in most other orientalist paintings of the period, fascination with Muslim women and their veils is invoked here through its opposite, the persistent desire to unveil, to uncover, to reveal. Muslim women were thus regularly represented through the metaphor of the harem or that of the veil: either a veil that hid women from view or, more often, a veil discarded to reveal more plainly what lay underneath it.

Delacroix played a central role in defining the parameters of representing Middle Eastern women artistically. In his works, like in the orientalist painting tradition as a whole, there was an unquestioned assumption that women who lived in the Middle East formed a homogeneous group of Muslims who shared certain stable characteristics. They were all thought to be overly sexual and seductive at the same time that they suffered at the hands of tyrannical men and an oppressive culture and religion. The prime symbols of Muslim women's eroticism and oppression were the veil and the harem. Any European or American artist had to repeat these themes if their work was to be successful.[2] Orientalism relied more on repetition than it did on originality.

Jean-Auguste-Dominique Ingres's *Le bain turc* (*The Turkish Bath*), completed in 1862 and today also housed at the Louvre, follows in the same tradition. Like Delacroix, Ingres depicts a scene he is unlikely to have witnessed: Turkish (Muslim) women's baths. Baths are of course as private as harems, if not more so. They are by definition off limits to *any* man, and certainly to any *foreign* man.

Ingres's depiction of the Turkish women, like Delacroix's of Algerian women, is striking because none of the women portrayed bears a traditional Middle Eastern phenotype: most of the painted Turkish and Algerian women have fair skin and blue eyes. While some Algerian and Turkish women certainly have such features, Ingres's and Delacroix's decisions to portray the women as fair with blue eyes cannot be attributed to cultural sensitivity or a desire to avoid homogenizing their subjects. Rather, this portrayal is most likely based on the fact that they, like other European artists, either did not use a live subject or used a European one, even as they endeavored to paint Oriental scenes.

Besides, Ingres, unlike Delacroix, never traveled to the Middle East, despite his multiple paintings on the subject. In that he is not alone. Many European and American painters did not shy away from painting the Middle East and Muslim women's private quarters without ever setting foot there. It was sufficient to reproduce the established metaphors and fixed motifs. That alone gave one authority to speak about, represent, and paint the Orient.

Ingres's *Turkish Bath* is based on a well-known account written by an English aristocrat, Lady Mary Wortley Montagu, in the early eighteenth century. Lady Montagu had traveled to Istanbul with her ambassador husband from 1716 to 1718 and from there had sent many letters to friends and family. Lady Montagu had written copiously to her daughter and described in great detail the customs of the Turks. She was reportedly the first European woman to truly have had access to Muslim women's private quarters, including harems and baths. Her letters thus became extremely famous and were a key source of inspiration to later male and female travelers to the Middle East and to orientalist artists generally.

Like most of his contemporaries, Ingres had read Lady Montagu's *Letters from Turkey*, and in fact copied some passages from her letters as early as 1825. Today, his *Turkish Bath* is considered an artistic rendition of Montagu's letter number 27 to her daughter, Lady Mar, on April 1, 1717, in which she depicts her own experience visiting a Turkish bath.

In her eyewitness account, Lady Montagu describes many fine-looking naked women "in different postures, some in conversation, some working, others drinking coffee or sherbet, and many negligently lying on their cushions while their slaves (generally pretty girls of seventeen or eighteen) were employed in braiding their hair in several pretty manners." Yet she is quick to point out that despite the presence of so many naked women, "there was not the least wanton smile or immodest gesture among them."[3] By this admission alone, Lady Montagu's observation and her depiction of Turkish women's baths differ strikingly from Ingres's painting.

Ingres indeed transforms Lady Montagu's description where there was "no wanton smile or immodest gesture" into a scene replete with precisely that. In his artistic rendition, the Turkish women are lying in sexually compromising positions with one another, and many engage in what appear to be lesbian sexual encounters. In the orientalist painting tradition, depictions of Middle Eastern women are conflated with suggestions of unbridled sexuality.

It is also interesting to note how in Ingres's painting, women's nudity contrasts with their elaborate headdresses. The contrast between the women's naked bodies and their veiled heads reminds us that nineteenth-century European *male* artists and viewers were less interested in the veil itself than in what lay underneath it.

The obsessive desire to paint the private quarters of Oriental women and to unveil both this private space and the women's bodies can be understood as a thinly veiled European desire to enjoy their sexual favors. The very shape of the *Turkish Bath* painting points to this unspoken yearning: the round canvas evokes a peephole, placing the viewer in the position of a voyeur who is penetrating a scene from which he was excluded. Looking at the women in their baths, we are in the same position as Shahzenan in *Arabian Nights*.

Veiled Muslim women were not just uncovered and exposed by European and American painters. They were treated similarly by *any* artist, no matter what medium he or she worked in. In other words, photography and film, despite their claims to capture more authentic and immediate moments and scenes, simply repeated and reinforced the same stereotypes and motifs we find in the orientalist painting tradition.

EARLY TWENTIETH-CENTURY PHOTOGRAPHS AND POSTCARDS

Muslim women and their veils remained an endless source of captivation and inspiration for artists at the turn of the twentieth century. Technological advances gave rise to new media that helped fuel, popularize, and spread stereotypes of Oriental women. By the 1880s, the postcard became one of the key new art forms through which images of the Orient circulated around the Mediterranean and soon thereafter across the Atlantic.

Because they were cheap to reproduce and purchase, light to transport, and easy to understand, postcards successfully reached a wide-ranging audience comprising all social classes. They visually communicated the supposed essences of colonial subjects and foreign people. They also focused on riveting differences between cultures, especially where women were concerned. In the process, they helped to reaffirm the hegemonic project of empire.

Like the nineteenth-century paintings that preceded them, postcards of the early twentieth century repeatedly reproduced images of veiled and, more often, unveiled North African women. An interesting group of such postcards was taken in Algeria between 1900 and 1930, during the heyday of French colonization, and sent back to France by French soldiers, colonizers, and tourists to report on their stay or vacations in Algeria.

In 1981, the Franco-Algerian scholar Malek Alloula compiled and published for the first time a selection of these photographs in a book titled *Le harem colonial* (*The Colonial Harem*). The collection is suggestively subtitled *Images d'un sous-érotisme* (*Images of a Sub-eroticism*). This is because most of the postcards conform to the leitmotifs that orientalist painters had established decades earlier. They represent Algerian women in some state of undress, of eroticism, and also as dominated and oppressed. Photos and postcards, which one may have expected to offer a more authentic view of their subject matter, in fact conveyed the same stereotypes as orientalist painting. Their goal was to objectify, homogenize, and titillate rather than to inform.

Postcards of hyperveiled women—that is, of women covered in layers of clothes from head to toe—circulated widely even as they appeared to defy the photographer's and the audience's voyeuristic gaze. Such images were as prevalent as those that depicted a woman whose veil had conveniently fallen off at the very moment the photographer took the picture. Many other postcards portray women behind bars, as though imprisoned in their homes and crying out to Europeans for help and liberation. The most disturbing image to me and to my students is unquestionably that of a woman entirely veiled but whose breasts shockingly and shamelessly protrude from her cloak.

There is little doubt that the large, sagging breasts of the woman in this photograph would have been considered at once pornographic and repulsive, seductive and dangerous by European audiences. They would have brought to mind visual representations of witches' and old women's breasts that had been common in Europe since at least the sixteenth century and that evoked danger and fear.[4]

For a European or an American who has never traveled abroad, who has never seen a veiled Muslim woman, and who is relying on the allegedly authentic depictions afforded by photographs and postcards, the unspoken message of this visual material is clear: Veiled Muslim women are imprisoned and oppressed. Yet they are also sexually available objects, prostitutes, or witches who do not hesitate to shed their veils to tempt and titillate a male audience. Their morality is in jeopardy; they need to be saved by an altruistic European Christian hand.

For many in Europe or America who received these postcards from loved ones abroad, it was undoubtedly difficult to think critically about

Colonial postcard 1 (early 1900s): hyper-veiled Algerian women circulating in public.

(left) Colonial postcard 2 (early 1900s): Algerian woman whose veil and dress have slipped, revealing a breast. No respectable Algerian woman would have posed in this fashion.

(right) Colonial postcard 3 (early 1900s): Algerian woman whose black *burqa* only serves to reveal her breasts, pointing to orientalist men's sexual interest in Muslim women.

this visual material and to realize that photographs, like paintings, can in fact be staged. The images they offered popularized stereotypes rather than giving a truthful representation of Middle Eastern or Muslim women.

In his book, Alloula points out that the women seen on the postcards were neither Muslims nor harem women. Most were prostitutes or orphans, as these were the only ones willing to pose unveiled or half-naked for foreign photographers for pay. The women portrayed on the colonial postcards thus do *not* offer an accurate representation of what Algerian Muslim women were like, even though they were understood as precisely that. They are nothing less than projections of European male fantasies.

Frantz Fanon (1925–61), the well-known psychiatrist and postcolonial thinker, offers us additional ways of understanding these postcards. Speaking about the early stages of the Algerian resistance movement in the mid-twentieth century, he reminds us that French colonial administrators intended to destroy the Algerian capacity to resist by first conquering Algerian women. By forcing Algerian women to unveil under the pretext of "saving them" from their allegedly barbaric and medieval traditions, French occupiers thought they could shame Algerian men, achieve power over them, and ultimately destroy Algerian culture.

In his essay "Algeria Unveiled," Fanon likens this forced unveiling of Algerian women to rape. He writes, "Every veil that fell, every body that became liberated from the traditional embrace of the *haïk*, every face that offered itself to the bold and impatient glance of the occupier, was a negative expression of the fact that Algeria was beginning to deny herself and was accepting the rape of the colonizer."[5] Looking back at the postcards produced from 1900 to the 1930s, we can say that the unveiled women depicted on them represent or foreshadow the rape of Algerian women by French colonizers.

Another series of photographs produced in Algeria in the 1960s portrays again the violence of the colonizers and the symbolic rape of Algerian women. In contrast to the postcards from the 1930s in which women were paid to pose, the photos from the 1960s were of Algerian women who were forced by the French authorities to pose without their head covers.[6]

These photographs, taken by the French photographer Marc Garanger, who was completing his military service in Algeria at the time, were not published as a group until 1982, in a book similar to Alloula's

Colonial Harem. Garanger's book, simply titled *Femmes algériennes 1960* (*Algerian Women, 1960*) was intended to uncover some of the strategies of control and objectification that the French used during their rule of Algeria. It was meant to pay tribute to the courage of the Algerian women whose photos were taken by force.

Garanger recalls thus the events and his own lengthy and forced photo-shooting sessions: "I photographed nearly two thousand people, mainly women, at a rate of two hundred a day. In each village, the postmaster would call up the residents. It was the faces of the women that struck me most. They had no choice. They were forced to unveil and be photographed. They had to sit on a stool, outdoors, in front of the white wall of a house. They glared at me from point-blank range; I was the first to witness their silent but fierce protest."[7]

The forced unveiling of Algerian women during this time serves as a powerful reminder that French colonization functioned through the objectification and silencing of its subjects, particularly its female subjects. Unveiling Muslim women, whether in painting, postcards, or state photography, was a tool of control, of domination, and of degradation. Muslim women were not oppressed by their male family members or by their affiliation with Islam. They were oppressed mainly by the European civilizing mission.

The mandatory unveiling of Algerian women in the 1960s remains a vivid memory in the minds of many Arabs and Muslims living in France today, and they consider the present-day legislation banning the veil and the *burqa* a reiteration of this violent history, a repetition of colonial policies and rule, and therefore an imperialist paternalistic gesture. Evidently, the past remains very much present in the experiences of many Muslims living in Muslim-minority societies today, while the power of photography and the violence of forced unveiling continue to haunt their memories.

EARLY HOLLYWOOD FILMS

Early Hollywood films, produced during the heyday of European imperialism, disseminated the same orientalist (mis)representations of Muslim women that had become established in colonial painting and photography. In film after film from 1900 to the 1950s, Middle Eastern (Oriental) Muslim women were regularly depicted as sensual, sexual, and subjugated by tyrannical husbands and an oppressive culture and religion.

In these films, Western men regularly played the role of saviors and liberators of Oriental women.

The theme of the harem beauty and the trope of "rescue" are central to early Hollywood productions, perpetuating further stereotypes about Muslim women. Douglas Fairbanks, who starred in *The Thief of Bagdad* (1924); Rudolph Valentino, who starred in *The Sheik* (1921) and *Son of the Sheik* (1926); and Bing Crosby, who appeared in *The Road to Morocco* (1934), are iconic figures of the genre and emblematic of the figure of the Western male hero who penetrates the harem to rescue the Oriental beautiful woman from her tyrannical husband. Elvis Presley played a similar role in *Harum Scarum* in 1965, while the 1992 Disney film *Aladdin* may be considered one of the latest renditions of earlier Hollywood stereotypes through its representation of the half-naked Jasmine (and, in fact, also of Aladdin himself).

Tania Kamal Eldin's 1999 documentary film *Hollywood Harems* and Jack Shaheen's 2001 monumental study titled *Reel Bad Arabs: How Hollywood Vilifies a People*, like his more recent *Guilty: Hollywood's Verdict on Arabs after 9/11* (2008), are based on a study of hundreds of Hollywood films from the 1900s until today that have contributed to the perpetuation of stereotypes about Muslims.

Kamal Eldin and Shaheen both point to a consistent pattern of stereotyping and vilifying Arabs and Muslims since the earliest days of Hollywood. The films they review confirm as a central theme the image of the overly sexualized beautiful (and presumably Muslim) woman saved by a heroic European or American man against a desert or harem background.

Shaheen has pointed out that Algerian independence in 1962, the oil embargo of the 1970s, the 1979 Iranian Revolution and hostage crisis, and the Palestinian Intifada of the late 1980s have led to a new image of Muslim women in Hollywood films. Veiled women were no longer the sexually tempting objects whose veils could so easily be cast off when they were rescued from oppression by white males. With increasing frequency, they now emerged as terrorists threatening national security. Underneath their veils, they hid bombs. Gillo Pontecorvo's 1966 neorealist documentary film *The Battle of Algiers* is noteworthy for transforming the traditional filmic representation of veiled Muslim women from sexual and passive objects of desire to active, political members of the resistance. Because veiled women were not subjected to the same invasive body searches as men, many became the *porteuses de feu*—literally,

Pontecorvo, *Battle of Algiers*, 1966 (Courtesy of Kevin Durst, Casbah Entertainment)

those who carried firearms or bombs during the urban guerrilla war that pitted the Algerian National Liberation Front against French colonizers.

The events of 9/11 exacerbated the association of Muslim veiling with violence and the emergence of a threatening, radical form of Islam. In fact, this association has been privileged over others and repeated in various forms in the media and in popular discourse. In film, even if the desire to unveil Muslim women did not entirely disappear, it often gave way to the urgent need to eradicate the danger and menace that Muslims and their veiling practices posed to democratic Western liberal values and societies.

In fact, in *Guilty*, Shaheen concluded that nearly all films produced after 9/11 reaffirmed earlier stereotypes. Post-9/11 films continue to portray Arabs and Muslims as enemies, villains, and quintessential Others. Even in films that have nothing to do with Arabs or Muslims, token characters are inserted to play the role of a villain. Films such as *The Kingdom* (2007), *American Dreamz* (2006), *The Stone Merchant* (2006), *Young Black Stallion* (2003), and *Black Hawk Down* (2002), are just some of the more recent blockbuster titles that have contributed to the further dehumanization of Arabs and Muslims and to a clash-of-civilizations perspective opposing Islam and Euro-American societies.

The impact of films and visual images is enormous. Because films are viewed by many people and because they allow easier access than paintings, for example, the stereotypes they convey are even more powerful. They become more readily internalized and end up becoming part of the collective unconscious that we inherit.

VEILS, HAREMS, AND THE MISSION TO CIVILIZE

Reflecting on the different meanings that veiling has had during the past two centuries in Euro-American societies, it is hard not to be struck by the fact that they are all products of fantasies and anxieties. Whether veiling denotes sexuality and eroticism, oppression and subordination, or threat and radicalism, it seems clear that these meanings have been created as a way of justifying Euro-American imperial projects and of coming to terms with a distinct foreign culture.

Viewing Muslim women as sexually obsessed, as oppressed, or as violent is an implicit strategy to establish the moral, cultural, and spiritual superiority of Euro-American societies where women are presumably liberated, peaceful, and independent. Viewing Islam as a repressive, backward religion justifies the call to combat it and to rescue those who live under its cruel domination.

In fact, the whole debate over the meaning of Muslim veiling and its indelible association with the oppression of women and the backwardness of Muslim societies is one that began in nineteenth-century Europe. Veiling was then one of the central arguments offered in justification of European (French and British) colonial expansion and soon afterward became the key rallying cry around which anticolonial factions formed in Muslim-majority societies.

While European colonizers could have invoked other aspects of Muslim women's lives that might perhaps have warranted an intervention (such as Muslim women's education, health care, poverty, or personal and political disenfranchisement), veiling was identified as the primary site of necessary European involvement. To validate their imperial mission and the colonization of various parts of the Islamic (Ottoman) empire, European colonizers invoked their concern for the lot of Muslim women. The main oppression from which a Muslim woman supposedly suffered was that from her *hijab*, that is, from her seclusion behind a veil and the gender segregation characterizing Middle Eastern societies.

Lord Cromer (1841–1917), who served as the British consul general of Egypt for almost a quarter century (1883–1907), is well known for his many pronouncements on the subject of Muslim women's veiling, on the evils of Islam, and on the alleged degradation of women that this faith promotes. In his view, the practices of veiling and gender segregation constituted "the fatal obstacle" to Egypt's "attainment of that elevation of thought and character which should accompany the introduction of Western civilization." It was, therefore, essential, he argued, that Egyptians "be persuaded or forced into imbibing the true spirit of Western civilization" to achieve "the mental and moral development which he [Cromer] desired for them."[8]

The imperial mission was thus an endeavor undertaken by "white men to save brown women from brown men," as the contemporary feminist Chandra Mohanty has sarcastically observed. By saving Muslim women from Muslim men and by helping them—at times forcing them—to shed their veils, European colonizers argued that they were helping bring about the industrial development of Middle Eastern societies and allowing them to "catch up" with the intellectual advances made by European civilization. The lot of Muslim women (i.e., primarily veiling) was intrinsically linked to the state of backwardness of Islamic societies, a situation that could be remedied only by abandoning native traditions (shedding the veil) and embracing European culture.

Ironically, even though some of the colonizers were critical of European women's rights, they often adopted the language of the emerging European feminist movement to establish a moral justification for the military occupation of increasingly larger segments of the Ottoman Empire. In fact, Leila Ahmed has aptly pointed out that Lord Cromer, who championed so wholeheartedly the unveiling of Egyptian women, was also well known for his opposition to women's suffrage in England.[9] Evidently, women's rights per se were inappropriate because threatening in Europe, but the language used to speak about women's rights was a valuable political strategy abroad.

These were the perspectives invoked to justify the civilizing mission yesterday. They are the same ones that continue to inform much of Euro-American domestic and foreign policy today.

◼ The stereotypes about veiled Muslim women that have been circulating at least since Galland's translation of *Arabian Nights* and echoed in painting, photography, and film (among many other media) continue to affect the lives of real Muslim women living in Muslim-minority societies today. The legislation developed in Europe that bans the Muslim headscarf and *burqa*, like cases of discrimination against veiled women in the United States, are not occurring in a vacuum. They can be considered a new form and an extension of nineteenth-century imperialism, a legacy of earlier orientalist thought. This is certainly how many Muslims often interpret them, as we will see in the following two chapters.

I will end by quoting a poem titled "If the Odalisques," written in 1994 by one of my favorite contemporary Arab American Muslim writers, Mohja Kahf. In it, she calls for the women depicted in orientalist paintings (called *odalisques* or slaves) to walk away from the artworks that have imprisoned them for more than a century and to leave the walls of European national museums barren. This is how she creatively envisions a solution to the ideological manipulation that Muslim women have suffered from Europeans and Americans:

> If all the odalisques
> in all the paintings
> in all the museums
> in all the capitals of Europe
> got up and left,
> they'd leave a big hole in the wall . . .[10]

This law has made my life miserable. I've been spat at, honked at from cars
and also beaten. I was assaulted while I was carrying my daughter in my arms.
—Ms. Ahmas, Muslim woman wearing the *niqab* in France (2002)

We've been very perturbed about the veil. To see those
very young girls veiled. . . . Perhaps the veil once said something religious,
but now it's a sign of oppression. It isn't God, it's men who want it.
—Anne Hidalgo, deputy mayor of the city of Paris (2004)

CHAPTER FIVE

Veiling in Western Europe Today

It is not easy being a veiled Muslim living in western Europe today. If
you are a Muslim woman living in France, for example, and you wear
any sort of veil, you have no chance of being employed in the public
sphere or government sector. If you are a school girl in France and you
decide to adopt *hijab,* you must basically forfeit your education. And if
perchance you happen to be a Muslim who wears the *burqa* or the *niqab,*
the face-covering veils, you are not allowed to circulate in public spaces
and so must stay at home. The irony of the latter policy, of course, is that
you do not need to wear any type of veil if you are inside your home with
your close family.

In 2004, a French law banned "all ostentatious religious signs" from
French public schools. This means that since 2004 for Muslim girls the
choice has been between removing their *hijab* and continuing school
or holding onto the *hijab* and leaving school. This is a choice that many
Muslim girls face as early as twelve or thirteen years of age. It is a decision that is agonizing to make.

In 2010, France became the second European country, after Belgium, to ban the *burqa* (the full-body and face covering that conceals the eyes behind a mesh) and the *niqab* (the full-body and face covering that leaves a narrow opening for the eyes) from all public spaces, including streets, shops, malls, parks, and sports arenas.

Under the French law, women found wearing a *burqa* or a *niqab* are forced by police to uncover their faces, required to attend citizenship classes, and risk a $190 fine. Men who are charged with forcing a woman to wear a *burqa* or *niqab* are more heavily punished: one year in prison, as well as a fine up to $38,000. Both penalties are doubled if the victim is a minor. In addition, the law makes it possible to revoke the French citizenship of any person accused of wearing the face veil or forcing a woman to wear it.

The precedent set by both Belgium and France to ban the *burqa* and *niqab* from public spaces has encouraged other European countries — including Spain, the Netherlands, Austria, Italy, and most recently Switzerland — to consider whether they too ought to ban the Islamic face veil from government buildings, hospitals, and even public transportation.

Just as there is no European consensus on how to deal with *hijab*, there is also no consensus within individual European countries on how to deal with the face veil. The divided views of British politicians on the topic offer an illuminating example. In 2006, the former British prime minister Tony Blair called the Muslim face veil a "mark of separation" and explained that it "makes people from outside the community feel uncomfortable."[1] His views echoed those of Jack Straw, the former leader of the House of Commons, who refused to meet with women in *niqab* because their face veils, he said, prevented communication and set their wearers visibly apart. In contrast, the schools secretary Ed Balls issued a statement in 2010 stating that a law opposing the wearing of the *niqab* would be contrary to the British tradition of embracing cultural differences.

Driving the debates among European policy makers on how and whether to legislate veiling is a general discomfort among the European population toward women who wear headscarves and face veils. In fact, the first study on Islamophobia published in France in 2012 revealed that 84.73 percent of all Islamophobic incidents in France are made against women who veil. Moreover, a Pew Global Project Attitudes poll, released in July 2010, showed that majorities in Germany (71%),

Britain (62%), and Spain (59%) would support a ban on face veils in their own countries. Most Americans (65%), on the other hand, indicated they would oppose such a ban.

Reading newspapers and witnessing the rapid movement calling for legislation to ban veils throughout Europe, one might think that Europe is experiencing an unprecedented increase in the population of veiled Muslim women, or that Muslims in Europe are becoming more radicalized and adopting more conservative practices. But the European obsession with Muslim women's clothing cannot be explained by numbers alone.

It is estimated that of the half million Muslims living in Belgium, only thirty women wear the *niqab*; in the Netherlands, which has a Muslim population of 1 million, it is estimated that no more than four hundred women wear *niqabs*; and in France, an estimated three hundred women wore the *niqab* when the debate over face veils began. Today, that number is believed to be one thousand, out of a Muslim population of 6 million. Given these statistics, it is difficult to believe that legislation banning the *burqa* is based on the number of cases involved.

My students have a hard time understanding European laws legislating women's dress. For them, such legal actions contravene freedom of speech and freedom of religious expression. They are thus by definition antidemocratic.

How can we understand the expanding legislations in Europe on Muslim women's dress, and what implications do they have for Muslims living in European societies today? Why does veiling matter so much to European countries, even though the total number of people donning the *hijab* or *niqab* is quite small? To what extent do debates and legislation on the Islamic veil in Europe intersect with larger social, economic, and political issues taking place nationally and internationally? To shed light on these important questions, I will focus in this chapter on France as a case study for what is happening in western Europe today.

France, the country with the largest and oldest community of Muslim immigrants in western Europe, offers an excellent case for this purpose. Today the Muslim population in France is estimated to be in the range of 6 million people, making up about 7–8 percent of the population and establishing Islam as the second-largest religion after Christianity.[2]

Debates about veiling in France started more than twenty years ago, well before any European countries began focusing on their Muslim population. In this respect, France occupies the role of unofficial European policy setter for Islamic issues. Debates and policies on veiling initiated by the French government have direct and indirect implications for other European nations. So, by understanding what happens in France, the attitudes toward Muslims there, and the various laws adopted toward Muslim veiling, we can better comprehend the various positions espoused by other countries in the European Union, as well as the stakes behind mounting European legislation against veiling.

THE VEIL DEBATE AND FRENCH *LAÏCITÉ* (SECULARISM)

The onset of the veiling debate in France can be dated to October 3, 1989, when three Muslim middle-school girls (two Moroccans and one Algerian) refused to remove their headscarves in school and were subsequently expelled by the principal, Ernest Chénière, for contravening the principle of secularism (*laïcité*) and the neutrality of the public school.

This event took place in the Gabriel Havez middle school in the town of Creil (Oise), a poor and ethnically mixed suburb of Paris with a large Muslim population. Rather than being dismissed as a random school disciplinary problem, this occurrence immediately became a major media event in France and a symbol of everything that challenged the unity and universality of the French Republic. This one incident involving only three girls put into motion a long series of events that ultimately led to the 2004 law banning *hijabs* from public schools and invited similar moves from other European countries.

For Americans who have trouble grasping how the French state can legislate Muslim women's dress, it is important to remember that the French Republican model differs from the American system. The French Republic is premised on the absolute equality of all its citizens. From the French perspective, this means that no individual or group may demand recognition for ethnic, religious, or social origin. In France, any such demand raises the specter of the dangerous American models of multiculturalism and affirmative action. It amounts to nothing less than communalism, the fracturing of the social fabric.

To counter the threat of multiculturalism, a series of laws on schools was passed in France from the July Monarchy (1830–48) to the third Republic (1870–1914) with the goal of creating "a new, universal social morality in the minds of French pupils."[3] Then minister of public instruction, Jules Ferry (1832–93), is credited for establishing the French school as a "space into which, for the first time in the history of the nation, the Church could not go." Such schools, Ferry thought, would turn "peasants into Frenchmen," assert the priority of national identity over the individual, and lead to the full assimilation of French citizens. The equality of French citizens and the indivisibility of the nation were thus premised on the rejection of all hyphenated identities and the eradication of ethnic, religious, or social difference.

Knowing that, it is perhaps easier to understand why the French media and the country's politicians perceived the Gabriel Havez incident as a very real threat to France's secularist principles and universal republican values. The timing of the incident made things especially pressing: it coincided with the bicentennial of the French Revolution, a period when the principles of the revolution and the pillars of French republicanism (including secularism) were celebrated, rehearsed, and reinforced in everyone's mind. Girls in headscarves exposed a crisis that would soon become more and more explosive throughout France, a crisis between the ideals of French universalism and the reality of an increasingly multicultural population.

The 1989 event also coincided with rising domestic concerns and international crises that centered around Islam. The late 1980s represented the height of a French economic recession with steadily increasing unemployment rates. Such domestic woes fueled the Far Right movement and its rising leader, Jean-Marie Le Pen. His party gained votes during the legislative elections of 1986 by developing a strong anti-immigration platform and blaming the Arab population for France's unemployment. The headscarf became the symbol of this threatening Arab Muslim community, the cause of France's social and economic problems.

The incident at the school also coincided with a number of international threats involving Islam that the media covered excessively. In 1989, the Ayatollah Khomeini of Iran issued his *fatwa* against Salman Rushdie for authoring *The Satanic Verses*; the first Palestinian Intifada against the Israeli occupation was underway (1987–93); and the Islamic Front in Algeria rose to power.

Islamist militancy preoccupied the international community and was heavily covered in the French news. French politicians from all political parties, like the population at large, felt anxious about what the rise in Islamist militancy abroad might mean for its Muslim population at home. It may not be an exaggeration to guess that behind the three middle-school girls in headscarves, France perceived and feared an Islamist takeover.

For many French politicians and public figures, Islamic scarves were a symbol of oppression, a sign that immigrants at home could not be integrated, that Islamists abroad threatened Muslims everywhere. They sensed a relationship between Iranian *chadors*, *fatwas*, book burnings, Palestinian violence, assassinations in Algeria, and scarf-wearing girls in French middle schools.

Though the girls themselves attributed their veiling to an effort to distinguish themselves from their parents (who did not veil) and to claim their own identity as Muslims, their views were dismissed as adolescent mischief. The Gabriel Havez incident was eventually resolved through accommodation, as ruled by the State Council, France's highest legal body. The State Council determined that wearing headscarves and signs of religious affiliation did not necessarily contradict the principle of secularism. Prohibiting them outright would be a violation of "the right to individual conscience." The State Council also ruled that headscarves would be incompatible with secularism only when accompanied by "acts of pressure, provocation, proselytism or propaganda," or when they interfered with regular classroom and school activities. The State Council thus entrusted local school authorities and teachers with interpreting, on a case-by-case basis, which headscarf was ostentatious and polemical and which one stood merely for religious conviction.

In 1994, the Ministry of Education appointed Hanifa Chérifi (a French woman hailing from the Kabylia region of Algeria) to assist school administrators in their task. As the official mediator between schools and pupils regarding problems arising from the wearing of headscarves, Chérifi was asked to devise firm rules.

Chérifi distinguished between two types of scarves depending on the way they were tied, ruling that a scarf tied in the back was a sign of family tradition and was hence non-threatening and acceptable. A scarf tied underneath the chin, on the other hand, was deemed a "fundamentalist scarf," one that had to be shed. This distinction has no basis in Islamic law, nor is it a common one in Muslim-majority societies. Nevertheless, because it was an easy rule to apply, it proved somewhat successful in resolving many cases and keeping most veiled girls in schools.

The number of veiled middle- and high-school girls dropped from about twenty-four hundred in 1994 to about one hundred by the late

1990s. Compromises were reached through the adoption of what were called "discreet scarves," which would let some hair and the earlobes show, and the use of bandanas to cover the hair, instead of more traditional scarves. Settlements were also reached by specifying those spaces on school grounds where veiling would be acceptable and those where the scarf had to be dropped to the shoulders.

Despite the relative ease of this simplistic solution and the small number of veiled schoolgirls, the debates surrounding veiling in public schools escalated, leading to legislation in France and throughout Europe. The 1989 incident had brought about an increased use of the term *voile* (veil), suggesting a more conservative style of covering, instead of the more general word *foulard* (headscarf) in the media. This change in vocabulary heightened the perceived threat of Muslims in Europe and the urgency that politicians had to deal with them.

FROM A DEBATE ABOUT HEADSCARVES TO A BAN ON VEILING

When the debate about veiling reawakened in 2003, it did not at first concern headscarves in public schools, but rather their presence on the photographs affixed to French national identity papers.

Then minister of the interior Nicolas Sarkozy insisted that veiled Muslim women should be required to pose bare-headed on these documents. For him, women's resistance to be photographed without a scarf represented their failure to embrace the French Republic and to assimilate to its central principles. A refusal to shed the headscarf was a sign that they could not be French citizens.

For many Muslims in France, the debate about photographs on national identification cards was reminiscent of the 1960s when, under French colonization, Algerian women had been forced to shed their *hijab* and be photographed (see chapter 4). It invoked the specter of French imperialism all over again. Not surprisingly, the debate on photographs on national identity cards revived the debate on headscarves in French schools.

In September 2003, Alma and Lila Lévy (sixteen and eighteen years old) were expelled from the Henri Wallon high school in the town of Aubervilliers, a suburb northeast of Paris, because they refused to take off their headscarves in school. They also refused the compromise offered by their school administration, that of substituting a *foulard léger* for their *hijab*. The term "foulard léger" is quite an unusual one. It may be translated as a "light" scarf, which, according to Chérifi's guidelines, may mean a scarf tied behind the head, leaving the neck, earlobes, and hairline unconcealed.

The case of the Lévy sisters is especially noteworthy because it challenges everything that French ministers, school principals, and teachers had been claiming all along about headscarves. The Lévy sisters experienced no familial pressure to veil. In fact, the two sisters were not born into Islam, but were converts. Moreover, they were the only Muslims in their family and the only ones to veil. Their father was an atheist Jew, while their mother, from Kabylia (thus an indigenous Algerian, not an Arab), had been baptized a Catholic. Both parents were secular; both were shocked at their daughters' conversion and disapproved their adoption of the headscarf.

But both parents also supported their daughters in what they saw as nothing more than an exploration of adolescent identity. They thus defended their right to wear a headscarf and to receive an education. The girls' father vehemently condemned his daughters' expulsion and decried French politicians, the staunch defenders of French secularism, whom he dubbed the "*ayatollahs* of secularism who have lost all their common sense."[4]

The incident with the Lévy sisters may have become so explosive in part due to the general climate after September 11, 2001. Concerns about national security loomed large in Euro-American societies, especially in light of the newly declared global war on terror. The debates about veiled girls in French schools became more and more intense, and a clear shift was perceptible in governmental attitudes, which henceforth favored less accommodation and called for a firmer stand in support of radical secularism.

In July 2003, the former president Jacques Chirac set up the Independent Commission of Reflection on the Application of the Principle of Laicism in the Republic, later known simply as the Stasi Commission, to resolve the question of veiling as well as larger ones of religious and social diversity in the French Republic. He charged prominent government officials, educators, and scholars with formulating a policy that would both clarify and strengthen the 1905 law on the separation of church and state (better known as the law of secularism). The responsibility of the Stasi Commission was to present a revised law of *laïcité*, just in time for the centennial celebration of the law.

After months of meetings, deliberations, and interviews, the commission offered dozens of recommendations to reaffirm the sacred principle of *laïcité*.[5] Of those, Chirac selected the one recommendation related to clothing, and it was signed into law on March 15, 2004, and implemented the following academic year.

The sole recommendation that Chirac deemed effective (and presumably sufficient) to strengthen French *laïcité* and to ensure the unity and universality of the French Republic was the outlawing of all conspicuous signs of religious affiliation in public schools. He heralded this new legislation as a means of erasing gender differences and of halting the threat of radical Islam on French soil.

Lest it appear discriminatory and risk being overturned by the European Court of Human Rights, the text of the law was written in a language that did not refer to any religion specifically. Its stated goal was to prohibit *all* ostentatious religious signs in public schools: "In public primary and secondary schools, wearing signs or clothes by which pupils clearly display a religious affiliation is forbidden."[6]

Officially, this law prohibited *all* ostentatious signs of religion, including large crosses, Islamic headscarves, Jewish skullcaps, and Sikh turbans, while still permitting smaller adornments, like a small cross, a Star of David, a hand of Fatima, or a small Qur'an. Despite the breadth of the law, politicians, the media, and the general public understood the law to be targeting the *hijab* and Muslims specifically. In fact, in popular discourse and in much of the media, it quickly came to be known and referred to as the law against the Muslim headscarf.

Since the passage of the 2004 law, Muslim girls living in France have been banned from wearing headscarves in any French public school whether inside the Hexagon or in its overseas territories. Only those areas with a significant Muslim population (such as the island of Mayotte in the Comoros, northwest of Madagascar) have been allowed to continue to make some accommodations with their veiled Muslim pupils (e.g., replacing the veil with a bandana or a "small" scarf).

Despite opposition from a number of politicians, activists, and feminists from all sides of the political spectrum, the law was voted in 276 to 20, and supported by roughly 75 percent of the French population surveyed in polls. As in 1989, the decreased tolerance for headscarves can be partly attributed to international events taking place shortly before the law went into effect.

In the early summer of 2004, two French reporters were held hostage in Iraq by a group demanding that France repeal its law against head-scarves. This hostage crisis became a watershed event. Not only did it revive French anxieties about the implications of international Islamic terrorism for its citizens but it brought unity among those in favor of the law and those who had challenged it. During the hostage crisis, claiming one's right to wear the veil became tantamount to supporting the terrorists.

When the law was implemented in the academic year 2004–5, some students challenged it by coming to school wearing wigs or with shaved heads. About 550 difficult cases were ultimately successfully resolved though the dialogue period recommended by politicians prior to expulsion. Ultimately, only 47 students were expelled for refusing to abide by the law.

While most of the French saw these numbers as a positive step toward the reaffirmation of secularism and the integration of the Muslim population, French Muslims viewed them as just another sign of how unwelcoming France was to its Muslim citizens. They continued to call for their right to be both French and Muslim.

BANNING THE *NIQAB* TO SUPPORT WOMEN'S RIGHTS

The 2010 law banning the *niqab* in France unquestionably represents an escalation and a hardening of the French governmental position toward its Muslim population. In fact, while the 2004 law had been vehemently debated, a surprising consensus existed around the 2010 prohibition. The ban on the *niqab* proved extremely popular with politicians, passing the Senate with 246 votes to 1 (and 100 abstentions coming mainly from left-leaning politicians); 7 out of 10 French people also approved it.

These approval rates are especially astonishing considering that the number of women actually wearing the *burqa* or *niqab* in France was quite small. One central reason why so many people approved the ban may have been because of the new arguments about national security and women's rights that surfaced to justify the proposed law. Members of Parliament in both Belgium and France argued that in the context of heightened global security alerts and the war on terror, it was imperative for police to be able to check people's identities. A person behind a face mask could be just anyone, posing a potential threat to the public and the nation. Thus, they argued, it was imperative for reasons of national security to ban face masks in all forms. The more convincing arguments, though, concerned women's rights, French notions of gender equality viewed as "universally desirable,"[7] and the oppressive nature of Islam and patriarchy.

These ideas had already been advanced by French politicians in 2003 when debating the Islamic headscarf. Joan Scott has demonstrated how "by banning the headscarf, French legislators [thought] they were removing the sign of women's inequality from the classroom and, in so doing, declaring that the equality of women and men was a first principle of the republic."[8] They had adopted a feminist discourse, denouncing the violence of the suburbs where young Muslim girls were harassed if they did not conform to the conservative sartorial code of their patriarchal community.

At the time, French politicians had lumped together veiling, polygamy, genital mutilation, and forced marriages, claiming that Muslim women, veiled ones especially, were subjected to them all. The French secular republic presented itself as the savior of Muslim women from the coercion they presumably suffered at the hands of their fathers, brothers, and husbands. For Muslims in France, this rhetoric uncomfortably recalled nineteenth-century civilizing missions and early Hollywood orientalist films (see chapter 4).

The French government borrowed feminist arguments from a newly established and influential Arab and Muslim feminist organization called Ni Putes ni Soumises (Neither Whores nor Submissive Women). Because the organization was headed by a French-born Algerian woman, Fadela Amara, many French people assumed that the views it espoused were "authentic" and that the association spoke for a majority of Arab and Muslim women.

Yet the group was by no means an advocacy group speaking on behalf of Arab Muslim women in France. In reality, the French government financed the group's operations, and the French National Assembly and the media recognized the group only because it supported official French doctrine. Members of Ni Putes ni Soumises did not embrace a feminism that supported women's choice or right to veil. Rather, and also in the name of feminism, they claimed that *hijab* was an unambiguous symbol of totalitarianism and fundamentalism and urged the French government to support Muslim women's emancipation. From their perspective, any tolerance for headscarves equaled cultural relativism, an unacceptable position concerning women's rights.

Strongly supporting the ban of the *burqa*, President Sarkozy advanced the same arguments put forth by Ni Putes ni Soumises. He too invoked a concern for Muslim women and for their utter subordination symbolized by the *burqa*. In an oft-cited speech made in the summer of 2009, Sarkozy pointed out that the *burqa* "is not welcome on the territory of the French Republic" because it "debased women"; therefore, "we cannot accept to have in our country women who are prisoners behind netting, cut off from all social life, deprived of identity." Amara, the founding member of Ni Putes ni Soumises and the newly appointed urban regeneration minister in the Sarkozy government, echoed the president's views. For her, the *burqa*, like the *hijab*, unequivocally stood for the "oppression of women"[9] and had to be banned.

In the name of feminism, the new legislation prohibits any "incitement to cover the face for reasons of gender." It claims to liberate Muslim women from their alleged oppression, symbolized by the face veil, and from their subjugation by their conservative families and culture. It promises to lead to their successful integration into the French Republic.

LEGISLATION OF VEILING PRACTICES AND SOCIOLOGICAL FINDINGS

The rhetoric of the 2010 law banning the *burqa* is disturbing for many reasons, not least because it perpetuates the much cherished myth of a "clash of civilizations." This myth constructs a stark opposition between the ideals of the secular French Republic and a faith-based, misguided Islam, between liberated French women and oppressed veiled Muslim women, between the specter of a violent, radical Islam and a more enlightened, peaceful, and gender-equal Europe. It normalizes through repetition various stereotypes and presents them as accurate portrayals of reality. Ultimately, it lulls people into believing that these myths and stereotypes are true and withdraws them from public scrutiny.

The rhetoric surrounding the ban on veiling and the ban of the *burqa* is also alarming because it has the very real potential of stigmatizing the entire French (and European) Muslim community for the practices of a few. Although some politicians have been careful to point out that wearing a veil is different from wearing a *niqab*, because the former is believed to be a religious obligation, while the latter is open to debate, most politicians continue to insist that women who wear *hijab* or the *burqa* are manipulated by radical forms of Islam or by their male relatives and are not wearing them of their own volition.

Scholars such as Étienne Balibar, Nacira Guénif-Souilamas, Sylvie Tissot, John Bowen, Joan Scott, and Alec Hargreaves, among others, have argued that French policies against Muslim headscarves and *burqas* serve primarily to divert the public's attention from the real social and economic problems that plague French society, problems particularly virulent in the suburbs where the majority of Muslim immigrants live.

The same scholars have also denounced the work of Ni Putes ni Soumises as an "ideological State Apparatus" that supports an Islamophobic right-wing political discourse,[10] underlining that this association's and the media's focus on acts of violence in the suburbs obscures the challenges that women everywhere continue to face, regardless of religious background.

In addition, they have deplored the sexism of French society, which focuses on sexism in Islam rather than looking at the gender inequality that pervades its own allegedly liberated culture. In that regard, Scott has shown how in France, "the veil became a screen onto which were projected . . . a mythic vision of the French republic," not only "racism, postcolonial guilt and fear, . . . secularism" but also "and especially, French norms of sexual conduct taken to be both natural and universal."[11]

Academics have published data indicating that the majority of *burqa*-clad women in France are *not* immigrants, as they have been referred to by the media and politicians, but French citizens of French descent. Not only are many of these women French by birth but they were educated in France and are fully integrated into the French Republic. These women are *voluntarily* adopting the *burqa*; they are not forced by anyone; often they have adopted that practice after their conversion to Islam and marriage to a Muslim.

Sociologists have reproved policy makers and the media for failing to take into account the voices of girls and women who wear the veil. Even during the hearings of the Stasi Commission, none of the young girls who had been expelled from their schools for veiling and none of the many scholars who had studied the question of veiling were among the interviewed witnesses. One of the members of the commission had even decried this omission, noting that "it was unfortunate that there was no one with sensitivity about Islam," no one therefore who could present "the views, experiences, and interests of the girls concerned."[12]

Yet if French politicians and the media had taken the time to study the changing composition of the Muslim population during the past decade, and if they had bothered to listen to the voices of veiled women or women adopting the *niqab*, they would have heard a very different message from the one that circulates about their presumed oppression.

THE CHANGING COMPOSITION OF THE MUSLIM POPULATION IN FRANCE

Continuing to view the Muslim population through the constricting grid of the veil or *burqa* (whether someone is wearing it or not) disregards the changing composition of the Muslim population in France during the past decade.

Today, the greatest proportion of Muslims in France are second-, third-, or fourth-generation immigrants of African, Turkish, and, increasingly, Eastern European descent. Most were born and educated in France. They speak French fluently and have French citizenship (or will acquire it at age eighteen). Those hailing from the Maghreb are culturally and geographically distant from their parents' Arab country of origin, where some have never set foot. They may not speak its language and are not torn by the same longing and nostalgia for their motherland as their mothers and grandmothers were.

The current generation of female Arab Muslims in France is the first to attain a high level of education, often times higher than that of their male counterparts or of other non-Muslim women of French origin of the same socioeconomic class, a phenomenon that has led some sociologists to refer to them as the elites of immigration.[13] They are also increasingly involved in mixed marriages. The Islam they practice is different from that of their partly integrated parents or grandparents. Some of them voluntarily choose to wear Muslim dress; others choose not to.

Although the French media and official discourses continue to ignore such critical changes in the composition and practices of the French Muslim population, they have been confirmed by recent statistics on immigrant Muslims of North African, Turkish, and African origin. Vincent Tiberj and Sylvain Brouard, researchers at the National Political Science Research Center (CEVIPOF) in Paris surveyed the ways in which Muslim immigrants in France do and do not share the attitudes of the majority French population. They systematically compared the "new French" Muslim immigrants, as well as their children and grandchildren born in France, with a sample of the French general population. Their study has revealed striking information about the different religious situation of French Muslims today, in contrast to earlier generations, thus indicating the need to revise our view of the Muslim population in France. We learn from their survey that 20 percent of the Muslims of North African, Turkish, and African descent reported being *without any religion*. Of those who practice, only 21 percent reported regularly practicing their Islamic beliefs, and more than two-thirds indicated they participated only in major holiday celebrations.

The findings further suggest that despite the group's identification as Muslim and despite some people's explicitly voiced commitment to some ritual practices (prayer, fasting, giving alms), this population was overwhelmingly in favor of French national values, including secularism, which they did not view as a hindrance to their own religious practice. In fact, the researchers concluded that "no matter how we approach the question of religion and secularism, it appears that French citizens, from African and Turkish descent, adhere in their great majority to the principle of secularism. It is all the more remarkable that they do not differ from the rest of the population from this perspective even as they are more attached to their religious background. The equation 'more religious = less secular' does not function for the French Muslim population."[14]

Moreover, Brouard and Tiberj have pointed out that the French media and political focus on Islam are responsible for erecting religion, especially the practices of Islam, as the main problems for French national values. They have decried the fact that a disproportionate attention continues to be given to a minority segment of French Muslims who may indeed be opposed to integration and to French core values. This minority has overshadowed what they called the "silent majority" of Muslims who are similar to the rest of the French population but whose voice has consistently been marginalized in mainstream, popular, and political discourses.[15]

Brouard and Tiberj conclude: "If a French person is not this well-known figure of the person wearing a beret and branding a baguette, even though such individuals do exist, the 'French citizen of African and Turkish descent' is not a practicing Muslim, staunchly opposed to secularism, anti-Semitic, misogynist, and demanding social benefits because of communalism (*communautarisme*)."[16]

Such findings indicate clearly that the policies that continue to be enacted in France with regard to Muslim dress and the assumptions that are made about Islam and Muslims are not borne out by scientific investigations. These policies do not take into consideration the majority of Muslims living in France who are integrated, secular, and very much part of the French landscape.

Despite increasingly stringent legislation on Muslim women's dress in France, the law banning the *niqab* is rarely enforced. In fact, since the law was enacted in 2010, only 425 women wearing full face veils have been fined up to 150 euros ($188) each, and just 66 others have received warnings, according to Pierre-Henry Brandet, spokesman for the Interior Ministry. In addition, a French businessman of Algerian origin, Rachid Nekkaz, has offered to pay any fine incurred for wearing the *niqab*. So far, he has paid 412 fines totaling more than $60,000, plus $16,000 in legal fees.[17] Evidently, the law devised by French and European politicians to integrate their Muslim population has had little direct impact on the daily lives of Muslim women.

EUROPEAN MUSLIM WOMEN AND THE POLYSEMY OF THE VEIL

One of the central and long-cherished myths concerning *hijab* and the *niqab* is that these items of clothing have a homogeneous meaning among Muslims and that all women who veil do so for the same reason: because they are forced to do so by a father or a husband. French and European policy makers (in a striking parallel to orientalists of the nineteenth century) assume and assert that they understand the practice of veiling better than Muslims themselves do.

That veiling has always had different meanings at different historical times, in different places, and for different people is never taken into consideration. And certainly the possibility that a veil could at times be chosen freely as an expression of identity or out of deep-seated religious belief is never taken into account.

In my research, I have found that an individual woman's choice to don the veil or not is due to a variety of reasons, including social, political, cultural, and economic, as well as personal and spiritual ones. Even if it is true that some women wear the veil because it is imposed on them by a family with a conservative reading of Islamic traditions, they unquestionably constitute a minority of the Muslim population.

Some women wear the veil proudly out of deep piety and the conviction that it is an Islamic prescription. Others adopt it as a political assertion of their national identity, as an expression of their disappointment with the failure of Arab nationalism, as a tool of resistance to Euro-American stereotypes and policies toward Muslims, or as a means of declaring their opposition to the commodification of women's bodies in Euro-American societies. Still others wear it for socioeconomic reasons, either because it allows them to forego the expense of new clothes and a hairdresser, or because it legitimates their ambition to hold a job outside the home and gain financial independence from their family.

Many veiled women participate in interfaith dialogues, shape new feminist interpretations of Islam and the Qur'an, and struggle to achieve policy changes and gender equality from within key Islamic institutions. Veiled women may appear conservative on the outside, but underneath their veil one often finds sociopolitically active citizens, assertive individuals engaged in personal, social, economic, political, and spiritual advancement. Indeed, many Muslim women living in Europe, like members of grassroots feminist organizations, are actively engaged in upholding women's rights and in protecting their choice to wear the veil, no matter how long it is or how much of the body it covers.

The voices of these women are usually heard only by scholars. They do not make headlines in newspapers and magazines. They are not heard on TV, and the women's experiences are certainly not taken into account by policy makers. Yet these voices are crucial for a better understanding of Muslim practices and are an essential tool in combating political and religious extremism in all its forms.

French politicians continue to treat women who wear *hijab* or *niqab* voluntarily in a paternalistic way, telling them that they are mistaken and that whether they realize it or not, they are actually being manipulated by an external authority. The specter of Islamic fundamentalism looms large in such thinking, leading to a simplistic formula that a critic has recently summed up as follows: "headscarf = female oppression = Islamicization = threat to freedom and democracy."[18]

The polysemy of the veil explains why an increasing number of veiled (and non-veiled) Muslim women are refusing to discuss their religious beliefs in public. Even though the veil is a visible sign of their identity and their faith, many Muslim women continue to assert that veiling is a choice and a decision that belongs in the private sphere. A high school student named Fariba summed up this desire for privacy when interviewed about her decision to wear *hijab*: "If I could wear the veil while hiding it I would do it. Because in religion it is clear that you should do things for God and not for people. It is not to show my affiliation with other people but my affiliation to God."[19]

VEILING IN EUROPE TODAY

The intensification of the debates on *hijab* and the *niqab* in Europe today reflect global fears of radical Islamism and Islamophobia more generally. These anxieties are mounting in the aftermath of the Arab Spring and the first democratic elections in various Arab Muslim-majority societies that have catapulted conservative Muslim groups to the helm.

The veiling debates in Europe are also convenient strategies that divert public attention from pressing national socioeconomic challenges. Joan Scott, like other scholars, has shown how "banning the veil . . . became a substitute solution for a host of pressing economic and social issues; the law on headscarves seemed as if it could wipe away the challenges of integration posed for policy makers by former colonial subjects."[20]

It is easier for many politicians to dictate what women are allowed to wear than to address directly some of the real problems facing their own countries. After all, a far greater number of Muslim women wear bikinis in Europe than women wear veils. Yet policy makers and the media have nothing to say about the former and everything to debate about the latter, regardless of how few they are.

Today, legislating Muslim women's dress has become a convenient platform for many European politicians when they want to show a tough stance in international matters and national security issues. Not surprisingly, the obsession with veiling coincides regularly with elections and appears on platforms aiming to garner votes by stigmatizing the Muslim population and espousing a hard line toward immigration. By perpetuating the long-cherished myth that Islam constitutes a national and global threat, the veil debates in France and elsewhere divert attention from the real economic and social problems facing countries today. Rather than shed light on the situation of Muslims in Europe, challenge radical Islamism, or champion the rights of Muslim women, the growing legislation against Islamic veiling instead exposes European anxieties about issues of integration, unemployment, social violence, and the crisis of a common currency. It highlights a true identity crisis running through Europe concerning the future of the European Union, the Eurozone, and individual nations within it.

The National Organization for Women got annoyed
After some of us put on *hijab,*
And wouldn't let us speak at their rally,
But wanted us up on their dais as tokens of diversity.
—Mohja Kahf, "*Thawrah des Odalisques* at the
Matisse Retrospective" (2003)

CHAPTER SIX

Veiling in the United States of America Today

When I ask undergraduate students enrolled in my "Arabs in America" or "Arabs and the West" classes at the University of North Carolina at Chapel Hill what comes to mind when they hear the word "veil," I am always struck by the changes in their response since the events of 9/11. Before these events, veiling systematically evoked orientalist fantasies, harems, sheer veils, Hollywood films, belly dancing, and erotic or sexual promiscuity.

These images have been prevalent in the United States since the nineteenth century. They are derived from memories of orientalist paintings such as those by Delacroix, Ingres, or Jean-Léon Gérôme, as well as by early Hollywood films set in the Orient. Both paintings and films depicted the erotic promise of the harem and the imagined sexual availability of Oriental women in veils (see chapter 4).

My students today are heirs to these artistic representations and to their more contemporary retellings, such as the Disney sensation *Aladdin* or the TV series *I Dream of Jeannie.* Veiling conjures up the character of the scantily clothed Jasmine, or the belly dancers in the film wearing transparent face veils.

Yet after 9/11, everything evocative of Islam and Muslims has also acquired a whole new set of associations. While images of belly-dancing women and women lounging in harems did not disappear entirely, they receded into the background. Now, new images propagated by the media and contemporary concerns come more readily to students' minds.

After a minute or two of uncomfortable silence, my students now respond that veiling evokes the oppressed women in *burqa* living under Taliban rule in Afghanistan. Veiling, for them, has come to mean the subordination and dehumanization of women, victims of Muslim male regulations and of tyrannical Islamic law. At best, a veiled Muslim woman is assumed to be socially, politically, and religiously conservative. At worst, a veiled Muslim woman is thought to be forced to veil and considered a victim of other forms of oppression, including genital mutilation, physical violence, polygamy, and stoning.

In addition, since 9/11, veiling for my students and for the American general public conjures up the specter of radical Islam, of terrorism, and of concealed weapons. If Muslim women are forced to veil, as most are presumed to be—why else would any rational person want to be covered like that, from head to toe, especially in the hottest months of the summer?—they are likely also made to submit to radical and political forms of Islam. Muslim women's perceived passivity is considered especially dangerous, not just because it violates women's fundamental human rights but because it means that women can be manipulated and required to behave in violent ways toward non-Muslims, Americans especially.

My students raise many questions about Muslim women's veiling practices. Even when they end up appreciating why a Muslim woman may cover her hair, most remain "disturbed," as they commonly report, by Muslim women who wear the full-body cloak and cover their faces. They struggle to grasp the meaning of what they perceive to be a disconcerting sartorial tradition, even as they attempt to be respectful of religious and cultural differences. They often wonder what a veiled woman might conceal underneath her cloak, and whether anyone could be sure who hid behind a woman in *burqa*.

The fact that suicide bombers (especially those involved in the Palestinian struggle) are often shown by the media dressed in a *kefiyyeh*, the large white-and-black checkered headscarf that conceals both the head and the face of the terrorist, only serves to alarm students and the general public, increasing their anxiety about veiled Muslim women on American soil. They tend to conclude that veiling masks violence and is thus something to be feared.

The heightened sensitivity toward any visible expression of Muslimness in the public sphere has fueled debates about the place of Muslims in America. It has helped displace the rhetoric of the global war on terror onto the *hijab*. The great emphasis placed on veiling practices in American media and popular discourse has ended up emphasizing the opposition between Euro-American secular democracies and Islamic traditions and making gender relations the focal point of divergence between Muslims and non-Muslims.

As one of the most visible signs of Islam, veiling and, by extension, veiled Muslim women have become the scapegoats for the anger toward the perpetrators of the horrific events of 9/11 and for the frustration of not being able to catch Osama bin Laden for almost a decade after the attacks. Muslim women's veils have become the easy target of anyone's concern about the alleged spread of Islamic terrorism, and a constant reminder that the American sense of security had been shaken to its core.

For many Americans, the events of 9/11 constructed a mental grid that predetermined the way they came to perceive Islam and veiled Muslim women. At the same time, few non-Muslims have had an opportunity to engage in discussion with Muslims about their faith or religious practices. In fact, a TIME poll of August 2010 revealed that 62 percent of those surveyed did not personally know a Muslim American. This chapter intends to be the beginning of such a conversation, one that many Muslim women living in America today are yearning to have.

VEILING AND DISCRIMINATION IN THE UNITED STATES

Compared to France, where the law on secularism and the separation of state and religion has led to an official ban on headscarves in schools and on *niqabs* in public spaces, secularism in the United States has not had similar effects, nor has it resulted in the legislation of Muslim women's dress. From this perspective, one could argue that Muslim women's right to wear religious attire in the public sphere is more protected in the United States than it is in France and in Europe. To some extent, it is.

At the same time, and at least since the turn of the millennium, Muslim women's clothing has come under increasing scrutiny in American civil society. In fact, despite the official separation of state and religion affirmed by the U.S. Constitution, and even though clothing worn for religious reasons is indirectly protected under the First Amendment, there are several documented disputes over headscarves in the United States and mounting discrimination against women who wear them.

In contrast to what we might have thought, there *is* a veil debate in America, just as there is one in France and Europe, though its contours and expressions are different. However, unlike in France, the question of *hijab* in the United States does not take center stage in public or political debates over the status of immigrants.

We know about cases of discrimination against veiled American Muslim women from a variety of sources. Sometimes they are reported informally to family, friends, and acquaintances. In these cases, they usually do not receive any media coverage and remain circumscribed to the group in which the incident has occurred. At other times, cases of discrimination against veiled women are reported to the Council for Arab-Islamic Relations (CAIR), the largest American Muslim civil liberties advocacy association, which keeps a tab on all such incidents that come to its attention. These incidents are the ones best known because they are reported or prosecuted in district, state, or federal courts. They also end up being abundantly covered by the media.

Not surprisingly, reported cases are fewer than the actual numbers of discrimination incidents. All of them are important, however, because they tell us a lot about the day-to-day experiences and challenges of women who wear the veil.

FOUR PLACES OF DISCRIMINATION
AGAINST VEILED MUSLIM WOMEN

When we review documented cases of discrimination against Muslim women living in America, we discover that veiled women encounter prejudice in four main areas: schools, the workplace, government agencies, and sports.

The threatened right to wear the *hijab* in schools is undoubtedly one of the most common cases of discrimination reported by veiled Muslim girls. In these instances, veiled girls are suspended from school for what is said to be a violation of the school's dress code policy.

Nashala Hearn, a sixth-grade veiled Muslim student at Ben Franklin

Science Academy in Muskogee, Oklahoma, was suspended twice from school in 2003 for contravening the school dress code banning all types of head covering, including bandanas and hats. In an article that partly summarizes the case, Kathleen Moore, a law professor, points out that Hearn's parents sued the school at the federal level with the support of the Rutherford Institute, an evangelical Christian public interest law firm.[1] This is interesting because it shows that in matters of free religious expression, Muslims in America (like those in Europe) get much support from other religious groups keen on protecting the freedom of religion. Christian and Jewish groups know that any ruling contravening religious freedom would ultimately affect them as well.

Discrimination against veiled Muslim girls in schools leads, not surprisingly, to feelings of depression, humiliation, and embarrassment. And this is what the young Nashala Hearn testified before senators in a U.S. Senate Judiciary subcommittee hearing. She described "a battle between being obedient to God by wearing [her] *hijab* to be modest in Islam versus school dress code policy."

Ultimately, the Hearn family, like most other families in similar situations, won their case. Their civil rights attorney clearly spelled out their constitutional right to religious identity and expression, and he reaffirmed the American federal government position in the matter, namely, that "no student should be forced to choose between following her faith and enjoying the benefits of a public education." This is of course a vastly divergent and happy conclusion from similar discrimination cases reported in French schools, as noted in the previous chapter.

The discrimination that some Muslim American girls face in school because they wear *hijab* clearly shows that despite the U.S. constitutional prohibition on the official establishment of religion and its recognition that everyone is entitled to their religious beliefs, Islamic practice is not *automatically* protected in public spaces. The right of individuals to religious expression is ultimately *accommodated*, however, after an appeal, with the support of other religious or civil groups, and through the intervention of state or federal justice departments.

Workplace discrimination is also common among veiled Muslim women. Some of them are admonished by their supervisors for wearing *hijab*, are advised or pressured to remove their head coverings, or fired from their jobs altogether simply for refusing to take off their *hijab*. According to CAIR, the number of documented cases of workplace discrimination against veiled Muslim women has more than doubled since the events of 9/11. This finding has been confirmed by the Equal Employment Opportunity Commission (EEOC) in Washington, D.C. According to David Grinberg, a spokesman with the EEOC, "the number of charges filed by Muslims alleging discrimination doubled from the four years before the September 11, 2001 terrorist attacks to the four years after."[2]

Similarly, a study by the Discrimination Research Center, a nonprofit research, advocacy, and public education organization, has found that job applicants with South Asian or Middle Eastern names were least likely to be hired by California temp agencies.[3] While we do not know whether the South Asian or Middle Eastern applicants mentioned in the study are all Muslims, the finding does suggest a broader pattern of prejudice toward foreigners including those of Muslim descent.

Veiled Muslim women often report that subtle and less subtle discrimination sometimes occurs during the interviewing process, rendered visible through the body language and overall attitude of the employer toward a prospective employee. In an article that appeared in the online version of the *Washington Post* (September, 25, 2005), Amy Joyce quotes an e-mail from an anonymous veiled Muslim woman in the D.C. area who endured this type of bias when looking for a job: "When I walk into interviews, I find that literally interviewers' jaws drop. They are excited on the phone, but in person they lose the energy." Even though this particular woman did eventually get the job she had hoped for, other veiled women report significant challenges to securing a job despite their qualifications and years of experience. Some of these Muslim women end up in unpaid, part-time, volunteer work simply because they cover their hair and wear modest clothing; others end up not being hired at all.

These cases of workplace discrimination occur despite the 1964 Title 7 of the Civil Rights Act, which requires employers to accommodate the religious needs of employees. In practice, however, and as a result of several 1977 court rulings, this requirement has been greatly relaxed, leading to instances of discrimination against veiled Muslim women that continue to go unpunished. Until today, every effort to reinstate the earlier civil rights requirement to accommodate the religious needs of employees has stalled in Congress.

Veiled Muslim women also face discrimination when they demand their right to wear the *burqa* or *niqab* on photos used for identification purposes at governmental agencies. Before 9/11, thirteen states allowed the delivery of identity cards and driver's licenses without any photo affixed to them at all (Arkansas, Indiana, Kansas, Minnesota, Missouri, Nebraska, New Jersey, North Dakota, Oregon, Pennsylvania, Tennessee, Washington, and Wisconsin). Some of the Muslim women wearing the *niqab* or *burqa* welcomed this option because it allowed them to forgo entirely the photo shoot that might involve a mixed-gender interaction.

After 9/11, however, national security concerns loomed large and took precedence over civil rights. Many states revised their policies and procedures concerning photos on identity cards and driver's licenses. Most determined that a photograph was required, and twenty-one of them asserted that it had to show the person's face. Many states offered accommodation in the actual procedure of photographing the individual concerned, allowing, for instance, that a veiled Muslim woman request another woman to photograph her. Nevertheless, the very requirement of a photograph for identification purposes (rather than fingerprints and other biometrics) indicated a tightening of the rules and has given rise to much protest in the Muslim American community concerning its right to religious expression.

Perhaps the most sensationalized court case on discrimination at an American governmental agency is the one that took place in Florida shortly after 9/11. Sultana Freeman, a Muslim convert, saw her driver's license suspended because the photo affixed to it showed her wearing a *niqab*, something considered legal when she had renewed her driver's license only months earlier, in February 2001. Even though the Florida court recognized that Freeman was not suspected of any terrorism, it nevertheless ruled in favor of national security interests, which in this case limited her right to religious expression. In other words, while admitting that Freeman was not herself a threat to national security, the court associated her with Islamic terrorism because she wore the *niqab*.

The right to wear *hijab* around swimming pools is another area of concern for Muslim women. Veiled Muslim women continue to be viewed with suspicion even when tending to basic parental tasks, such as accompanying their children to the community pool. One such case was in the news incessantly in June 2004. A lawsuit had been brought by the Nebraska American Civil Liberties Union (ACLU) against the City of Omaha defending the right of a Muslim mother dressed in a headscarf and cloak (but not a face veil) to accompany her children to the municipal pool. The pool directors argued that the mother's attire did not adhere to pool regulations, even though other mothers were admitted dressed in regular street clothes. Ultimately, and only after the case was taken to court, was a settlement reached to accommodate the religious (and medical) needs of the pool patrons.

A similar controversy arose in January 2008 when Muslim women at Harvard University requested women-only hours (six hours per week) at one of the university's three main recreational facilities to exercise in private, away from the eyes of men. Even though the Harvard College Women's Center supported this request since it was considered attractive to other women as well, it was met with much frustration by critics on and off the campus. Critics of Harvard's women-only recreational hours argued that such a request was unfair to men, constituted an invitation to discriminatory practices, and could possibly be a precursor to cooperating with terrorism. This is what Michael Smerconish, a talk show host and the author of *Muzzled: From T-Ball to Terrorism—True Stories That Should Be Fiction*, implied when he asserted that Harvard's policy amounted to nothing but "political correctness."[4]

Until today, the right to accommodate religious needs (and Islamic ones especially), like the right to wear Muslim attire at recreational facilities, is never a given but must be renegotiated by each woman, in each city, and with the directors of each facility involved.

Finally, veiled Muslim women often encounter resistance to their right to wear *hijab* when they participate in organized sports activities. Muslim girls are at times barred from competing in sports tournaments while wearing headscarves because of safety concerns: the headscarf, it is argued, could pose a safety hazard to the girl playing sports, or to one of her teammates. This safety argument is advanced despite the development of new sports head covers made from breathable fabric and Velcro closures that have been tested and meet the highest standards of quality in the market.[5] Yet safety, like concerns for national security, is an area where accommodation must be negotiated.

Veiled Muslim girls are thus often forced to choose between playing no sports at all or creating teams with others from the same religious group. Frequently they end up playing with other veiled Muslim girls. Many of them end up on the sidelines of those activities considered the foundation for developing lifelong skills such as team culture, trust, and basic communication. For many veiled Muslim American girls, sport is a sphere of heightened discrimination and failed cross-cultural communication.

The lifting of the ban on *hijab* that the Soccer World Cup Association (FIFA) voted for in the summer of 2012, like the permission given for the

Carolina Cyclones, Charlotte, North Carolina, 2009,
Esse Quam Videri Series (Courtesy of Todd Drake)

first time to veiled Muslim women athletes to compete in the London 2012 Olympics, may in time produce changes in the situation of Muslim girls playing sports in schools. For now, the popular reaction to the loosening of clothing regulations in major sporting events has been one of resistance and accusations of giving in to pressures from the Gulf governments. Only the future will tell us how such regulations will affect Muslim girls in America and around the world.

As these cases of discrimination illustrate, the United States, even as it is a haven for religious and individual freedoms and a bastion of First Amendment Rights, does not *automatically* protect American Muslim women's right to veil. While most instances of discrimination against veiled Muslim women and girls do ultimately end with *accommodation* (except in cases where safety and national security concerns are invoked), such accommodation is never routine and often requires the intervention of a court of justice, be it local, state, or federal.

REASONS FOR WEARING THE VEIL

While we might have assumed that the climate of discrimination and the mounting anxiety in American civil society toward any visible expression of Muslimness might have led to a decrease in the adoption of *hijab* among American Muslims, quite the opposite is true. Sociologists and cultural geographers have measured an increase in veiling practices since the events of 9/11, especially among second- and third-generation American Muslims.

This finding is striking because it reveals that Muslims living in the United States are not following the expected trajectory of assimilation emblematic of other immigrant groups who over time shed many of their parents' cultural and religious practices. Rather than becoming *less* religious, American Muslims are becoming *more* observant, especially since 9/11. Many are choosing to veil to affirm their identity, even though their mothers and grandmothers may have never adopted this religious and cultural sartorial practice. And many are adopting conservative Muslim clothing in spite of their family's wishes.[6]

There are multiple reasons why American Muslim women are increasingly adopting veiling and insisting on the public display of their Islamic identity in the face of expanding Islamophobia, discrimination, and familial objections. Piety, spirituality, and modesty are undoubtedly crucial reasons for wearing *hijab* in America, as they are elsewhere, but as the preceding chapters have made clear, they are not the only explanations for this practice. Various people regularly advance different rationales for veiling, and often there is more than one reason for donning *hijab*.

VEILING, DEMOCRACY, AND AMERICAN ISLAM

Many of the veiled women I spoke with over the years report that they started wearing *hijab* in solidarity with the many Muslim women around the world who are struggling and facing discrimination. Some began veiling to express their support of other veiled women who experienced Islamophobic incidents after the first Gulf War. Others began veiling to champion Muslim women in Turkey and European nations who are banned from wearing *hijab*, or those living in Saudi Arabia, the Sudan, Afghanistan, or Iran who are forced to adhere to a strict Islamic dress code.

The adoption of veiling as an expression of support mostly characterizes Muslim women living in Muslim-minority societies. In an interview with the anthropologist Homa Hoodfar, Mona, an Egyptian Canadian woman born and raised in Montreal, affirmed this point: "I would never have taken up the veil if I lived in Egypt. . . . But since the Gulf War, seeing how my veiled friends were treated, I made a vow to wear the veil to make a point about my Muslimness and Arabness."[7] According to Mona, minorities must present a united front to become visible and fight stereotypes. Wearing the veil is a key feature of this unified front. Her view was confirmed by a Muslim leader in an interview with Yvonne Haddad, the well-known scholar of American Muslims from Georgetown University, who pointed out, "If they do not wear the *hijab*, how will Americans recognize that there are American Muslims?"[8]

Furthermore, Mona added that people often asked her why she veiled when living in Canada. Her reply emphasized the preservation of her rights: "I want to exercise my democratic rights, just like they do." Veiled Muslim women living in Muslim-minority societies want to be seen primarily as citizens, as individuals with the same intrinsic rights as everyone else.

Many veiled Muslim women, like Mona, are choosing to veil despite the discrimination and stereotypes because of their profound trust in the American (or Canadian or European) democratic system. For them, veiling is a public demonstration of their freedom of choice and thus of the freedom of religious practice guaranteed by the laws and constitution of the Muslim-minority country in which they live. Muslim women living in America (or Canada or Europe) express pride and empowerment because they live in a country that allows them to make their own religious choices. If, at times, they are critical of some of its foreign policy toward Muslim-majority societies and the Middle East in general, they are also at the same time patriotic citizens and staunch supporters of the U.S. Constitution, of American multiculturalism, tolerance, and secular values. In fact, a number of scholars and a growing number of Muslim women and activists consider veiling a symbol of an emerging *American* Islamic identity (as opposed to simply an Islamic identity), precisely because of the American constitutional protection of religious expression.

VEILING AND ADAPTIVE STRATEGIES

An increasing number of American Muslim women, younger ones especially, are adopting the veil as a way of creating a cultural space for themselves, one independent from their parents' traditions, and of negotiating more successfully their hybrid identity as Muslim Americans.

Because veiling, in the eyes of the Muslim community, functions as a nonverbal symbol that grants its wearer moral authority and respectability, its adoption reassures some parents that their daughters are maintaining religious and cultural values. Muslim parents, seeing their daughters veiled, tend to ease some of the restrictions that they might otherwise impose on them and grant them a degree of freedom from traditional and conservative family practices that may be unimaginable under different circumstances.

Veiling thus allows some Muslim American women to demonstrate their solidarity with their religious, racial, ethnic, and familial background, while adapting to the Muslim-minority culture in which they live. It permits them to publicly display their religious affiliations while safely participating in American popular culture. It authorizes them to interact with non-family males without compromising their reputation. Therefore, veiling grants Muslim women living in America the possibility to participate in two worlds at once, that of their Muslim parents and that of their non-Muslim friends. Seen from this perspective, veiling is an effective adaptive strategy deployed by some Muslim American women to connect the American side of the descriptor to the religious, social, and cultural background of their family of origin.

Despite some parents' objections and fear that their daughters might be targeted or discriminated against because of their *hijab*, some adolescent and college-age women choose to wear modest clothing and cover their hair because of peer pressure and the particularly vital need at that age to fit in. This is precisely what Rhys Williams and Gira Vashi discovered during their interviews with Muslim American women between eighteen and twenty-five. One of the young women explained: "If I don't wear the *hijab*, the Muslim girls [at the Muslim Students' Association, MSA] will not acknowledge me," while another pointed out, "I don't like [her college's] MSA because all the girls want you to wear the *hijab* or else they are rude to you."[9] Such statements indicate that many Muslim women imitate their friends' sartorial practices lest they be ostracized by their Muslim friends and face alone potential bullying by non-Muslim students. In this case, veiling is a means of displaying their in-group belonging, maintaining their friendships, and avoiding social isolation.

VEILING TO CHALLENGE STEREOTYPES

Many Muslim women are veiling to challenge the persistent stereotypes weighing on them since the period of early orientalist productions (see chapter 4). Orientalist paintings and Hollywood films may date to the nineteenth and early twentieth century, but many of the parameters they had set continue unabated and predetermine the way many Americans perceive veiled Muslim women. The fictions they established have been relayed by Disney and Hollywood and have displaced any sort of reality about Islam or Muslims. Rather than being understood for what they are—fantasies—these artistic representations have been taken as accurate reflections of Muslim women's lives.

Muslim American women, veiled ones especially, thus find themselves continuously explaining, justifying, and defending their choice of dress. They feel pressured to constantly clarify that they are not oppressed victims of patriarchy or religion who are forced to wear their *hijab* or *niqab*, but active leaders of their lives and in their communities who are *choosing* to wear modest clothing. For them, as they must incessantly repeat, embracing veiling as a practice does not imply the approval of an ideology of female subordination.

Many feel a special responsibility to act as diplomats of Islam, to offer positive images to American society, and thus to counter the negative views emphasized by the media and discernible in the violent actions perpetrated by a few in the name of Islam. For them, adopting the veil becomes not just a private religious and spiritual decision but a political, activist choice intended to change people's perception of Islam, of Muslims, and of veiling.

In her brief autobiographical narrative "Hijab and All: She Lives the Good Life in Pasadena," published in a collection titled *Voices of American Muslims*, Amira al-Sarraf, a Muslim American woman from California, observes that although she, like the majority of American Muslims, leads "a very normal kind of life," she is perceived otherwise by non-Muslims. This is because "how Muslim women dress is probably the most distinctive feature that non-Muslims pay attention to."[10]

The battle veiled Muslim women are waging is not just to combat general societal presuppositions about the meaning of *hijab* and Islam but surprisingly also to challenge the views of some Euro-American feminists. Many still remember how first- and second-generation American feminists did not always support Muslim women's right to choose, including to wear *hijab*. This first wave of European and American feminists had fought so hard for the right to shed corsets and bras, to wear short skirts and pants, that the notion of some women choosing to adopt clothing that limited their freedom of movement seemed extraordinary. Many Muslim women, whether they wear *hijab* or not, have expressed their dismay at finding themselves the unsuspecting victims of British and American feminists in the 1980s.[11] They learned, often at their own expense, that some Euro-American feminists did not consistently hold a nuanced view of Muslim women or did not consider them equal partners in the feminist struggle. In fact, many Muslim women discovered that in practice feminism was not always a global call for women's liberation and that they at times faced bias and racism from their assumed partners in the struggle. The brief citation of one of Mohja Kahf's poems in the epigraph of this chapter expresses the tense relation that can sometimes characterize the relation between Muslim and Euro-American feminists.

Azizah al-Hibri, a professor at the University of Richmond Law School and the founding editor of *Hypatia: A Journal of Feminist Philosophy*, has written an eloquent piece about what she calls the "blindness" of white, middle-class European and American feminists where the question of veiling and Islam are concerned. In a brief essay published in a collection of Arab American and Arab Canadian writings titled *Food for Our Grandmothers*, she surprises readers by associating veiling not with Muslims but with Euro-American feminists. In fact, her essay is aptly titled "Tear Off Your *Western* Veil" (emphasis mine).

Al-Hibri decries the fact that "Western feminists" are concerned only with two main topics related to Muslim women, clitoridectomy and veiling. They view both these practices as definitive proof of the backwardness and inferiority of Muslim societies, and also as "proof that Islam, as well as Muslim and Arab societies (which the West often conflates into one) are inherently patriarchal and oppressive." Al-Hibri thus calls on "Western feminists" to tear off their "Western veil" because it is blocking their "insight" and preventing them from hearing the actual voices of Muslim women and the real issues that they are facing. She writes that the attitude of Western feminists has resulted in "silencing Muslim/Arab-American women, not through coercion, but rather by their astounding inability to hear us regardless of how loudly we protest."[12]

This difficulty of hearing the voices and concerns of actual Muslim women and of moving beyond the issue of veiling is something that many American Muslim women regularly decry. Many of my veiled Muslim American acquaintances and colleagues, like a number of my veiled American students, report being exhausted by having always to speak of the veil, as though there were nothing else that mattered about them in the eyes of non-Muslims. Many look forward to a future when wearing the veil or not will no longer be a divisive issue, or a topic of discussion, fascination, or prejudice between Muslims and non-Muslims.

In an essay titled "The Arab Woman and I," also published in *Food for Our Grandmothers*, Mona Fayad describes her feeling of being "haunted" by the "Arab Woman" who is a symbol invented by the West that takes two main forms: first, "the Faceless, Veiled Woman, silent, passive, helpless, in need of rescue by the West"; second, the "Arab Woman" as the "exotic, erotic and seductive [woman] that follows [me] in the form of the Belly-Dancer."[13] Fayad explains that this "two-in-one Arab Woman" is always imposed on her by others, including her own students at Salem State College in Massachusetts, displacing her own sense of self, ultimately drowning her voice and true experiences as a (Muslim) Arab American woman.

The imposition of prefabricated images on Muslim women, the assumption that they are all passive, silent victims of a tyrannical religion, and the refusal of many non-Muslims to listen to their real stories are some of the reasons given to explain the decision to veil. Some Muslim women adopt *hijab* because they refuse to be labeled and placed as an object inside a box that Fayad has ironically labeled the "Organic Arab Woman."

Veiling in America can thus at times be considered a form of resistance to stereotypes and an active step to demonstrating the multiple facets of veiling practices among Muslim women. Veiling can mean that, yes, you can wear modest clothing including a headscarf or a face veil, and lead an ordinary life, like everyone else: shop, work, cook, dance, and go about your business. A young Muslim American woman I recently interviewed summed it up beautifully: "I'd really just love for people to be able to look at us as people and not as an alien creature with a scarf on our head."

DE-VEILING; OR, DECIDING TO TAKE OFF THE VEIL

The rise in prejudice, intolerance, and Islamophobia after the events of 9/11 has led some Muslim women to make the difficult decision to stop wearing the veil after having worn it for a long time, some for as many as fifteen or twenty years. For these women, wearing *hijab* had become a burden, a responsibility too heavy to continue carrying.

The conscious and self-made decision to remove *hijab* is an act that some have dubbed *de*-veiling, in contrast to *un*veiling, which describes the forced and violent removal of the veil by an outside agent. Much less is known about American Muslim women who decide to remove their face veils. De-veiling is a very emotional choice. Many compare removing their veils to going about naked in public, without a shirt on, stating that they feel embarrassed, exposed, vulnerable, and utterly immodest.

In a series of interviews aired by National Public Radio (NPR) in 2011, several American Muslim women explained the numerous reasons that led them to de-veil.[14] One of them described her decision this way: "When you put the scarf on, you have to understand that you are representing a community. And that is huge. That's a huge responsibility. And I don't know if it's for everyone." For this Muslim woman, the burden to be a public spokesperson for Muslims at all times and to represent the entire community led her to remove her *hijab*.

Another American Muslim decided to de-veil because her heightened visibility in public spaces made her always appear suspicious. She commented: "When you wear *hijab* and you walk into a room, everyone notices you; everyone stares at you; everyone makes assumptions about you." If *hijab* drew attention to her, she reasoned, it defied the original intention of veiling, which was to make women *less* noticeable. Removing the veil, especially in the context of Muslim-minority societies, is considered by some as an act of obeying the *spirit*, rather than the letter, of the Qur'anic injunction to veil.

Other Muslim women decided to take off their *hijab* because they feared for their own safety after being spat at, yelled at, and generally intimidated while walking on the street. Many veiled women throughout America have reported such incidents of intimidation both before and increasingly after 9/11, including on college campuses.

In fact, the events of 9/11 marked the onset of a long period when Muslims generally, and veiled Muslim women in particular, were perceived as somehow implicated in acts of terrorism or in sympathy with them. Many Muslim advocacy groups urged veiled women to exercise care when going out in public, while some *imams* advised Muslim women to remove their headscarves for their own protection. Veiled Muslim women's only choice was blending in or risking potential violence: "Walk the walk or go under cover," as an article in the *Atlanta Journal-Constitution* stated on September 11, 2001.

Similar incidents have been reported by many non-Muslims, male and female, whose clothing or phenotype vaguely evoked the "Middle East" or "Islam." This means that Hispanics and Italians were also targeted after 9/11, as were Sikh men whose turbans were mistaken for Muslim head coverings. In fact, the first hate-crime victim of the 9/11 events in the United States was not a Muslim woman but a Sikh man. Balbir Singh Sodhi was murdered on September 15, 2001, in Mesa, Arizona. Evidently, the killer perceived any clothing that resembled a Muslim-style covering worn by a person with a Middle Eastern phenotype as inherently threatening.

Such events occurred before 9/11 too. I, for one, was victim of similar suspicions toward veiled Muslim women and the tendency to intimidate and bully them. This happened in the summer of 1990, shortly after the beginning of the first Gulf War while taking an evening stroll in a small town in New Jersey with my cousin who was wearing *hijab*. The event stands out in my mind not only because it traumatized us but also because it took place well before 9/11, and thus prior to the general anxiety floating around the nation toward anything having to do with Islam and Muslims.

I remember walking down the street with my cousin who had just arrived in the United States from Egypt to join her husband. We were enjoying ourselves, as we had countless times before, talking about various everyday matters and paying little attention to our surroundings. Suddenly we heard a group of teenage boys who were standing on the other side of the street and yelling "go back home" while throwing stones at us. I grabbed my cousin's hand and began running, pulling her behind me. Luckily, the stones did not reach us and we were not physically hurt. But I was emotionally scarred by the incident.

My cousin, luckily, did not speak English. She did not understand what the boys had said or why we had started to run. She kept asking me what the boys had said and why they were throwing stones at us. I kept pulling her away, repeating "hurry up, hurry up," until we were at a safe distance. I knew, of course, that the boys' anger was directed at my cousin's *hijab*, which set in motion a series of simplistic associations in their minds: veil, Islam, terrorism, American war in the Gulf. Having lived in the United States for almost a decade by then, I had never before experienced outright racism and violence toward Muslims and veiled

Muslim women, not even when I myself veiled in the early 1980s while living in Pennsylvania.

This event has remained firmly anchored in my mind throughout the years. Not only had I witnessed firsthand the effects of ignorance and fear but I understood more clearly than before the cost of wearing *hijab* for so many Muslim women. Women who wear *hijab* in Muslim-minority countries often face an enormous amount of ignorance from many non-Muslims. This lack of understanding can become a veritable safety hazard at times. The women must be very brave and hold firmly to their faith to continue wearing *hijab* in the face of stereotypes and assumptions.

I would be remiss if I did not also acknowledge that de-veiling in America is also associated with some American Muslim women's increased knowledge about Islam, Muslim history, and the range of ways sacred texts have been interpreted over time. Many of the American Muslim women I interviewed, like those featured on the NPR program, explain that they decided to stop wearing the *hijab* because they no longer considered it a requirement of Islam. In this regard, these Muslim women may be considered part of the global movement of progressive Muslims described in chapter 2. These women are no longer satisfied with having the meaning of the Qur'an and the rules of Islam dictated to them. They are re-reading the Qur'an, uncovering the layers of meaning that have been attached to it throughout the centuries, and recognizing the extent to which the open-ended and flexible verses of the Qur'an have been displaced in favor of conservative interpretations.

As they peel away these imposed interpretations, Muslim women are embracing the elasticity of the Qur'anic text with its spirit of gender equality and message of universal social justice. The growing religious and spiritual awareness of American Muslim women is leading many to de-veil to be true to their newly discovered spiritual selves and to their evolving identities that are no longer tied down by culturally specific injunctions and rules.

This spiritual awakening comes at a great cost for many American Muslims. On the one hand, de-veiling makes them less of a perceived threat and able to blend in more easily with non-Muslims. On the other hand, de-veiling, whether it occurs for political, personal, or spiritual reasons, often leads to a backlash from Muslim family and friends. Some of those hailing from conservative backgrounds are blamed for allegedly betraying their Islamic roots and culture, for not standing firm against their detractors, or for succumbing to American values. In close-knit American Muslim communities especially, whenever a woman decides to de-veil, she is censured for daring to question what many consider "God's will." Evidently, the whole topic of veiling is as much a controversy among Muslims as it is among non-Muslims.

■ American Muslim women must thus fight two battles at once: one against stereotypes and assumptions from their non-Muslim neighbors, and another against conventional interpretations of Islam espoused by conservative members of their community. Both constitute the two sides of the same challenge that American Muslim women face to assert their right to religious expression.

Contrary to what some may believe, wearing the veil in Euro-American societies is rarely, if ever, the sign of an imposed dress code or an indication of submission to patriarchy. Rather, it is a mark of inner strength, courage, and faith precisely because it is so misunderstood. Women who decide to de-veil teach us a great deal about the very real challenges that women who wear the *hijab* face in America on a daily basis.

PART THREE

Veiling in the World and Words of Women

Understanding Muslim women's veiling cannot be complete without a consideration of Muslim women's own voices, modes of expression, and cultural practices. What does veiling mean in the life of a Muslim woman and how might she express her own style or assert her resistance to this sartorial tradition? These are some of the central questions I explore in this third and final section of *What Is Veiling?*

Each of the following three chapters addresses one aspect of Muslim women's veiling and shows how attitudes toward veiling have varied during the past century. Chapter 7 examines the two main voices of feminism in Muslim-majority societies and describes how some feminists have rejected veiling because it allegedly oppresses women while others have embraced it because they see it as a means of liberating women. Chapter 8 focuses on the recent development of the Islamic fashion industry and on how some women have adopted fashion as an expression of individuality or as a strategy of resistance toward conservative readings of Islam. Chapter 9 surveys a selection of poetic and artistic responses by Muslim women that point to the great heterogeneity of voices and standpoints on veiling. Taken together, these three chapters reveal that for some Muslim women, veiling is a practice that sits squarely at the crossroads of religious, political, feminist, economic, and sociocultural traditions.

Feminism is not bound to one culture. It is no more Arab
than it is American, no more Mediterranean than it is North European.
—miriam cooke, *Women Claim Islam* (2001)

Feminism is a movement to end sexism, sexist exploitation, and oppression.
—bell hooks, *Feminism Is for Everybody* (2000)

[Islamic feminism is] a feminist discourse and practice articulated within
an Islamic paradigm. Islamic feminism, which derives its understanding and
mandate from the Qur'an, seeks rights and justice for women, and for men,
in the totality of their existence. Islamic feminism is on the whole more
radical than Muslims' secular feminisms.
—Margot Badran, interview published by Al-Ahram Online (2002)

CHAPTER SEVEN

Veiling and Feminism

Can veiling really be an outward sign of feminism? This question is often posed with much skepticism, if not downright irony. The mere suggestion that one might associate traditional Islamic dress—the alleged symbol of Islamic patriarchy and the oppression of women—with feminism, a movement that many value as a hallmark of Euro-American civilizational advances, is perceived as an oxymoron. Many Muslims and non-Muslims think it is simply impossible that a veiled Muslim woman could consider herself or be considered a feminist.

After all, in the view of many, the principal goal of feminism is not only the liberation of women from patriarchal, familial, sexual, political, and/or economic power dynamics but also their liberation from imposed cultural traditions, including sartorial customs. Let us remember that as early as the 1850s, American feminists fought hard to shed corsets and demanded their right to wear pants and short skirts. In the early part of the twentieth century, Euro-American feminists asserted their personal freedoms by cutting their hair short or letting it hang loose.

Until recently, there has been a tendency in Euro-American societies to associate the amount of clothing worn with the extent of a woman's liberation and at times to measure it against her commitment to feminism. A short skirt, a tank dress, and shorts are, for some, indicative of a liberated woman, a feminist one.[1] From this perspective, a Muslim woman who wears a head cover, at times a face veil, and who goes around in a long *abaya* or wears long-sleeved shirts and maxi skirts *cannot* be a feminist. Often people assume that the only women who dress in modest and traditional Muslim garb are those forced to do so.

And yet many Muslim women who veil do not believe that their veil or other modest sartorial choices limit their movement or their agency. In fact, many assert just the opposite and consider anyone who believes otherwise a neo-orientalist who is rehearsing the familiar nineteenth-century Euro-American rhetoric of the civilizing mission (see chapter 4). At that time, Euro-American rulers had justified their military expeditions by claiming to rescue Muslim women from their so-called subjugation. They thus encouraged, and at times forced, Muslim women to shed their veils.

The desire to liberate Muslim women from their allegedly oppressive religion and veiling practices is not limited to the nineteenth century with its particular political and ideological configuration. It continues to circulate today among many secular Muslims and non-Muslims who are concerned about the rise of Muslim veiling practices around the world. And yet shedding the veil or putting it back on defies simple binary categories of emancipation and oppression. Whether a woman wears *hijab* or not is *not* directly associated with her level of independence and feminism or with the amount of oppression she presumably suffers.

Amina Wadud has recently summed up the impossibility of assigning *hijab* a singular meaning, be it of liberation or coercion, of piety or resistance, by writing that "the *hijab* of coercion and the *hijab* of choice *look the same*. The *hijab* of oppression and the *hijab* of liberation look the same. The *hijab* of deception and the *hijab* of integrity look the same. You can no more tell the extent of a Muslim woman's sense of personal bodily integrity or piety from 45 inches of cloth than you can spot a fly on the wall at two thousand feet."[2]

A richer and more culturally sensitive understanding of Muslim veiling must take into account the history of veiling practices during the past century and the development of feminist debates about veiling in Muslim-majority societies during that time. While the label of feminism is contested among Muslims (and non-Muslims), some embracing it wholeheartedly and others rejecting it, it is important to examine the two extreme ends in the debate to understand the range of feminist perspectives: On one end, the perspective of those feminists who consider veiling an oppressive tradition that must be shed, and at the other end of the spectrum, those who embrace veiling in the name of Islamic feminism and of women's true liberation.[3]

THE EARLY FEMINIST MOVEMENT: HUDA SHAʿRAWI AND SHEDDING THE VEIL IN MUSLIM-MAJORITY SOCIETIES

In May 1923, on their return from the International Women's Alliance Conference in Rome, the Egyptian delegation made up of Huda Shaʿrawi, her protégée Saiza Nabarawi, and Nabawiyya Musa (the first Egyptian woman to obtain a secondary school diploma) surprised the Egyptian population and the world at large by shedding their *hijab* as they stepped off the train in Cairo. As is clear from photographs of the event widely disseminated in contemporary newspapers, and despite the use of the phrase of *rafʿ el-hijab* (shedding the *hijab*), which is what their act has been called, the veils that Shaʿrawi and her two colleagues shed were actually face veils, not their head covers, which they maintained and continued to wear for several more years. Nevertheless, the decision to appear in public without a face veil was interpreted as an unmistakable act of defiance against solidly entrenched customs. This moment marked the official birth of the Arab feminist movement.

Following *rafʿ el-hijab*, the feminist movement quickly spread to other Arab countries and across Muslim-majority societies. Upper- and middle-class urban women first in Egypt, and then in Turkey, Iran, Tunisia, and elsewhere began casting off their veils in imitation of the revolutionary actions of a few women in Cairo. In cities, Egyptian Copts, Arab Christians, and Arab Jewish women who had been veiled for centuries were among the first to follow suit. Rural women, on the other hand, who had never traditionally worn a face veil because such attire would have greatly interfered with their farmwork, seized the opportunity to adopt the very same veiling practices that urban and aristocratic women were discarding.[4]

Peasant women appropriated veiling because, at the time, the veil symbolized primarily women's upper-class, non-working status, rather than their religious background. In the early twentieth century, a Middle Eastern woman who veiled could be a woman of any religion whose family or husband could afford to have her stay at home and not work. For rural women who were accustomed to hard work outside the home, the adoption of *hijab* represented urbanization and the hope for upward social movement.

I should emphasize that the type of feminism that Sha'rawi introduced in the 1920s was primarily political and secular, not religious. In other words, challenging Islamic traditions was not Sha'rawi's principal goal. Rather, she was chiefly interested in liberating Egypt from British colonial rule, achieving national independence, and encouraging women to get involved in the reconstruction of the new Egypt. When she established the Egyptian Feminist Union (EFU) in 1923, Sha'rawi wanted to promote women's rights in a variety of political, social, and cultural spheres. She also desired the end of British colonization and supported the Palestinian cause. Casting off the veil was perhaps a by-product of these activities, but it was certainly not the main platform of her feminist activism. Yet many Euro-American feminists today tend to reduce Sha'rawi's feminism to a religiously motivated action, that of liberation through the act of casting off the veil.

REASSESSING SHA'RAWI'S ACT OF SHEDDING THE VEIL

Wherever the act of shedding the veil stood in Sha'rawi's overall feminist program, it signified much more than just liberating Muslim (as well as Coptic and Jewish) women. Recent scholarship in early twentieth-century Egyptian cultural and gender studies has uncovered the extent to which Sha'rawi's act of shedding the veil, even as it was a watershed event for Muslim-majority societies, was also a valorization of and a concession to the colonizers' perspective.

If for Sha'rawi veiling marked the inferiority and subordination of Muslim women, it was because this was precisely the way it had been construed in the logic of European colonial domination (see chapter 4). The rhetoric of European colonizers and the association they had established between the lot of Muslim women, the oppression of the *hijab*, and the backwardness of Muslim-majority societies became part of the core arguments of the nascent Arab feminist movement.

This means that when Sha'rawi shed her veil in 1923, she was not just making a heroic gesture that challenged her own society to bring about women's social and cultural liberation. She was also putting into practice what British and French colonizers of Egypt had been advocating for at least a century, thereby unwittingly enacting an imperialist agenda. Ironically, the first symbolic act of Arab feminism is above all a tribute to European colonial doctrine.

That Sha'rawi's feminism reproduced perhaps subconsciously one of the main tenets of imperialism and its negative views of indigenous women ought perhaps not to be all that surprising. After all, Sha'rawi, like all upper-class women of the time, had been given a European (French) education. In fact, in her own autobiography, she acknowledges her love of French literature, and the role that her French education, and her European friends played on her political and feminist activities. Sha'rawi's European education had taught her not just the complexities of the French language and the beauty of French literature but also the innate superiority of European over native culture. The act of shedding the veil is an example of such teachings, of the superiority of unveiling (and of European women) to veiling (practiced by native Egyptian women).

In a brilliant book titled *Women and Gender in Islam*, Leila Ahmed suggests that Sha'rawi's symbolic discarding of the veil was most likely an action instilled in her since childhood by her French friend and mentor Eugénie Le Brun. This Frenchwoman who lived in Egypt after her marriage to an Egyptian had transmitted to the young Huda the commonly held European belief that "the veil stood in the way of their [Egyptian women's] advancement." Le Brun's words are reminiscent of those uttered by the British consul general of Egypt, Lord Cromer. They reveal the extent to which colonial views were shared by Europeans and the Egyptian upper classes.

THE FIRST EGYPTIAN FEMINIST WAS A MAN: QASIM AMIN

Sha'rawi was not the first Arab person to promote women's unveiling in Egypt, though she may have been the *first woman* to do so. The first advocate of Arab feminism and of unveiling was an Egyptian *man* by the name of Qasim Amin, and the first Arabic feminist manifesto is his hugely controversial book of 1899, *The Liberation of Woman* (*Tahrir al-Mar'a*). The publication of this text marked the onset of the first battle over the veil in the Arabic mainstream press.

Like Sha'rawi, Amin was thoroughly Europeanized. Also like her, he was French educated and belonged to the more privileged classes. Even more explicitly than does Sha'rawi in her autobiography, Amin lavishes praise on European civilization in his *The Liberation of Woman*. He sees it as superior, and he virulently condemns Muslims and Egyptians, whom he paints as lazy, dirty, and backward.

Muslim women in particular are harshly disapproved of in the text, with Amin calling for their education, their unveiling, and the end of gender segregation, arguing that learning comes precisely from such gender mixing. He writes that the veil constitutes a "huge barrier between woman and her elevation, and consequently a barrier between the nation and its advance."[5]

Amin's *The Liberation of Woman* sparked a heated debate, a great deal of anger, and much passion. His argument that Arab society needed to undergo a major cultural transformation and to reform some of its basic practices, above all the veiling of women and gender segregation, was received differently by members of different social classes. Generally speaking, the aristocratic, upper, and upper-middle classes, who had gained many advantages from the colonial presence through their various collaborations and mutual economic interests, were predisposed to favor European ways. They tended to be European educated, to have interacted with European expats in Egypt, to have traveled abroad on a regular basis, and to have had less direct contact with the Egyptian population as a whole. Their education led them to believe in European cultural superiority and in Arab backwardness. Many members of the Arab upper social classes were already convinced of Amin's views even before he published his book. Thus they tended to agree with his call for social and cultural reform and favored the unveiling of women.

On the other hand, many lower-class Egyptians had been utterly disenfranchised by European colonizers, who had limited their access to education, to advanced government positions, to health, and to opportunities of upward social mobility in general. For them, Amin's views were controversial primarily because they echoed British colonial discourse. These Egyptians loudly criticized Amin's call to reform and his invocation to shed the veil. In the end, their voices were drowned out by those of the upper, more Europeanized classes.

Amin's call for major cultural and social reform paved the way for Sha'rawi and the first waves of feminism in Egypt and throughout the Middle East. This was the beginning of profound sociocultural transformations, especially concerning women's sartorial practices and female sociopolitical activities. Starting in the 1920s, Muslim and non-Muslim women throughout the Middle East began taking off their veils, first the ones covering their faces, and soon the ones that covered their heads. Sleeves and hemlines became shorter, and European-style attire (skirts and blouses) became popular in the race to become modern and catch up with European civilizational advances.

At first, these changes were adopted only by those urban women who had some affiliation with European culture, but soon they were taken up by women from a wide range of socioeconomic backgrounds. We could say that Amin's book, well before Sha'rawi's public unveiling in a Cairo station, set the stage for women shedding their veils and adopting European dress.

A WAVE OF UNVEILING: MODERNIZATION AND PROGRESS SWEEP MUSLIM-MAJORITY SOCIETIES

While the call to shed the veil, to reform in order to achieve progress and partake in European industrial and cultural advances, began in Egypt, it quickly spread to other Middle Eastern societies. The cases of Turkey and Iran are especially interesting.

In Turkey, Mustafa Kemal Atatürk (1881–1938), the founder and first president of the Republic of Turkey, undertook Westernizing and secular reforms, some of which affected women's dress (see chapter 3). Like those of Qasim Amin, Atatürk's views reflected his European affinities and reproduced colonial discourse with its binary opposition between Europeans (advanced) and natives (primitive and backward). In an oft-cited speech from 1925, Atatürk explicitly expressed his profound contempt for traditional Muslim women's dress, which, he claimed, made them (and by extension, traditionally dressed men) appear uncivilized. He reportedly said: "In some places I have seen women who put a piece of cloth or a towel or something like that over their heads to hide their faces, and who turn their backs or huddle themselves on the ground when a man passes by. What are the meaning and sense of this behavior? Gentlemen, can the mothers and daughters of a civilized nation adopt this strange manner, this barbarous posture? It is a spectacle that makes the nation an object of ridicule. It must be remedied at once."[6]

Atatürk's remedy to the perceived backwardness of his society was to ban from the new Turkish Republic all overt signs of religious affiliation. In 1925, Atatürk introduced the Hat Law, which forced all male civil servants to adopt a Western-style hat instead of the traditional fez or turban, and later he forced Turkish men to abandon their traditional clothing in favor of European suits. Contrary to what is often believed, Atatürk never introduced legislation to ban specifically the *hijab* or headscarf. Nevertheless, the veil was strongly discouraged in the name of modernizing Turkey, that is, of Westernizing and secularizing it.

Similarly, Reza Shah Pahlavi (1878–1944), the imperial monarch of Iran from 1925 to 1941 and a staunch Westernizer, also introduced legislation between 1920 and 1930 that was intended to modernize his country and make it appear civilized. As one of his many reforms, Reza Shah proclaimed a law banning *hijab* and cracked down on any disobedient woman and businesses that catered to her. Because Reza Shah's unveiling law echoed European perspectives, the Europeanized secular Persian upper classes strongly supported it, while members of other social classes and of conservative religious groups resented its colonial flavor. For them, the veil signaled not backwardness but respect, a protection of women, and a profound symbol of cultural belonging.

The examples of Egypt, Turkey, and Iran demonstrate that the history of the feminist debate about Muslim women's veiling throughout Muslim-majority societies is one inscribed within the history of colonial domination and of the growing class divisions promoted by colonial powers. Despite the return to veiling that we have witnessed throughout Muslim-majority societies since the late 1970s, some Muslims remain suspicious of any feminism that calls on women to cast off their veils because they remember that unveiling was an ally to colonialism, Western imperialism in disguise, not too long ago.

Reading Arab feminism and the call to unveil without a sensitivity to this history of colonization and the Europeanization of the Arab upper classes leads us to interpret unveiling (and de-veiling) simplistically as a symbol of female autonomy. Such an analysis, as attractive as it may be, actually derives from European notions of progress established and disseminated during the period of colonialism.

ISLAMIC FEMINISM: EMBRACING VEILING

According to Leila Ahmed, shedding the veil served as the chief feminist platform in Muslim-majority societies throughout the twentieth century. Yet she also points out that there has always been an alternative voice of resistance to this pro-colonial feminism. This alternative voice was audible even in the early years of the twentieth century, though it remained, until recently, marginalized. Championed by Malak Hifni Nassef (1886–1918), this alternative movement sought to oppose what it considered a hasty rush to modernize without a thoughtful consideration of local customs and traditions and without taking the time to establish the building blocks of a modern society. Nassef's views stemmed from her deep mistrust of men and of their alleged quest to liberate women.

As the first woman to publish in the mainstream Arabic press, Nassef wrote a series of articles responding to Amin's book and to his call to unveil women. In one of them, cited in Ahmed's *Women and Gender in Islam*, she denounced the corruption and arrogance inherent in men's claims that they wanted to unveil women to liberate them: "The majority of us women continue to be oppressed by the injustice of man, who in his despotism commands and forbids us so that now we can have no opinion even about ourselves. . . . If he orders us to veil, we veil, and if he now demands that we unveil, we unveil, and if he wishes us to be educated, we are educated. Is he well intentioned in all he asks of us and on our behalf, or does he wish us ill? There is no doubt that he has erred grievously against us . . . in decreeing our rights in the past and no doubt that he errs grievously . . . in decreeing our rights now."[7]

Nassef's distrust of men's intentions and behavior, coupled with her own observations and knowledge about women's experiences, led her to regard unveiling as an unwise solution to the myriad problems facing Egyptian society. In her view, given "a collection of men such as we have at present, whose abuse and shamelessness a woman should not be exposed to, and a collection of women such as we have at present, whose understanding is that of babes, for women to unveil and mix with men would be an innovation that would lead to evil."[8] Nassef denounced those Egyptian women who were already appearing unveiled in public. According to Nassef, these were all upper-class women interested only in looking fashionable, pursuing neither liberty nor knowledge, which were, for her, the only worthy goals. Instead, Nassef called for the reformation of men's moral character and for the education of women as the necessary prerequisites for a healthy nation. Only once these building blocks had been established could a debate about women's veiling take place. And only at that time could women be left to choose what to wear.

Nassef's call to maintain *hijab* as a practice is thus not based on traditional, conservative reasons. Nassef did not believe that Islam dictated a specific dress code for women, nor did she believe that modesty could be measured by the presence or absence of a veil. She was simply wary of the indiscriminate adoption of European ways in the name of modernization and questioned the suitability of unveiling for Egyptian women of her time. Much more pressing in her view was the reformation of men's attitudes and the education of women.

The examples of Sha'rawi and Nassef reveal that the relationship between the veil, feminism, and religious and social conservatism in the Arab context is much more complex than generally assumed. For despite their opposite views on the veiling of women, Sha'rawi and Nassef were both feminists who agreed on the importance of female autonomy and agency. Both spoke out in favor of educating women to the highest degree of their ability, and both strove to reform marriage laws and establish women's liberation. Both also expressed clear political goals and struggled to end British colonial occupation to help Egypt gain political and economic independence. Sha'rawi and Nassef diverged only in their attitudes toward European culture and, conversely, toward Egyptian culture (admiration or denunciation). It is this point of disagreement that led them to adopt opposite attitudes toward *hijab*. Emulating European ways led Sha'rawi to support women's unveiling, while her suspicion of European ways led Nassef to support veiling and to call for women to freely choose their own style of clothing.

Because Nassef's narrative of resistance favored *hijab*, it has been for the greater part of the twentieth century considered antifeminist, that is, anti-Western, antimodern, antisecular, anti-Amin, and anti-Sha'rawi. Only today has this alternative eclipsed that of Sha'rawi and Amin and emerged as the dominant voice of Arab, Middle Eastern, and Muslim feminists. In fact, the rise in women's adoption of *hijab* throughout Muslim-majority societies today may be considered one of the contemporary legacies of Nassef's version of Islamic feminism and her pro-choice position toward veiling.

FROM UNVEILING TO RE-VEILING: ISLAMICIZATION AND THE RESURGENCE OF VEILING PRACTICES SINCE THE 1970S

The type of feminism prevalent throughout the greater part of the twentieth century in Muslim-majority societies has meant that until the late

1970s, urban women from all socioeconomic classes no longer wore any type of veil and that they had adopted European fashion. In fact, any woman wearing any type of head or face veil between approximately the 1940s and the late 1970s could safely be assumed less educated or rural. No educated, sophisticated, or modern woman would be caught wearing what was then considered an outdated peasant's outfit.

Watching Egyptian films of the 1940s to 1960s, I am always struck by women's outfits (short-sleeved dresses and skirts), by their European lifestyle, common use of alcohol, and mixed-gender dancing. There are no veils in these films except as erotic accessories in belly-dancing scenes or to portray an uneducated village woman. My own mother's wedding pictures from the early 1960s, like those of all her friends, show women wearing sleeveless and low-cut dresses. This is thirty years before they all began wearing *hijab*.

It is only in the early 1980s that I began to notice an increasing number of Muslim women covering their hair with a scarf (a small one at first, and one or two decades later it became a larger, longer, and darker one) and adopting first longer skirts, then full-length dresses. Veiling was at first embraced by twenty- and thirty-year-olds; a decade later, women of all ages followed suit. I was shocked to say the least. Today, and in the aftermath of the Arab Spring, very few women go out on the streets without a headscarf, and those who are unveiled are automatically assumed to be Copts.

The words of an Egyptian woman interviewed by the anthropologist Fadwa El Guindi in the late 1970s gives a sense of the shockwaves that the new veiling trend sent to a large segment of the Egyptian population. This woman commented: "That a young woman goes on pilgrimage to Mecca two or three times, this is not a phenomenon, this is good, it is being a good Muslim; but to dress like these college girls and cover with a veil, now that is a phenomenon. It is not even Islamic."[9]

The religious revival that began in the late 1970s and 1980s and the visible signs of piety that became the hallmark of this period were especially bewildering to many Muslims and non-Muslims because the women who had begun to veil were educated, professional, and modern.[10] The presupposition at the time was that veiling signaled a backward individual, while unveiling meant being modern. The women concerned were decidedly modern, but they had chosen to veil. How could that be possible?

VEILING AND POLITICAL RESISTANCE

El Guindi has dated the resumption of veiling throughout Muslim-majority societies to Egypt's 1973 war against Israel. According to her, the widespread espousal of *hijab* at that time symbolized the population's disillusionment with the political regime and a feeling of profound humiliation in the face of Zionist advances.

The "newborn Muslims" of the 1970s, whose main action and recruiting grounds were college campuses, believed that Arabs had erred when they turned to Arab nationalism and followed the leadership of Egypt's first president and hero, Gamal Abdel Nasser. For them, only Islam and a strict observance of Islamic rituals could restore the sense of security and self-esteem they had lost. They vied to re-create an Islamic empire to replace Arab nationalism, called for the youth to identify as Muslims rather than as Arabs, and supported the reestablishment of gender segregation. They also insisted that men lower their eyes and grow their beards and that women adopt veiling as a marker of identity and a visible sign of their adherence to Islamic principles.

The veiling of the 1970s and 1980s was thus not due to religious fervor and piety alone. Rather, it was also associated with the rise of political Islam and a strategy of resistance against authoritarian regimes.[11] The anthropologist Carla Jones, for instance, has argued that the new veiling that occurred in Indonesia during the 1980s was far from marking a simple resurgence of spirituality. She found that Indonesian Muslim women who began veiling in the 1980s and 1990s were no longer those who had completed the pilgrimage to Mecca. Rather, an increasing number of younger women had begun adopting *hijab* as an expression of resistance and as a safe means of critiquing Suharto's corrupt government (1965–98). The type of *hijab* these younger women began wearing differed noticeably from the traditional *kerudung*, a gauzy, loose-fitting overcoat. Instead, they adopted the *busana islami* (Islamic dress), which consisted of a flowing dress or a long skirt with an oversized tunic and some type of head cover.

More recently, some Indonesian Muslim women have started wearing the *jilbab*, a fashionable piece of attire. This type of dress, reminiscent of Arab women's *hijabs*, gives Indonesian women a sense of belonging to an imagined global Muslim community and serves to symbolically include them in the growing movement of piety and resistance to local corruption and global American political, economic, and cultural encroachment.

VEILING, FEMINISM, AND SOCIOECONOMIC INDEPENDENCE

Piety and politics alone do not explain why an increasing number of Muslim women around the world have decided to veil since the late 1970s. New social and economic conditions in many Muslim-majority societies have also come into play and are partly responsible for the rise in veiling practices.

The number of Muslim women with college degrees has been steadily rising. Many of them are professionals, having entered the workforce in fields and occupations traditionally monopolized by men. Moreover, because of poor economic conditions among the middle and lower middle classes in all Muslim-majority societies, women have had to take on jobs outside the home to help support their families. These conditions have created an entirely new situation in which Muslim men and women have to work side by side in public spaces traditionally gendered masculine.[12] Some modifications have thus had to be introduced to accommodate the growing number of women coming into regular contact with men outside of their families. Many Muslim women resorted to *hijab* for the protection they felt they needed to circulate comfortably in public and hold jobs alongside men.

The new veiling thus allows some conservative women to maintain traditional gender segregation while observing various local conventions of modesty and community customs when interacting in public, non-segregated environments. It allows them to be modest and maintain a personal subjective space while actively fulfilling their civic, social, and individual responsibilities.

The *hijab* allows some Muslim women to maintain a public image of respectability, to dissociate themselves from prevailing assumptions about modern (European or American) women—such as that they are sexually and morally loose. Many Muslim women have told me that they have decided to veil to deflect unwanted flirtations and harassment from men on the streets. When they go about veiled, these women feel safer and less likely to be harassed, although this is certainly changing today.[13]

Other women state that veiling gives them greater mobility, even allowing them to date without compromising their reputation. Because a veiled woman is often assumed to be morally conservative and chaste, she is less likely to be disparaged if she is unmarried and seen in public with an unrelated man. When veiled, a woman accompanied by a man is typically assumed to be in a legal relationship.

Thus veiling, far from confining women, as many non-Muslims might hastily assume, instead sometimes allows Muslim women to assert themselves as active individuals and citizens, to compete with men on equal terms in the workforce, and to exercise their human right to a satisfying public and personal life. If veiling is on the rise in Muslim-majority societies today, and it certainly is, it is because for many the veil is a sign of and means to female autonomy.

Many Muslims around the world are eager to make known that the veil can be *independently and willingly adopted* by Muslim women. Reflecting this assertion of women's agency, a linguistic shift has occurred in Egypt in the past two years, and a new term has been coined to refer to veiled women. It has been adopted by some specialty *hijab* shops as part of a new marketing strategy, and it is one gaining currency in some media outlets. Rather than cater to *muhajjabat* (covered women), some *hijab* specialty shops thus now use the related *mutahajjibat* (women who cover). Even though the form and style of the clothing sold is the same for both, the new term emphasizes women's agency. The difference between *mutahajjibat* and *muhajjabat* is therefore the difference between the active and the passive adoption of *hijab*. Today's Muslim women are the dynamic *mutahajjibat*—professional, independent, and self-assertive women who are active in society even as they appear to many non-Muslims as stereotypically conservative and passive.

■ We can therefore say that in contrast to the early wave of Middle Eastern feminists who called for shedding the veil, many Muslim feminists today see no contradiction between female equality and wearing *hijab* or even *niqab*. This is precisely why we increasingly see the re-adoption of veiling and modest dress that had all but disappeared forty years ago in cities. Though it appears counterintuitive, the increase in veiling practices is partly a result of the rise of Islamic feminism. Many Muslim women today are wearing *hijab because* they are pious feminists, *not* because they are oppressed or subjugated.

The rising numbers of active, well-educated, and veiled Muslim women around the world has been accompanied by a growth in the number of businesses catering to their needs. These businesses, which I describe in the next chapter, claim to encourage Muslim women's pious self-image through the consumption of Islamic goods and new fashion lines. They provide another angle from which to view and understand why many Muslim women choose to veil today.

My little cousins were referring to the *hijab* as an ugly cover and disliked it because it did not go well with their colorful dresses.

I think they [Muslim customers] are interested in buying Turban because it allows them to dress up, mix and match, express their personal style, all while remaining within the acceptable borders of Islamic dress code.
—Rand AlBassam, Saudi fashion entrepreneur, founder of T4Turban (2012)

Hijab makes me an original Inspector Gadget. It is a Bluetooth-,
age- and bad-haircut hider; protects me from germs, UV, bees, slimy guys and
surprises like poop and sudden changes in the weather; it's low maintenance,
nonconformist and nuns say hi to me.
—Mona Ebrahim, *101 Reasons Why I'm Glad I Wear Hijab* (2013)

We want to change the way this product has been sold for centuries. Our vision is to cheer up the world of *hijab*. —Tarik Houchar, owner of Hijab House (2013)

CHAPTER EIGHT

Islamic Fashion, Beauty Pageants, and Muslim Dolls

In the past decade, each time I travel to the Middle East, I find myself eagerly anticipating the new styles and colors of *hijab* that Muslim women will be wearing. I am struck, every time, by the new veiling fashions, the growing complexity in the way headscarves are wrapped around the face and neck, the creative layering of the clothes, the colors that are becoming more and more vibrant, as well as by the detailed embroidery, multicolored pins, and shiny stones that decorate the fabrics of *abayas*, jackets, and headscarves. I am also always impressed by the perfect color coordination between clothes, headscarves, makeup, and accessories including handbags and shoes.

I am especially humbled by how much everyone I encounter seems to know about the names of the most recent fashion brands, accessories, and colors of the season, something that I, living in the United States and traveling regularly to Europe, have never seemed to master. The fashion statements on the streets of Muslim-majority countries are up to date with the most recent developments in Europe and the United States, even as they are often also an adaptation of Euro-American trends to suit the tastes and requirements of Muslim women living in Muslim-majority societies. Yet increasingly, many Muslim women also show a creativity undaunted and unrestricted by any Euro-American fashion trend. They have themselves become trendsetters of new styles that are gaining popularity and quickly spreading among Muslim women of all socioeconomic classes around the world.

My elder family members and my most conservative relatives often feel irritated by these new veiling fashions. For them, as for many conservative Muslims in general, veiling and seeking to be fashionable are contradictory practices. The very concept of "fashionable veiling" is viewed as an oxymoron. After all, isn't the goal of *hijab* to be modest and to go unnoticed? And isn't the goal of fashion the exact opposite, to draw attention to the self, incite desire, and at times even flaunt social status and economic capital? For many, a person who seeks to be fashionable is someone who cannot be truly pious.

For many conservative Muslims, the development of a booming new industry of Muslim haute couture attests to the growing appeal of Euro-American fashion and consumer culture to younger Muslim generations. The very idea of Muslim fashion is viewed by some as a threat both to the practices of devotion and to Islamic core values, signaling surrender to Western capitalism, materialism, and their allegedly corrupt moral values.

A conservative Muslim website recently posted a rant against Muslim haute couture that speaks eloquently to the frustration that puritanical Muslims feel toward the growing appeal of Euro-American fashion: "Every day, we see our Muslim sisters proudly displaying names and initials on their clothing. . . . What are they advertising? CD, YSL, D&G [Christian Dior, Yves Saint Laurent, Dolce & Gabbana]. How ironic that the most modest of dressing—the cloak and scarf—should become contaminated by advertising the names of some of the most shameless and perverted people in the world."[1]

Muslim fashion is not just criticized from within conservative segments of the Muslim community. It is also met with great skepticism and condescension by many Muslim secularists who advance arguments strikingly parallel to those of conservative Muslims. They, too, denounce Muslim women's interest in fashion as deceitful, tasteless, and pretentious. This is of course counterintuitive, as we might have assumed that secularists would support Muslim women's interest in fashion as a posi-

Muslim woman wearing a *niqab* with YSL logo (Jodi Cobb/National Geographic Stock)

tive expression of cosmopolitanism and modernity. Yet this is not always the case. Some Muslim secularists indeed believe that veiled women ought not to be attracted to fashion. If they are, it must be because they are being manipulated by a fraudulent industry that uses religion to cover up its commercial interests. These Muslim secularists, like conservatives, blame designers of Islamic fashion for exploiting Muslim women's conflicting ambitions and persuading them that they can be both modest and beautiful.

As if this were not enough, Islamic fashion has also met mounting scrutiny from the mainstream Euro-American fashion industry, which considers Muslim fashion a failed fashion, if it recognizes it at all. Do Muslims know *anything* about fashion and are Muslim women even *permitted* to wear anything but a *burqa* when venturing outside? And in any case, if they are going to be wearing an all-encompassing cloak and possibly a face veil, *who cares what they wear underneath*? This is what countless non-Muslim friends have asked me. And this is what a number of non-Muslim fashion professionals wonder.

THE EMERGENCE OF THE ISLAMIC FASHION INDUSTRY
AND THE RISE OF THE MUSLIM MIDDLE CLASS

Since the 1980s, a whole industry of Islamic fashion has emerged, despite internal criticism and external challenges. Its goal is to demonstrate that Islam and fashion are not contradictory practices, that Muslim women can be pious and trendy. In addition, and since the events of 9/11, this industry has attempted to present itself as an emissary of social change, proving to non-Muslims in particular that veiled Muslim women are modern, active, well-integrated members of society whose contributions must be highlighted.

But of course the main ambition of this Islamic fashion industry, like that of any industry, is to be a successful capitalist enterprise, a flourishing business venture. Savvy entrepreneurs understood early on that there was a business opportunity to be had with the marketing of *hijab*. Because veiling means so many different things to different people and because it is worn differently around the world, it has become an empty signifier, one that can be invested with new social meaning and sold at a dear price. Understanding and catering to the desires and needs of a rising international Muslim middle class and a very wealthy Gulf clientele became the way for many up-and-coming businessmen and businesswomen to make money.

Ironically, the rise of the Islamic fashion industry is a by-product of the emergence in the 1970s of revivalist Islamic movements throughout Muslim-majority societies. These movements sought to promote faith-based communities opposed to secular and Westernized lifestyles. They were the early proponents of a return to Islamic veiling, a practice that had been all but abandoned in major Muslim-majority cities since the 1930s and 1940s (see chapter 7). The Islamic fashion industry established itself primarily to address the needs and increasingly sophisticated tastes of the emerging Muslim bourgeoisie. The new Muslim middle class itself developed as a result of increased migration from rural areas to urban centers. The migrants were lured by new labor opportunities made possible by liberal economic policies that encouraged foreign investments. The Muslim middle class also flourished because of job openings abroad, in Saudi Arabia and in the Gulf region in particular, which permitted entire families to rapidly climb the socioeconomic ladder and form the new class of nouveaux riches, now firmly entrenched in Muslim-majority nations.

In the 1970s, the availability of Islamic modest dress in stores to serve the needs of this new and rising Muslim middle class was limited. Any woman who wanted to don *hijab* had to sew it at home or commission it with a tailor who would skillfully adjust and cut to measure any design from the very popular European fashion magazines (*Burda* being the most heavily circulated one throughout my childhood). Any advice about veiling or the adoption of an Islamic lifestyle in general was passed down in private circles, from mother or aunt to daughter and neighbor.

Growing up in the 1960s and 1970s in North Africa, I do not remember seeing anyone in my immediate family or friends who wore *hijab*. My paternal grandmother was the only person I knew who added a long and narrow black or white transparent chiffon scarf over her head when going out of the house. Since my grandmother always covered her head with a small scarf, even when inside the house, we attributed the addition of the long scarf to two main factors: First, we thought that she was simply wearing the conventional clothing from her village in Upper Egypt, following a residual Ottoman custom. Second, we thought that this conservative attire was appropriate for someone her age who had completed the *hajj* (the pilgrimage to Mecca and one of the pillars of Islam). It was a sign of piety, certainly, but also of cultural standing. We never thought of it in terms of required Islamic clothing, and certainly not as fashionable veiling.

It was only in the 1980s, and especially in the 1990s that a specialized industry flourished, one that designed, manufactured, promoted, and distributed Islamic clothing to the rising Muslim middle class. This industry did not just seek to fulfill the needs of (newly) devout women but it also endeavored to create a new identity for these Muslim women.

The newly veiled Muslim woman was promoted by the Islamic fashion industry as someone who was at once modern and religious. She chose *hijab* voluntarily, not because of coercion. This new Muslim woman was also and especially one who regularly and avidly consumed the latest commodities that the emerging Islamic industry began selling (e.g., Islamic toothpaste, Islamic weddings, Islamic beach vacations, Islamic banking). The image of the modern and modest Muslim woman was attractive. It quickly gained an impressive following and established itself solidly as the ideal female Muslim subject, one at once devout and avidly consumerist of an Islamic lifestyle.

It is this model Muslim woman that I encounter everywhere when

I have returned to Egypt since the 1990s. Each time, I am speechless at the sight of the increasing number of women of all ages and backgrounds on the streets wearing *hijab*, as well as by the diversity of styles that have become appropriate. I am amazed by the many cuts and colors of Muslim clothes and headscarves, and by the new specialized ready-to-wear boutiques that cater to veiled women. It has become quickly evident to me that many women veil not simply because they are expressing a newly discovered spirituality but because this is the new fashion, the trendy way to demonstrate one's modernity and personal style. Girls imitate cousins; friends imitate neighbors; and women in villages imitate those living in the city.

When I adopted *hijab* in 1983, I was imitating my paternal cousin who was just three years older than me and the first one in the family to veil. By the time I took off my *hijab*, one year later, most of my cousins had adopted it. My mother, aunts, and all their friends started veiling several years later, in the 1990s.

What was deemed fashionable Islamic clothing in the 1980s looks very different from what is considered trendy Muslim dress today. Throughout the 1970s and 1980s in Turkey, for example, being covered meant wearing a long, blue, loose-fitting overcoat and a large, usually patterned headscarf. Such an outfit is dismissed today as unwearable, out of fashion, and described as "grandma" style by the veiled women between the ages of eighteen and fifty that Banu Gökarıksel and Anna Secor interviewed in the cities of Istanbul and Konya in the summer of 2009.

These Muslim women recognize that what they choose to wear today would have been considered sinful only ten or twenty years ago. As Nesrin, a forty-four-year-old housewife, explains: "If you had said to the covered community twenty years ago, 'You'll wear pants, a skirt and on top of that, a headscarf,' they would have booed you. But now this is the fashion."[2] Fashion and time have clearly rendered the unacceptable acceptable and, in fact, trendy.

Many new terms have been coined to describe this most recent wave of trendy Muslim women. They are referred to fondly (or ironically, depending on the speaker and context) as "hijabistas" or "fashionable fundies" (as in fundamentalists) to draw attention to their commitment to being visibly both Muslim and fashionable. They are also called "makeuphijabs" and "muhajababes," words that associates the English terms "makeup" or "babes" to the Arabic *muhajjaba*, a woman who wears *hijab*. These terms serve as apt reminders that we cannot make any assumption about a woman wearing the *hijab*. She can be, and often is, as much of a "babe," and might wear as much (if not more) makeup, as any other non-Muslim or non-veiled woman.

Titles of new Islamic fashion blogs are equally evocative: Hijabulous, Muslim Style Queen, Fashionably Modest, Modest Plus, Hijabs High, We Love Hijab, or Hijab Style. Similarly, online retailers catering to women who wear *hijab* stress the importance of fashion. Interestingly, some of their names do not even include any reference to Islam or veiling, such as Yaz the Spaz, House of Blush, Rebirth of Chic, Silk Route, Sixteeenscarves, Shukr, BlackDiiamonds, and Splashgear.

VEILED WOMEN GO SHOPPING

In striking contrast to the veiled women of the 1970s, who had to stitch their own Islamic clothes, or to the Muslim women of the 1980s and 1990s, who had to go to specialized stores to buy their *abayas* and scarves, the muhajababes of today can simply walk into any of the new malls that have sprouted in all metropolitan areas to find what they need to build their *hijab* wardrobe. In shopping malls throughout Muslim-majority societies, one finds branches of major luxury and mainstream Euro-American boutiques adjacent to those recently opened by a growing number of local designers. Muslim women living in Muslim-majority societies are thus just as likely to shop at Christian Dior, Hermès, or Gucci as they are at Abercrombie & Fitch, Gap, the Tie Rack, or H&M.

In these stores, veiled Muslim women shop side by side with non-veiled (in fact, non-Muslim) women, and each of them can find everything she needs for any occasion (professional, casual, evening wear, or sports), from the most risqué to the ultraconservative, from the most fashionable to the most sober styles. In these shops Muslim women can choose whether to buy their *hijab* outfit piecemeal—a skirt here, a blouse there, and the scarf in yet another store—or they can purchase an entire matching outfit including all accessories in one boutique. Being veiled today has become an entirely different experience from what it was forty or even twenty years ago.

EURO-AMERICAN FASHION DESIGNERS
ADAPT TO ISLAMIC FASHION

Today, Muslim women are widely recognized as a new, until recently un-tapped, demographic that can make the fortune of haute couture labels anywhere. Marketing research has indeed revealed that Muslim women around the world, but especially from the Emirates and the Gulf region (Dubai, Kuwait, Qatar, and Saudi Arabia) are among some of the most fashion-conscious consumers to be had, and with much dispos-able income to boot. They are young, well educated, widely traveled, watch fashion television and read fashion magazines, are open to Euro-American culture, all while being devoted to their own social, cultural, and religious traditions. Today, they are counted among the leading con-sumers of Euro-American luxury retail whose loyalty every designer is vying to win.

Thanks to the consumption patterns of affluent Muslim women, Is-lamic fashion has today become a 100 billion dollar industry. France in particular has recognized the privileged place it occupies in the imagi-nary of many Middle Eastern women and has been entrepreneurial in en-suring that it maintains and augments the 30 percent of luxury business it already makes in the Gulf. It has thus been actively pursuing market-ing strategies and cultivating business opportunities in Muslim-majority countries to sell its haute couture scarves, suits, and makeup to rich Muslim women. This is of course ironic since France is also the country that recently banned both the *hijab* and the *niqab* in public schools and government institutions on its own soil (see chapter 5). The *hijab* and *niqab* may be challenges to French secularism, as French policy makers like to repeat, but they certainly also present an economic boon.

To meet the demands of this highly discriminating and affluent Mus-lim consumer, Euro-American luxury designers have not shied away from adapting their collections to the tastes and sizes of their wealthy Muslim clientele. Many are systematically making longer (and wider) versions of the dresses they show on catwalks to accommodate Islamic requirements and tastes.

Marigay McKee, the fashion and beauty director of London's exclu-sive Harrods department store, reports that Diane von Fürstenberg, for instance, designs a version of her well-known elastic wrap dress spe-cifically for the store's Muslim clientele. The dress is made floor-length, with long sleeves, and is often embellished with black crystals. According to McKee, the dress retails at 2,500 pounds, is exclusively sold at Harrods, and sells out every season.[3]

While non-Muslims often assume that all *abayas* look the same, there are in fact many nuances and details that can escape the untrained eye. *Abayas* can have elaborate trimmings and embroideries; they can be slim or wide fits, and they can have wide or slim sleeves that confer much individuality to the item and to its wearer. Euro-American luxury designers often work with famous artists to exploit the endless variations in the design of *abayas* and thus to attract and maintain the loyalty of their wealthy Muslim clientele.

What most distinguishes the adaptation of Euro-American fashion to Muslim women's tastes and requirements is perhaps the fact that affluent Muslim women demand more vibrant colors, additional embroidery, extra gold, Swarovski crystal buttons, beads, and precious stones, as well as wild prints, on their accessories. For them, plain means poor and must therefore be avoided. Or perhaps it is precisely because some of the women who are seeking out Islamic haute couture most are those who must also don a dark *abaya* over their trendy clothes. And as so many Muslim women have pointed out to me throughout the years, it is because they wear dark *abayas* that they want to be colorful and unrestrained underneath them.

Affluent Muslim women are prepared to pay top dollars not only for designer clothing that will be worn underneath their *abayas* but also to ensure that they will be alone among their friends to wear a particular item from a luxury brand. It is often difficult for non-Muslims, as well as for non-fashion-obsessed Muslims, to understand the yearning for exclusivity that marks the consumption patterns of some Saudi, Emirati, and other Gulf women.

Many friends working with Emirati women have confirmed what Harrods' McKee has observed in her dealings with affluent Muslim women. Some of these women, they report, directly order pieces from catwalk collections, and they are prepared to buy the two or three copies of the item that have been prepared for a particular fashion show. They do so to ensure that they are the first and only one among their friends to don the most recent dress of a much coveted label, carry the latest bag or accessory from the hottest designer, or wear the trendiest seasonal color from the makeup collection of an exclusive brand.

While luxury Euro-American designers are eager to adapt their styles (and at times their advertisements) to the tastes and requirements of their wealthy Muslim clientele, they are much more reticent to reach out to middle-class clients and to the mainstream Islamic lifestyle and fashion magazines that cater to them. They are known for their reluctance to send Muslim lifestyle magazines products for photo shoots, or even to advertise and be associated with them, preferring to retain their exclusive labels for the more lucrative opportunities afforded by their elite clients. From their vantage point, any affiliation with middle-class Muslims, that is, with mid-price-range customers, is viewed as an undesirable association with a parochial venture, whereas linkages with affluent Muslim clients are considered for the golden economic prospects they potentially mean.

THE NEW MIDDLE EASTERN, AFRICAN, AND ASIAN ISLAMIC FASHION INDUSTRY

Since the turn of the millennium, Euro-American luxury designers no longer have a monopoly in the field of fashion in general, or in that of Islamic fashion in particular. New Muslim, Middle Eastern, African, and Asian designers have emerged, recognizing the economic advantages that could be derived from serving the discriminating tastes not only of wealthy women but of middle-class ones as well. These new designers have capitalized on the fact that they are Muslims and as such are better suited than non-Muslim designers to understanding and catering to the specific sartorial needs of the Muslim community. Moreover, a new generation of Muslim *women* designers has also emerged who proclaim themselves more able than even their male Muslim counterparts (and business competitors) to understand the meaning of religiously appropriate garments and to come up with designs in tune with the needs of Muslim women.

Today, Muslim fashion designers have become regular attendees of international fashion shows and fairs where they get the latest information on styles, fabrics, and colors and gain inspiration for their own garments. They then *adapt* Euro-American trends to the tastes of their local clientele. Most of the new styles they develop are characterized by cross-cultural hybridity, a fusion of Middle Eastern and Euro-American trends.

The most common strategy adopted by Muslim designers to remedy sleeveless dresses and short skirts common in Euro-American fashion is called layering. It consists of wearing one garment over or underneath another so that no skin remains visible, allowing Muslim women to observe *hijab* while keeping up with the most recent international cycles of fashion. Fashionable Muslim women are hence encouraged to wear the same items of clothing as non-Muslim women, but to wear them differently.

In both the March and April 2011 issues of the Egyptian Islamic fashion magazine *Hijab Fashion*, this layering style is the first topic covered, immediately following a presentation of the main trends in the spring and summer 2011 international fashion season. In both issues, we find a page-long article titled, in translation, "Your *Hijab* as Inspired by International Fashion." In the March 2011 issue, this is the advice offered to magazine readers:

> Many women assume that *hijab* diminishes their elegance. And most veiled women believe that they cannot follow the trends of international fashion, and that they are limited by well-rehearsed styles considered to be the only modest ones that are suitable for veiling. However, these ideas are completely wrong. For many of the styles that are presented by the most famous designers can also be appropriate for women who veil, either as is or with small modifications in the way the clothes are worn. The woman who veils, just like the one who does not, can therefore find what suits her in most, if not all, fashion styles.
>
> And to prove this, we present to you here a few models created by some of the most famous designers for the Spring–Summer 2011 season. These styles correspond to the latest fashion trends that we described in the previous pages, and they are appropriate to wear with your *hijab*. This is so you can get inspired for your clothing this season and relish in the fact that you are "fashionable."

These introductory paragraphs give a sense of the creativity and flexibility in veiling practices in Muslim-majority societies. Veiled Muslim women need not shy away from the latest international designs, but are encouraged instead to embrace them to be fashionably veiled.

The remainder of the article in *Hijab Fashion* gives three examples of luxury clothing (Fendi, D&G, and Alberta Ferretti) that can be easily adapted and worn with *hijab*. The author of the article suggests wearing Fendi's short dress as a tunic over pants. In the same spirit of layering, D&G's sleeveless dress can become suitable for *hijabi* women simply by adding a small jacket over it, while Ferretti's low-cut dress can be worn

حجابك من الموضة العالمية

| Fendi | D & G | Alberta Ferretti |

Advertisement for luxury *hijab* styles from *Hijab Fashion* magazine, Egypt March 2011

with a turtleneck underneath it, or with additional scarves. By advising women to layer their clothes, to wear short dresses over jeans, turtlenecks underneath sleeveless or short-sleeved tunics, and thick tights underneath short skirts, the article's author shows that every Euro-American fashion garment can easily become *hijab* friendly.

The technique of layering is clearly not limited to designer clothing. In fact, it has become the strategy of choice for veiled Muslim women from all socioeconomic classes. This strategy allows veiled Muslim women to shop at the same stores as non-veiled women. Muslim and non-Muslim women, veiled or non-veiled, thus shop with equal frequency at Zara, Topshop, Gap, Forever 21, or H&M. Despite the small modifications necessary to some garments to make them suitable for a *hijabi* wardrobe, veiled Muslim women have the same lively conversations and discus-

sions about cuts, fabrics, and colors. Their main objective, like that of non-veiled women, is to look trendy and hip.

Perhaps because the editors of *Hijab Fashion* know that the adaptation of Euro-American fashion often invites easy allegations of Westernization and a loss of national or Islamic cultural values, they devoted an article in the March 2011 issue to what I call "patriotic fashion." Inspired by the Arab Spring, and specifically by the Egyptian revolution of January 25, 2011, which led to the ouster of President Hosni Mubarak, the editors of *Hijab Fashion* indicate that wearing *hijab*, expressing patriotism, and being fashionable are compatible goals. An article titled "5 New Ways of Wearing the Egyptian Flag" describes this new fashion through a series of images and brief descriptions to explain each style.

The author of the article suggests that the Egyptian flag can be worn as a tunic, a dress, a shawl, a belt, or a scarf, thereby allowing veiled Muslim women to display at once their patriotism, their piety, and their sense of fashion. Islamic fashion can thus be enlisted to promote patriotism just as, inversely, national pride might encourage some women (whether veiled or unveiled) to adopt fashionable dress.

Wearing a flag to display both patriotism and piety is a strategy commonly adopted by Muslims living in Muslim-minority societies. In the United States and Europe, for example, images of Muslim women covering their hair with the French or American flag are often seen on the covers of news articles, books, flyers, and they circulate on the Internet. The message of such images is always to demonstrate that Muslim women can have both Muslim and secular allegiances, that the adoption of the much debated *hijab* in no way contravenes their full integration into or respect for the laws of the Muslim-minority country in which they live.

What we have in the *Hijab Fashion* article is something slightly different. First, the flag covers more than the woman's hair. Moreover, and equally important, the flag used in this new patriotic fashion is an Arabic (in this case, the Egyptian) flag. The promotion of the Egyptian flag as a fashionable and suitable Islamic cover for the body and head affirms a renewed sense of national pride lost in Arab societies since the heyday of decolonization and the uprising against European powers from the 1920s to the 1950s. It introduces a new link in the association between Islam and fashion, thus demonstrating the magazine's commitment to the revolutionary movement under way. By adding patriotism to the equation and by affirming a seamless connection between fashion, Islam, and patriotism, the Islamic fashion industry becomes more difficult to criticize, since its goals are allegedly aligned with those leading the revolution. Criticizing Islamic fashion would thus here mean criticizing the uprising and challenging national identity.

NEW ISLAMIC FASHION BRANDS

Muslim and Middle Eastern designers are participating in the growth of the Islamic fashion industry not only by adapting global fashions but also by developing their own fashion lines, brands, and styles. Some of them are reinterpreting traditional styles and aesthetics, revisiting ethnic attire with their culturally meaningful patterns and colors, and creating an updated sartorial tradition.

This is the case with Muslim convert Jamesa Fields Nikiema, for instance, an American designer and the owner of Rebirth of Chic, an online retail clothing store for trendy Muslim women. In an interview titled "Wrapped Up in Style," she explains that she founded her online business because she had discovered that "most of the *hijab* clothing that was available [in America] for Muslim women was imported from Pakistan or Arab countries." While she could certainly wear them, she felt that they did not correspond to her sense of being an American, which called for "different fabrics and a wider variety."[4]

Interestingly, the modest and trendy clothing available on Rebirth of Chic does not satisfy American Muslim women only, but has also inadvertently attracted another clientele: Orthodox Jewish and modest Christian women. Evidently, *hijab* fashion is considered appropriate and fashionable by *any* conservative woman, regardless of her religious background. This of course reminds us that women who seek modest clothing have all kinds of religious affiliations and tend to search for similar cuts and designs. Ironically, fashion may well be an area where Muslim, Jewish, and Christian women come together in their quest for conservative yet fashionable outfits.

Similarly, Iranian designers Simin Ghodstinat and Parissa have become well known in the Islamic fashion industry for anchoring their designs in Iranian history while using fabrics coming from elsewhere (*saris* from India and Pakistan mixed with materials from Europe and Asia). The combination of traditional designs from various regions of Iran with heterogeneous fabric types, colors, and borders is what lends Ghodstinat's and Parissa's clothes their particular type of chic.

Such clothing, resulting from a reinterpretation of local traditions with a careful selection of global materials and peppered by the aesthetic genius of the designers, is becoming more prevalent in many Muslim-majority societies. It is especially coveted by European expatriates (often working at embassies or in similar positions), by tourists, and increasingly by upper-class women.

The success of such outfits lies in their ability to rouse nostalgic feelings and establish a symbolic link with the homeland while at the same time being solidly anchored in contemporary styles and modern cuts. Their other source of success resides in their capacity to represent suitable Islamic attire and evoke ethnic (not religious) fashion depending on the consumer. They can thus easily be worn by veiled and non-veiled women, at home and abroad. Not least, because such garments do not blindly follow Euro-American fashion, they never go out of style.

VEILED WOMEN GO SWIMMING: THE BURKINI

Another fashionable invention from the past decade came to the rescue of those veiled women who wanted to continue enjoying water activities. The options previously available to them were quite limited: swimming in privately owned pools, finding a pool with women-only hours, locating isolated beaches and anxiously swimming in the wee hours of the morning, or wearing a long dress or a long-sleeved shirt with leggings that either ballooned or conformed to the women's bodies the moment they got wet.

None of these were comfortable solutions until the creation of modest and fashionable swimwear and sportswear for veiled Muslim women. The *Burkini* (also spelled *Burqini*) is a term that refers to the creative combination of a *burqa* and a bikini, and the *Hijood*, a hybrid between a *hijab* (head cover) and a hood, are the first and most widely available products, created by the Lebanese Australian Aheda Zanetti. Similar types of modest and fashionable swimwear include the *Veilkini* (from veil and bikini) and the *MyCozzie*. All these items are available online only.

This modest and fashionable swimwear was initially marketed specifically to veiled Muslim women who wanted to observe their religious and cultural traditions while participating in sports and community activities. According to Zanetti, the *Burkini* line seeks to provide Muslim women with the freedom to engage in sports, the comfort and confidence that they are dressed modestly, and the knowledge to easily care for their sportswear.[5] Interestingly, the line has become increasingly popular among non-veiled women from other faiths looking for a modest swimsuit (the British food writer Nigella Lawson allegedly owns one). Testimonials posted on the Ahiida website give a sense of the satisfaction that both veiled and non-veiled women find in the *Burkini*.

Christine L., for example, writes about her reaction to seeing women in *Burkinis* on a beach in northern Virginia: "The *burkini* looks fabulous! I'm going to tell my Orthodox Jewish friends about it! Plus I like the ¾ style myself! (I'm very fair skinned and am waiting for skin cancer!) Mazel tov! Salam! Pax!" Another commentator exclaims: "I have even received compliments from non-Muslim friends at our town pool!" Clearly, the quest for modest swimwear, even one associated with Muslim women, unites women, regardless of faith.

Ironically, and despite the popularity of the *Burkini* among women from various religious backgrounds, some European five-star hotel chains in the Middle East do not allow it in their pools. This is most likely a marketing strategy geared toward making non-veiled, non-Muslim guests feel comfortable on the property while at the same time presenting the hotel as liberal, secular, and pro-Western.

VEILED WOMEN GO TO THE HAIR SALON

Veiled Muslim women today have a wide range of sartorial options, from the very high-end, exclusive brands to the made-in-China outfits.

In addition, every city in Muslim-majority countries now boasts numerous hair salons with a section specifically catering to the special needs of veiled women.

In fact, about ten years ago, my male hair dresser in Cairo, who had been cutting and styling my hair since I was a child, dedicated a new room in his salon to veiled women. He explained to me that now that an increasing number of women in Egypt veiled, he (like many other hairstylists) had seen a drop in his business and thus had to modify his salon to suit his changed clientele. He taught his wife to cut and style women's hair so that she could be in charge of that part of the business.

When I go to get my hair styled in his salon, I regularly witness a delicate dance taking place between veiled women and my hairdresser. Veiled women enter the salon from the street and quickly and nervously cross the shop's front section to reach the back room reserved for women in *hijab* or *niqab*. My male hairdresser still works in the front section, so he must avert his eyes or pretend to be occupied by some other important matter while the veiled women head to the back section of the shop, partitioned off with a thick, black curtain.

Some continue to allow my male hairdresser to style their hair, even though this contravenes the strict rules of *hijab* that dictate that a woman not show her hair to a man who is not a close relative. These women, invoking the hairdresser's unmatched skills, maintain that he knew them in their pre-*hijab* life and hence does not strictly count as an unrelated male. While such arguments are questionable from a strict religious perspective, they reveal that being stylish and maintaining a perfect hairdo are top priorities for some women even if they veil. Simply because they do not show their hair (or face) in public does not mean that they neglect their hairstyle or hair color. For that, some flexibility in the interpretation of *hijab* and some negotiations must be allowed.

ISLAMIC FASHION SHOWS

Muslim designers are not content to just create new lines of clothing for their growing middle- and upper-class clientele. They are now also actively participating in the global fashion industry by organizing fashion shows specifically tailored to veiled Muslim women.

The first such event took place in Turkey in 1992 and was organized by a prominent Islamic fashion company, Tekbir Giyim, whose motto is "to make covering beautiful." Tekbir featured famous Turkish models, known for the swimwear, lingerie, and secular clothes they typically showcased, but who for the purposes of the Islamic fashion show donned headscarves, overcoats, long dresses, and suits. Muslim conservatives and secularists alike immediately attacked this show, but it was so successful that it has been regularly repeated by the same company and imitated by many others.

Today, several countries host an Islamic fashion festival, including Turkey, Indonesia, Malaysia, Pakistan, Dubai, and, perhaps surprisingly, Iran. Because of the growing number of Muslims living in Muslim-minority societies and because of the economic boon that the Islamic fashion industry represents, Islamic fashion festivals are now hosted in these countries as well. While London included an important segment on fashionable *hijab* in its first Arabian Fashion World event in April 2009, Monaco became the first country in Europe to host an Islamic fashion show in August 2010, and Paris did the same in December 2011. Islamic fashion has now become a truly global phenomenon.

Because of the denigration that anyone involved with Islamic fashion often faces from many Muslims, Muslim fashion designers must take active steps to placate critics. Some (in Asia especially) are careful to display and prove their Islamic values and sensibilities by following a lunar fashion show calendar, corresponding to the Islamic lunar year. They therefore often release their new lines and schedule major fashion shows in the month preceding Ramadan. While this schedule means that Islamic fashion shows may take place in different months of the Gregorian calendar each year, it has the advantage of anchoring Islamic fashion within Islamic cultural traditions, thus forging a link between piety and fashion.

In Iran, most fashion shows, either public or private, take place just before *Norouz* (the Iranian New Year), in mid-March, because this is when most people are prepared to buy new clothes. By presenting their collections at that time, Iranian designers indirectly affirm their commitment to local customs and government traditions, thereby evincing any potential censorship from the Commission of Islamic Guidance, which must approve public fashion shows.

Other Muslim designers appease their Muslim critics by focusing on the economic benefits that could derive from the Islamic fashion industry. They argue that Islamic fashion can benefit a nation's economic growth since it supports a whole new professional universe including creators of clothing, styling salons, and makeup artists. These designers also argue that Islamic fashion relies on inexpensive labor, something readily available in Muslim-majority countries. However, unlike non-Muslim fashion, they rush to point out, Islamic fashion does not rely on outsourcing work, but actually supports local economies. It thus has a noteworthy role to play in activating national economies and offering Muslim-majority nations a new source of wealth and development. This line of reasoning has become especially powerful among a growing audience of politically engaged Muslims concerned with the global rise of poverty and labor exploitation.

ISLAMIC LIFESTYLE AND FASHION MAGAZINES

The emergence of a sartorial industry catering to veiled Muslim women has been accompanied by the creation of Islamic lifestyle and fashion magazines. These magazines began appearing in the 2000s and were intended primarily for the growing urban and heterogeneous international Muslim middle class. Most are published monthly or quarterly in different languages. Some circulate only locally; others have a global presence and an international readership base. Most are widely available on the Internet. Some of the best-known titles include *Hijab Fashion* (Egypt), *Muslim Girl* (Canada), *Azizah* (USA), *Muslimette* (USA), *NooR* (Indonesia), *Emel* (United Kingdom), *Sisters* (United Kingdom), *Alef* (Kuwait), and *Lotous* (Iran). These magazines have endeavored to cultivate the same Muslim female subject that fashion designers have created, that of the devout and attractive Muslim woman who is true to her religion, to her sociocultural background, and at the same time is a well-integrated global citizen. This Muslim woman is assumed to work outside of the home while being dedicated to her husband and children. She is aware of fashion trends beyond her native culture, and her purchasing power allows her to seek and buy both beauty and modesty. This figure of the pious and feminine Muslim woman is heralded as the ideal whose image, accessories, imagined lifestyle, and cosmopolitanism can be acquired and purchased by magazine readers.

The image of the piously dressed Muslim woman, modest and attractive, that graces the glossy covers and pages of Muslim lifestyle and fashion magazines throughout the world has generated much anxiety. Like the topic of Islamic fashion, it has been the site of debates over the relation between true piety and material consumption. Muslim critics of Islamic lifestyle magazines, and especially of their fashion pages, have blamed its editors for promoting the performance of piety, rather than truly experienced piety, as well as for encouraging desire and immorality. They have accused the publishers of camouflaging their capitalist interests with an Islamic facade and of misusing religion for economic gain.

Editors of Muslim lifestyle magazines continuously struggle to justify their mission and to affirm their own commitment to core Islamic values. They repeatedly stress that their main intent is to educate and provide Islamic guidance to their readers. Circulating images of veiled, pious Muslim women, as they do, is necessary, they say, only because such women have long been considered utterly unfashionable and hence been left out of the fashion media. The publishers claim that they seek to give a voice to veiled Muslim women, to alleviate their sense of isolation from the global Muslim and fashion community, and to combat rampant misunderstandings about their cultural specificities.

Editors of lifestyle magazines also strongly deny that they are imposing a new subjectivity onto their readers. In fact, they claim just the opposite, namely, that they are simply allowing already devout Muslim women to develop their personal image, to express their piety in new (fashionable) ways, and to actualize their spiritual potential. The mission statement of the founding editors of the Indonesian lifestyle magazine *NooR* is based on the assumption that the public expression of a Muslim identity remains a deeply personal choice. Once this choice is made, the role of magazine editors becomes that of supporting and encouraging it. Fashionable piety, in their words, is a liberating kind of piety, one described as "so beautiful it makes you want to fly."[6]

Editors of the booming Islamic media also insist that the images they circulate, whether reflecting the reality of already devout women or not, are ultimately morally edifying. After all, just by imitating the purchasing trends of women featured in the magazines, some readers may be inspired to become even more pious. From this perspective, appearing and acting more devout could lead one to actually becoming more devout. Fashion is performative and can support, they argue, the overall spiritual betterment of the nation.

In their effort to convince their detractors that the proliferation of an industry of fashionable Islamic dress is not contrary to the pursuit of genuine piety, some editors of Islamic fashion magazines have endeavored to cultivate an image of strict adherence to conservative interpretations of Islam. Some thus publish articles written only by Muslim women (*Sisters, Azizah*). Others only profile clothes designed by Muslim women or carried by Muslim businesses (*Azizah*), while others still give priority to the advertisement of Islamically permissible accessories such as *halal* makeup (*NooR*).

Some of the magazine editors have also attempted to devote space in their pages not only to Islamic guidance columns but also to stories of highly successful Muslim women, or of former models and celebrities turned pious (*Azizah, Emel*). By portraying such women, highlighting their achievements, family background, and status, the editors seek to present them as role models for their readers. Muslim women, they claim, can be veiled, thrive professionally, and be completely trendy. In contrast to what some may think, fashion is not necessarily inconsistent with core Islamic teachings; fashionable piety does not pose a threat to Muslim women's reputation.

Moreover, and initially at least, some of the editors sought to avoid professional models as the magazines' cover girls, featuring instead white-collar professionals who have chosen to veil. In the same spirit, others attempted to employ only female, preferably veiled, stylists, photographers, and technicians to appease the pious sensibilities of their readership, as well as in the belief that a Muslim tech crew is better qualified to select poses and light compositions that do not contravene interpretations of modesty according to different Muslim communities.

Despite these good intentions and efforts to establish moral authenticity, such policies have failed in most cases. Editors of Islamic magazines soon discovered the reality of the fashion industry, which is dominated by men and where attempts to find a team of pious female photographers, stylists, and technicians are challenging. They have also come to recognize that pious women felt uncomfortable posing as cover girls and ended up costing the magazines much time and money. So editors of Islamic lifestyle magazines, like designers in the fashion industry, continue to rely on professional unveiled (often non-religious) women as models to create an atmosphere of stylish Islamic dress to be consumed by affluent and pious Muslim women. Carla Jones, in her article on the Indonesian fashion magazine *NooR*, has summed up this paradox: "It is not uncommon to see models in tank tops and short denim skirts weave their way through a crowd of well-to-do, piously dressed women as they exit a five-star hotel lobby after working the Islamic fashion show."[7]

TO PICTURE OR NOT TO PICTURE
HUMAN FACES AND BODIES

The most controversial question that editors of Islamic lifestyle maga- zines confront is that of whether to represent women's faces and bodies in their fashion pages and, if so, how. For it is important to recall in this context that many conservative Muslims believe that picturing the human body is not permissible in Islam.[8]

The challenge that these editors must resolve is therefore how to publish fashion pages and present trendy veiling styles without offend- ing the conservative segment of their readership. Their responses and strategies vary from one magazine to another, demonstrating the com- plexity and sensitivity of the topic, the potentially explosive allegations that could result from particular choices, and the negotiations that con- tinually take place in decisions about fashion and Islamic modesty.

At one end of the spectrum, some editors have opted to not show the face of any woman in their magazine. This is what Naʿima Robert, the editor of the British quarterly magazine *Sisters*, and Mahla, the edi- tor of the Iranian magazine *Lotous*, have done. In fact, cognizant of the fact that her readership consists primarily of conservative women who wear either the *hijab* or *niqab*, Robert has made the restriction on repre- sentations of the face and body her main selling point. In an interview with Reina Lewis, she has explained: "People expect to find more reli- gious content in *Sisters* and they expect us to follow religious guidelines much, much more than those other magazines. Just the fact that [they use] images and we don't use images, for example. That's one of the big- gest differences between us."[9] In *Sisters*, fashion coverage is restricted to product shots. If at times a revealing product is featured (a tank top, a sleeveless dress, a short skirt, or tight jeans, for example), a note is added to clarify that the item is for *hijab*-free environments only, in the home, or at single-sex parties. This statement is included to make sure that readers do not doubt the magazine's commitment to respecting gen- der segregation and strict rules of *hijab*.

Sisters is not the only Muslim lifestyle magazine to have adopted this policy about human representation. In fact, the decision not to show women's faces was a well-established practice in the emerging Islamic fashion industry's advertisement campaigns of the 1980s in Turkey. Catalogs of Islamic fashion from that time, like advertisements in the contemporary Turkish designer magazine *Selam*, refrained from showing women's faces. In all photos displaying fashionable Islamic cloth-ing, the face is camouflaged by a black and white space, or the photo is cropped so only the bottom part of the headscarf is visible.[10]

The quarterly American magazine *Azizah*, like the monthly British magazine *Emel*, has followed a similar, if slightly less restrictive strategy. *Azizah*'s editor, Tayyibah Taylor, has asserted that she is less interested in Islamic fashion per se than in supporting and making visible the di-versity of Muslim American women. Her policy has been to allow the portrayal of human faces and bodies to counteract the homogenization of Islam by mainstream Euro-American media. The decision to show faces and bodies also derives from Taylor's primary mission to highlight the achievements of Muslim American women; for that, their faces must be made visible and known. However, because *Azizah* is also on the con-servative side of the spectrum, all women featured in it are veiled. The types of veil seen in its pages differ, but only veiled women are included.

The choice to represent human forms but to consistently show them veiled gives a sense of the dance that editors of Islamic lifestyle maga-zines must perform to convince their readers of the Islamic values they profess while giving voice to the diversity of practices behind these values. As Taylor has pointed out in an interview with Lewis: "[We're] trying to educate the community [that] Islam in general doesn't have to look exactly the way you're doing it, [that] unity doesn't dictate uni-formity."[11]

The British magazine *Emel* has adopted a more nuanced position than either *Sisters* or *Azizah*. Like *Sisters*, the magazine does not por-tray any faces or human forms on any of its fashion pages. Yet in pages with editorial content or news items about a named individual, a pic-ture of the featured Muslim woman is shown regardless of whether or not she wears *hijab*. Sarah Joseph, the magazine's editor, justifies her approach thus: "When you're dealing with a model . . . you're objecti-fying that person and presenting that person as you want them to be. . . . [It's] incredibly important that we present women [in features and interviews] according to what they have to say, what they're doing . . . not according to how they look. . . . We don't make any changes to that. They present themselves with a scarf . . . without a scarf, that's up to them."[12] Joseph's words sound familiar to many conservative Muslims. They echo one of the main justifications of veiling, namely, that it forces others (read men) to focus on women's ideas, on their intellectual abili-ties, rather than on their bodies.

At the other end of the spectrum, the Canadian magazine *Muslim Girls* has reached a different decision concerning human representation and veiling even if its editor is also committed to portraying the diversity of Muslim women. In contrast to all the other magazines mentioned here, Ausma Khan is committed to presenting *hijab* as a choice rather than a mandate. For this reason, and even as her fashion pages display a range of trendy veiling styles, her magazine front cover alternates between featuring a girl wearing *hijab* and another without. This flexible approach to *hijab* in an Islamic lifestyle magazine is unusual, one that continues to draw criticism. In fact, Khan reports that she has to restate on a regular basis the magazine's commitment to *hijab* as a choice in response to the numerous letters of protest that she receives.

In this debate about the moral and ethical justifications of the Islamic fashion industry and lifestyle magazines, trendy Muslim women themselves remain the best and ultimate source of validation. As women with substantial purchasing power who are continuously seeking to express their modernity through their consumption of fashion, they constitute the most solid reason for continuing to develop new lines of modest trendy clothing and lifestyle magazines to advertise them. As affluent and middle-class women, they represent the industry's livelihood. And as Muslims, they are better positioned than anyone to affirm the connection between devotion, modesty, and beauty. To conservative Muslims, websites, and general critics who decry the growing vogue of Islamic haute couture, trendy Muslim women respond by invoking the modesty of the soul, rather than secular modesty. Many cite a well-known *hadith* that states: "God is beautiful and He loves beauty." For both fashionable and devout Muslim women, veiling is intended to radiate God's magnificence through attention to one's own human beauty. For some, therefore, *hijab* fashion is adopted as an outward expression of a Muslim woman's spiritual beauty, and by extension as a symbol of God's glory.

The focus on spiritual beauty has become today the main alternative discourse deployed by the Islamic fashion industry to counter criticism. This argument is compelling since it allows virtue to coexist with the active quest for beauty. It validates women (and designers) who are working hard to achieve and align inner and outer beauty. And by referencing a well-known *hadith*, they are able to challenge their critics on their own terms.

ISLAMIC BEAUTY PAGEANTS:
CROWING "MISS BEAUTIFUL MORALS"

Ironically, it is this interest in spiritual beauty that has led to the recent development of Islamic beauty pageants, held in some Muslim-majority societies, though they remain little known to most Muslims and non-Muslims.

Islamic beauty pageants differ from Euro-American pageants in that their focus is not to identify the most physically beautiful girl but to recognize the girl with the most beautiful Islamic soul, with the most praiseworthy Islamic morals. Khadra al-Mubarak, the founder of the first Islamic beauty pageant in Saudi Arabia, an event that has received much media coverage, explains that the pageant's primary goal is indeed "to measure the contestants' commitment to Islamic morals. It's an alternative to the calls for decadence in the other beauty contests that only take into account a woman's body and looks."[13]

The Saudi beauty pageant claims therefore not to be interested in outer beauty but to reward instead Muslim women's inner beauty. This inner beauty is defined specifically as the devotion and respect that a contestant shows her mother. No men are involved in the contest, and the judges' role is to find the girl who will be crowned "Miss Beautiful Morals." The contest has been so well received that participation has more than doubled since the pageant was created in 2008: from seventy-five to more than two hundred young women between the ages of fifteen and twenty-five.

While women who compete in the Saudi pageant all wear *abayas* and cover their faces in observance of local traditions, this is not the case in all beauty contests. Lebanon lies at the other end of the spectrum and features non-*hijab*-wearing contestants and women participating in swimwear competition, just like in beauty contests in Euro-American societies. In Egypt, on the other hand, which hosted the first Miss Arab World Beauty Contest in 2009, both veiled and non-veiled women were invited to participate, and the winner of that contest was a veiled Saudi woman, Mawadda Nour.

Despite the differences between Euro-American and Islamic beauty contests, the very existence of Islamic beauty contests is worth noting as they reveal the efforts made by some Muslims to participate in an established Euro-American tradition. In Muslim-majority societies, these new pageants are as controversial as they are in Euro-American societies.[14] They are at times heralded as a positive sign of Islamic feminism, of modernity, and progress. At other times, however, such pageants are derided for being a facile imitation of, and surrender to, Euro-American popular culture, a capitulation to materialism, and a self-imposed distancing from Islamic core values.

MUSLIM DOLLS BECOME FASHIONABLE

Islamic fashion is not just a grown-up affair. After all, Muslim children are not immune to the development of the fashion industry. They learn early on that they too can, and should, dress and act fashionably, while holding onto modesty as defined by their families and community. In fact, as all savvy business entrepreneurs know, children are prime potential clients, the ones to be enticed and educated today so that they may become the avid consumers of tomorrow.

The introduction of Muslim children to the Islamic fashion industry begins with play, that is, role play with Muslim dolls. In fact, Muslim dolls have become a multi-million dollar industry, and promoters are advocating the dolls' important educational function, especially for Muslim children living in Euro-American societies. They claim that they want to teach children growing up in Muslim-minority societies what it means to be a good Muslim, how to hold onto one's culture and religion, while being fully integrated into the community of non-Muslims in which they live.

While the development of the Muslim doll industry started in the 1990s, after the Saudi ban of Barbie,[15] the growth of a fashionable line of clothing for each of the new Muslim dolls is a more recent phenomenon. When the first Muslim doll, Razanne, was created in the United States in 1996, for example, she came with two outfits only: some indoor apparel, which was fashionable and in line with what any non-Muslim girl would be wearing at the time, and some outdoor attire, consisting of a long overcoat and a headscarf. Today, Razanne has been given not only a whole series of identities such as Muslim Girl Scout, a teacher, and a doctor but also three ethnic variations for each: Caucasian, Pakistani-Indian, and black. Moreover, each ethnic variation comes with its own set of fashionable and color-enhancing clothing.

Similarly, the most successful Muslim doll, the Syrian Fulla, has witnessed an even bigger explosion of fashionable clothing, accessories, and lifestyle items around her name since she was introduced in 2003.[16]

Like other Muslim dolls, Fulla at first had only two sets of distinct clothing, one for the outdoors and the other for the indoors. For the outdoors, Fulla wears an *abaya* and a scarf. While these were both black in the doll's first edition, newer collections soon emerged offering *abayas* in different colors and with matching scarves. Moreover, Fulla, as a budding consumer of Islamic fashion, has been given a growing line of fashionable indoor clothing that continues to be updated with the seasons and fashion cycles. She has clothes that are appropriate for various activities including prayer, sports, or role play as a teacher or doctor. Any attire that reveals some skin is clearly labeled on the box as "indoor fashion," clarifying the manufacturer's allegiance to Islamic sartorial rules in an effort to placate any conservative parent's concerns about the morality of the doll.

A range of accessories are now available for Fulla, reminiscent of Barbie or Disney product lines and coveted by young Muslim girls around the world. They extend beyond all kinds of indoor and outdoor clothing, matching handbags, and jewelry (which were the company's original focus) to religiously non-specific accessories such as cell-phone cases, CD players, pink bicycles, sewing machines, furniture, beach toys, and tennis rackets.

As I was browsing the complete Fulla product catalog online, the most unusual items that caught my attention for a doll initially intended to serve as a role model for Muslim girls living in the diaspora are probably the Fulla chocolate egg maker, the ice cream and slushie maker, and the trash can. There is no Fulla bikini, although there is a Fulla swimming mask and snorkel set. Evidently, anything that has the Fulla logo on it is deemed fashionable and sells; in fact, it is guaranteed to become an instant success. And perhaps because it is associated with the brand name Fulla, it is also assumed to somehow inculcate Islamic values and be suitable for Muslim girls.

Despite the proliferation of fashion accessories, producers of Muslim dolls insist that fashion is secondary to their main intent, which is to uphold traditional family and religious values. The Fulla webpage explains clearly that Fulla is "the little girl that wears modest outfits, her top priorities are respect for herself and all around her and being kind to her friends and peers. We take pride promoting virtues to help girls be the very best today so they will grow up to be the women who make a difference tomorrow."

Despite the growing list of Fulla's fashionable clothing and accessories, many conservative Muslim mothers, those wearing the *hijab* or *niqab*, remain loyal consumers of the doll for their daughters. They confirm the words of Mohammed al-Sabbagh, a manager at Space Toon, Damascus's leading toy store: "Fulla is one of us, but Barbie is still a stranger," and also, "Fulla is my sister, my wife, my mother. She comes from the same culture. The other thing for me, as a parent, is about what I want for my child. Barbie has a boyfriend and a bikini and so on, which is not our style in the Middle East."

◼ It is undeniable that fashion has become an integral part of the lives of Muslims, young and older, around the world. Whether they are in favor of or consumers of Islamic fashion or against it, they can no longer avoid it. Whether living in Muslim-majority or Muslim-minority societies, both conservative and secular Muslims evolve in communities solidly anchored in fashion. The growing appeal of Islamic fashion today among Muslim women of all ages may partly result from the fact that such clothes can challenge conservative Islamist views of appropriate Muslim women's clothing and the strict governmental regulations imposed on women's dress in some Muslim-majority countries. In many ways, Islamic fashion is a contesting type of fashion.

In her interview with Alexandru Balasescu, the Iranian haute couture designer Parissa confirms this view. She admits that her bold use of color, for example, inspired by traditional Iranian women's clothing in rural areas, is intended as her own resistance to clothing restrictions and color limitations imposed on Iranian women after the Islamic Revolution. Like her, many Muslim women resort to Islamic fashion as a strategy to own what is considered in many societies a religious mandate to veil. By adopting fashionable veiling, some Muslim women stage their own revolution, at once following and subverting the sartorial rules of their community. Islamic fashion, like the voices of contemporary Muslim artists and poets to whom I will now turn, and despite its commercial implications, is a form of resistance to univocal, essentialist, and conservative interpretations of Islamic veiling.

Hijab is the one thing that has so much meaning.
—Miss Undastood, Muslim African American rapper

I'm tired of carefully picking outfits, colors, accessories, silks, every day for
public relations purposes to ensure that I look approachable, yet modest, rather than
withdrawn and oppressed, when really, some days, let me tell you,
it is so much easier for me to throw on my linen shawl and my *abaya* over my
pyjamas. —Linda Sarsour, *The Hijabi Monologues*

CHAPTER NINE

Veiling through the Arts

Muslim artists from around the world are increasingly participating in contemporary debates about the veil and taking up the subject of Muslim women and veiling. In their artistic productions, they use the veil as a forum to actively challenge the homogenization of Muslim women and to contest the prevalent view held that veiled women are oppressed, silent, and that they lack subjectivity and agency. As they voice their double struggle against common Euro-American stereotypes, on the one hand, and against conservative Islamist discourses, on the other, these artists help combat intolerance and invite us to consider veiled Muslim women from new perspectives.

Through poetry, stand-up comedy, storytelling, painting, photography, and music, contemporary artists are refusing to have their experiences dictated by others, their stories told by someone who does not know what it is like to be a Muslim, a woman, or a *veiled* woman in the world. They are asserting their right to be known and recognized as complex human beings. These artistic voices add fresh perspectives on the subject of veiling and invite us to engage in a creative dialogue about the multiple meanings of veiling for many Muslim women living in different societies, cultures, and continents. They call on us to look at veiling in new ways, to leave our assumptions behind, and open our eyes, ears, and hearts to the diversity of meanings that veiling has, as well as to their new artistic expressions.

HIJAB POETRY

Since the mid-1990s, a new type of poetry penned by progressive Muslim women poets has emerged. I call it *hijab poetry* because *hijab* is its central theme. In it, poets describe their sense of peace, blessing, freedom, and empowerment when veiling. They also express their frustration with the stereotypes that some non-Muslims often have on the subject of veiled Muslim women, as well as with conservative Muslims' obsession with women's proper attire.

In a long poem entitled "A Day in the Life" (2005), Su'ad Abdul-Khabeer, an African American Muslim poet and a scholar of anthropology and African American studies, describes a day in the life of a veiled Muslim woman.[1] Veiling and prayers punctuate her daily routine and constitute the central themes of the poem.

Abdul-Khabeer's poem is divided into sections, each headed by an hour of the day as though they were a series of regularly occurring prayers (3 A.M.; 5 A.M.; 1 P.M.; 5 P.M.; 7 P.M.; 10 P.M.; 11:45 P.M.). While observant Sunni Muslims pray five times a day, Abdul-Khabeer's "Day" is marked by seven prayers, inviting us perhaps to expand our understanding of prayers. These need not be limited to fixed rituals and outward expressions of religiosity, but might take into account one's spirituality and personal expressions of faith. Rather than a poem just about observant Muslims, her work reads like a universal mystical chant.

In this poem, Abdul-Khabeer describes herself as a free Muslim woman who cannot be made to conform or to remain "unseen and unheard" either in the name of male-centered traditions or of Euro-American assumptions. She asserts that her "scarf / is about / claiming space" for herself in the world. Veiling is here primarily about freedom, choice, individuality, agency, and personal expression. But of course the poet also knows too well that veiling is never just a private matter. Veiling is never just a neutral dress. Rather, as she suggests, veiling has become a public matter. It is a piece of attire that elicits, at times, judgment and fear and attracts unwanted attention or negative comments from Muslims and non-Muslims alike.

To Euro-Americans and non-Muslims who feel threatened by Muslim women in scarves, Abdul-Khabeer boldly responds by writing in both French and English, perhaps to ensure that she is fully understood by the two Muslim-minority societies with the largest Muslim populations and in which stereotypes of veiled Muslim women permeate public debates.

She denounces that the three central principles of the French Constitution (liberty, equality, and fraternity—words all written in French in the poem) have been trumped in the name of security and democracy. French legislative actions against the veil (2004) and the *burqa* (2010), Abdul-Khabeer points out, ultimately undermine the core principles of the French Republic. These laws do not uphold the liberty, equality, and fraternity promised to all citizens. Rather, French legislation against the *hijab* and the *burqa* are nothing less than antidemocratic projects.

Abdul-Khabeer also decries American feminists' desire to free Muslim women from their veils, or from what some wrongly perceive as "the tyranny of Faith." Non-Muslim American women, according to Abdul-Khabeer, seek to replace Muslim veils with "thongs," when "thongs" are nothing but another, worse type of "chain." Faced with the choice between dressing modestly (a veil) and dressing scantily (thongs), Abdul-Khabeer proudly and freely chooses the former because it liberates her from the dictates of the fashion industry and respects a woman's body, upholding its sanctity.

Just as she condemns Euro-American anxiety about veiled Muslim women especially in the post-9/11 world, Abdul-Khabeer also castigates, and perhaps even more vociferously, conservative Muslim women obsessed with criticizing others who do not espouse or conform to their own view of modest dress. To those Muslim women who claim that her own shirt could be longer, her scarf tighter, her pants looser, and the color of her clothes less provocative, Abdul-Khabeer ironically responds:

I grinned
and calmly
took off
my lavender-purple-plum scarf
my purple sweater tunic
my perfect sandblast jeans
placed them neatly in her hands
and said . . .
"you know, you're right."

You see I figured
if they were going to treat me like a whore,
I might as well dress the part.

Abdul-Khabeer pushes to its extreme the logic of the obsession that some Muslims display about proper Islamic clothes. She seems to be cautioning the most conservative members of her community about the consequences of their fixation on "modestly colored *jilbabs* and *khimars*." She warns them of the very real possibility that some potentially devout Muslims may abandon Islam and its rituals because of this continuous preoccupation with petty details of clothing.

Rather than concentrating on outward details of dress (length, looseness, color), Abdul-Khabeer urges Muslims to shift their focus inward, to their spiritual relationship with God, to prayers offered with humility and sincerity. For, she suggests, it is not the clothes one wears that matter, but the humility one exhibits when praying to God that makes a person a truly believing Muslim. It is the modesty of the soul that matters because this is precisely what returns to Islam the spirituality, principles of gender equality, and inclusiveness that are part of the faith. In the name of this spirituality and inclusiveness, the narrator continues to wear proudly her "lavender-purple-plum scarf" and "purple sweater tunic."

For Abdul-Khabeer, only once clothing is no longer the focal point of debates among Muslims and non-Muslims can Muslim women hope to be recognized for their intellect, be officially welcomed into the Muslim community, and be allowed to celebrate their beauty. The haunting refrain "To cover or not to cover / Is not my battleground" that punctuates one of the poems in the "A Day in the Life" series serves to remind the reader that the topic under discussion (*hijab*) is misplaced and that the real "battleground" for Muslims lies elsewhere, namely, in their internal struggles to become the best persons they can be.

Facing criticism from both non-Muslims and Muslims either because she veils or because she does not veil conservatively enough, Abdul-Khabeer courageously pledges her commitment to remain true to herself, her firm intent to uphold her faith regardless of others' discomfort and fears:

If you had asked me
I would have told you
I am a woman

and this is my scarf.
I believe in God
and freedom
and work for a world
where that is possible,
Invincible.
And if that frightens you
Be Afraid.

Equally evocative are Mohja Kahf's *hijab* poems included in her collection *E-mails from Scheherazad* (2003). Reading them, I am always struck by the extent to which the experiences and challenges of being a Muslim Syrian American (Kahf) parallel those of a Muslim African American woman (Abdul-Khabeer). The terse irony, playfulness, and humor that characterize Kahf's poetry always prove a big success in the classes I teach on Arabs and Muslims living in America.

Kahf's poem titled "My Body Is Not Your Battleground" is a prayer for the total emancipation of the Muslim woman's body from stereotypes, judgments, and even praise:

My body is not your battleground
My hair is neither sacred nor cheap,
neither the cause of your disarray
nor the path to your liberation
My hair will not bring progress and clean water
if it flies unbraided in the breeze
It will not save us from our attackers
if it is wrapped and shielded from the sun.

Like Abdul-Khabeer, Kahf decries that Muslim women's bodies and hair have become a "battleground" for both Muslims and non-Muslims. She reminds us that veiling and unveiling have both held contradictory meanings at different times in history and in different regions in the world. At times, veiling was considered the only path toward cultural and political progress. At other times, unveiling was a synonym of a society's liberation, the measure by which progress and development were judged. Yet, as Kahf points out, hair is just hair. Covering one's hair or not, she reminds us, does not produce political or social change.

The obsession with the proper coverage of a woman's hair and body ultimately divides the Muslim community and provides much fodder for

Islamophobic attitudes in Euro-American societies. Kahf calls for a truce between what she calls "the eastern fronts and the western," between the expectations of Muslims and non-Muslims. She envisions a "new age of lilac and clover," a space where peace reigns supreme, where Muslim women can live, occupied only with spreading love and beauty throughout the earth:

> My body is not your battleground
> Withdraw from the eastern fronts and the western
> Withdraw these armaments and this siege
> so that I may prepare the earth
> for the new age of lilac and clover,
> so that I may celebrate this spring
> the pageant of beauty with my sweet love.

In her poem simply titled "*Hijab* Scene # 2," the shortest one in *E-mails from Scheherazad*, Kahf denounces the contradictions inherent in the assumptions about Islamic veiling held by some non-Muslims. Muslim dress is not as restrictive as some might believe, at least compared to what some Euro-American women choose to wear to follow the dictates of the fashion industry. This is one of my students' favorite poems because of its brevity and the ironic twist in the last line:

> "You people have such restrictive dress for women,"
> She said, hobbling away in three-inch heels and panty hose
> To finish out another pink-collar temp pool day.

The "three-inch heels and panty hose" in this poem remind me of Abdul-Khabeer's "thongs," that is, items of clothing that some feminists consider a symbol of liberation. For such feminists, high heels, panty hose, and thongs seem liberating because they display a woman's body. Veiling, in contrast, is often considered a symbol of female oppression precisely because it hides women's bodies. This binary logic is expressed in the derogatory tone of the first line of the poem. Yet Kahf playfully reverses this type of logic in her last line. Those who are wearing "three-inch heels and panty hose" are "hobbling away" and are associated with a "pink-collar temp pool day," in other words, with a secretarial, temporary job assignment. Kahf thus reminds us that what some may consider liberating dress can be viewed by others as constraining and uncomfortable. Muslim women's dress, described as "restrictive" in the first line of the poem, becomes the more liberating form of dress in an unexpected reversal in the last line, the one not just fit for "pink-collar temp" jobs, but rather for stabler, more serious, and permanent employment and social standing.

In "Hijab Scene # 7," written six years before the attacks of 9/11 in 1995, Kahf tackles a question that will become central after this tragic time in America's history, that is, the perception that American Muslims are not as "American" as the rest. For veiled Muslim women, the question is perhaps even more pressing: Can a veiled Muslim woman be truly American? Can she be patriotic?

Kahf answers this question with a resounding yes, and the result of such a Muslim American identity is not a weak, divided individual, but a strong-willed woman who powerfully challenges Euro-American stereotypes about veiled Muslim women. This has regularly been another one of my students' favorite poems. I will quote it in its entirety:

> No, I'm not bald under the scarf
> No, I'm not from that country
> Where women can't drive cars
> No, I would not like to defect
> I'm already American
> But thank you for offering.
> What else do you need to know
> Relevant to my buying insurance,
> Opening a bank account,
> Reserving a seat on a flight?
> Yes, I speak English
> Yes, I carry explosives
> They're called words
> And if you don't get up
> Off your assumptions,
> They're going to blow you away.

Kahf points here to the irrationality of some "assumptions" and anxieties propagated by the media and prevalent in American society about veiled Muslim women. *Hijabi* women are not necessarily immigrant women from nations with limited rights for women ("Where women can't drive cars"), Kahf reminds us. Their loyalty to and patriotism for the United States are not to be doubted ("No, I would not like to defect"). Their linguistic skills and integration into American culture are strong ("Yes, I speak English"). The real threat to American security, according to Kahf, is not women in scarves, but rather the assumptions and stereotypes that continue to circulate and divide citizens from one another. A *hijabi* woman, Kahf points out, is often just a scarf-clad American woman trying to live, drive, buy insurance, or open a bank account. The only "explosives" she carries are her words. Her only weapon against those who mistrust her is her poetry.

VEILING, STAND-UP COMEDY, AND STORYTELLING

Since 9/11, many Muslim Americans have turned to stand-up comedy to broach social, cultural, and political issues such as the status of Islam in America, racial profiling, terrorism, and cultural stereotypes. Male and female comedians have resorted to laughter to invite discussion of these sensitive subjects with their audiences and to build bridges of understanding and solidarity among groups.

Some female stand-up comedians have addressed the topic of veiling specifically and deliberately chosen to dress in visually conservative clothing while performing comedy to challenge common stereotypes and unfounded claims about Muslim women. Through their appearance, they hope to shock their audiences and create dissonance in their minds between the clothes they see and the jokes they hear.

Here is an example of some of the jokes that Shazia Mirza, a British Pakistani comedian, told her audience in one of her performances: "People ask me: why does my mother walk five steps behind my father? I say, well, he looks better from behind. . . . But actually these days, the women are walking five steps in front of the husbands. That's because of the landmines."[2] Though this joke does not address the question of veiling directly, it comments on one of its associated stereotypes, namely, that Muslim women are oppressed and held in subordinate positions, forced to walk behind their husbands. Mirza turns this assumption on its head. Walking behind their husbands no longer confers a position of inequality or inferiority, but rather one that highlights Muslim women's complexity and sexuality. If they walk behind their husbands, it may be to better flirt with them. The second part of Mirza's joke about women walking in front of their husbands because of landmines reminds us that if Muslim women do suffer some prejudices in their societies, these have nothing to do with veiling, but everything with politics and warfare.

Later in the same comedy act, Mirza spoke directly about *hijab*, saying: "I am very lucky because in England, the women in my family, they are all Muslims and they all wear the *burqa* and it is great because they all use the same passport. In fact, we saved a lot of money and my brothers have started to use my mother's passport now." Mirza here associates positive terms such as "lucky" and "great" with the one item of clothing that evokes so much fear and anxiety in the minds of many non-Muslims (and Muslims)—the *burqa*. In contrast to what many may think, wearing a *burqa* need not be scary or oppressive; it can also be associated with happiness and family union.

In fact, the *burqa* here brings about unexpected benefits for her family. They can, she claims, all use the same passport. In this way, Mirza forces us thus to reconsider the rapid and facile invocation of security concerns that have been used to justify limiting the rights of Muslims and of veiled women in particular. Perhaps some Muslims do indeed use the *burqa* to hide their identity, she says, but they do not do so because they are terrorists, but perhaps for more pragmatic reasons such as saving money on passport applications.

Other artists address the question of Muslim women and veiling through storytelling. One of the most notable recent examples is *The Hijabi Monologues*. In the United States, *The Hijabi Monologues* were developed in 2007 by three University of Chicago graduate students. Sahar Ullah, one of the original creators, explains the goal of the project: "With *The Hijabi Monologues*, we are trying to move people's focus away from the headscarf and on to the personal stories of Muslim women. The characters of each monologue wear the *hijab*, but the *hijab* is not actually the focus of any story. Although many of these stories resonate with other Muslims and women in general, they do not claim to tell every story or speak for everyone."[3]

The series of vignettes that make up *The Hijabi Monologues* give voice to Muslim women's daily lives, from their joys and challenges to their sexuality. This encourages viewers to see that Muslim women cannot be defined simply by their clothes, but that they are complex individuals with a variety of experiences and backgrounds.

In a vignette titled "I'm Tired," the performer Linda Sarsour speaks of her frustration with the misunderstandings and assumptions held by many non-Muslims. She says it is "exhausting" and "heavy" for Muslim women to represent more than 1 billion people, to be perceived as an embodiment of a "whole world religion," instead of being simply seen for themselves, as individuals like others around them. Sarsour gives the example of the following double standard to which Muslim women are held in Muslim-minority societies: "I am tired of not going to class because I did not do my assignment. And if I do not say something incredibly brilliant, my silence will be attributed to being inherently oppressed by my religion, men, clothing, rather than the fact I didn't do my homework because I was screwing around on Facebook the previous night, like 90% of my class."[4]

Sarsour here points to the tremendous pressure that Muslim women feel because any one of their personal failings tends to be automatically attributed to a deficiency in the entire Muslim community. Sarsour asks her imagined non-Muslim audience: "Do you not see me? Do you not happen to see that I am standing here, right in front of you and that I am not wielding a sword?" In an assertive voice, she ends her performance by demanding her right to be seen as just another human being: "I'm not another angry Muslim. I'm not a bad example; hell, I am not a good example. I'm just not representation. I'm a human being; and my name is Linda."

The story Sarsour tells here resonates with many Muslim women living in Muslim-minority societies. But her story resonates also with other women (or men) whose individuality at times gets trumped by the fact of belonging to a particular group, be it religious, political, sexual, or any other. Sarsour invites us thus to consider that Muslim women, despite the heterogeneity of their lives, are more similar to other women than different from them. The audience leaves a performance of *The Hijabi Monologues* with a sense of shared humanity, a deeper understanding of, and a greater connection to Muslim women.

VEILING IN THE FINE ARTS

Since the early 1980s, visual artists from around the world have added their voices to the debates about Muslim veiling. They too have sought to combat stereotypes about veiled Muslim women through their artistic productions.[5]

Visual artists have focused especially on those images that have been circulating in Euro-American cultures at least since the early period of European colonization (the mid-eighteenth and nineteenth centuries). This period, known for its important production of orientalist paintings and made famous by artists such as Delacroix and Ingres, depicted Muslim women lounging lazily in exotic settings, having cast away their veils, sitting in erotic postures, and staring directly and invitingly at the viewer (see chapter 4). These nineteenth-century orientalist artistic representations of Middle Eastern women have greatly contributed to the creation and persistence of stereotypes about veiled Muslim women. A persistent assumption today holds that veiled Muslim women are oppressed, subservient to their husbands, voiceless, and forced to wear conservative clothing. At the same time, many continue to associate Middle Eastern women with belly dancing and erotic movement.

Many Muslim visual artists strive to challenge such orientalist representations and the impact of their stereotypes about Muslim women and veiling. Combating these stereotypes is pressing, because they inform a number of contemporary Euro-American views about Islam and Muslim women and because they recall arguments that some conservative Islamist regimes invoke to subordinate women.

A number of art exhibits have been organized around the theme of veiling in an effort to combat misperceptions of Muslims and Arabs. The majority of these exhibits have taken place after the attacks of 9/11 and most have toured Europe, Australia, and the United States. A large number of emerging and established international artists, male and female, Muslim and non-Muslim, have participated in these exhibits. The diversity of the artists' backgrounds is matched only by the variety of their approaches and techniques. Some have chosen to denounce veiling as a form of oppression and political manipulation, while others are working to transform orientalist stereotypes into new artistic forms. Taken together, these artistic voices open a new window that makes more complex, deepens, and enriches our understanding of Muslim women's experiences and practices.

Art That Denounces Veiling as a Form of Oppression

Some Muslim artists are using their work as a forum to denounce veiling as a form of oppression and as an imposition by some Middle Eastern governments. Their goal is to give voice to the lived experiences of veiled Muslim women who are forced to wear the veil and to invite viewers to understand intimately what some of the veiled women may be feeling.

Fahda bint Saud's watercolor painting *Three Women* is a poignant example illustrating the meaning of forced veiling for some Muslim women. The artist (b. 1953), the daughter of King Saud (d. 1969), the second ruler of Saudi Arabia, presented this work in the context of an ex-

Fahda bint Saud, *Three Women*, 2008 (Courtesy of
Dr. Khalid Kreis of the Jordan National Gallery of Fine Arts)

hibit curated by Princess Wijdan Al Hashemi and Aliki Moschis-Gauguet
and organized by the Royal Society of Fine Arts in Jordan and the Pan-
Mediterranean Women Artists Network of Greece. The show premiered
in 2008 at the Interfaith Centre of Melbourne and was titled *Breaking
the Veils: Women Artists from the Islamic World*. Saud's painting depicts
three women whose faces and entire bodies are concealed by a bright
blue veil and cloak (*abaya*) sitting cross-legged in a desert landscape
with mountains in the background. One of the women is covering her
eyes, the other her ears, and the third her mouth. At first sight, the painting brings to mind the proverbial three wise monkeys who see no evil,
hear no evil, and speak no evil. Could this be an Islamic rewriting of the
Buddhist code of conduct that invites viewers to approach the painting
with humanity and without stereotypical presuppositions about Muslim women?

The desolate setting of the painting and the yellowish-reddish color
of the desert heat accentuate the isolation of the three women sitting

in the foreground. Their portrayal as faceless figures who reject any sensory input focuses our attention on the feelings of loneliness and remoteness that emanate from them. The three women indeed appear very much disconnected both from their background and from each other. They cannot, or perhaps they refuse to see, hear, or speak. Could this be the everyday life experience of some women who are forced to veil and who hence find themselves cast aside by their society and cannot even find comfort in each other's presence? Could veiling lead to disenfranchisement and the absence of subjectivity? Could veiling cover not just the body but also the soul and individuality of women? These are some of the questions that continue to haunt me as I look at this painting. But rather than accentuate the otherness of these women, the painting invites me instead to share in their apparent sadness.

An even stronger sense of isolation and oppression emanates from Halida Boughriet's performance video entitled "Les illuminés" ("The Visionaries," 2007). Boughriet (b. 1980), a contemporary artist of Algerian descent who lives and works in Paris, takes us literally inside the *burqa* to film what a woman's eyes see from behind the face veil that masks her eyes. The video begins with an image of a busy Paris subway station on which are superimposed what appear to be crossbars. It soon becomes clear, however, that these are not bars at all, but rather the crocheted eye holes of a *burqa*. The viewer suddenly realizes that this is how women wearing the *burqa* must see the world. They look out as though from inside a prison cell. They can only see it as an incomplete space, discontinuous and fragmented. The more the video advances, the more claustrophobic I feel.

Not only does the woman in Boughriet's video see the world as a disjointed place broken up into squares but she also experiences it as a hostile environment. Throughout the video, the woman in *burqa* from whose perspective the entire video is shot endures the looks of shock, terror, worry, and even voyeurism of passersby. The video documents how people in the subway station turn back to stare at the woman, unaware that she is holding a camera inside her veil that films their reactions.

From Boughriet's performance video, not only do we see a woman isolated from the world but we are also invited to witness, if only briefly, the hostile stares and misunderstanding she endures daily. As viewers, we cannot help but feel uncomfortable. Have we too been guilty of a similarly unfriendly gaze toward women in *hijab* or *burqa*? Have we

Halida Boughriet, *Les illuminés*, 2007 (Courtesy of Halida Boughriet)

too turned back to stare at those who look different from us? Boughriet denounces here the oppression of complete veiling as a practice that isolates women from their social environment, and simultaneously she decries the unsympathetic attitude of outsiders toward veiled women.

At the same time, it becomes evident that for the brief time of the video, the tables are also turned, the power dynamics reversed: the viewers become the viewed, the objects of our gaze. The allegedly powerless, faceless, silenced, and fully veiled Muslim woman is the subject, the director of this uncanny scene. The oppression of the veil is here temporarily transformed into a veil that empowers.

Art That Transforms Traditional Representations of Veiling

Another group of artists seeks to challenge conventional artistic representations of veiled Muslim women as they have evolved since the nineteenth-century orientalist period and as they persist today. These artists decry the difficulty of their project because the meaning of Muslim veiling is so complex that it cannot be reduced to a singular representation. Their project is challenging also because of the weight of a long artistic Euro-American tradition that has pre- and overdetermined the parameters of the representation of Muslim veiling.

Zineb Sedira (b. 1963), a contemporary Algerian British artist who conceived one of the earliest art exhibits on Islamic veiling in the mid-1990s, describes the difficulties of attempting to represent Muslim veiling in this way: "How do you represent the unrepresentable, unrepresentable due to over exposure or lack of exposure? How do you represent that which has been drained of meaning, misrepresented to the point of over saturation, yet under-appreciated and neglected to the point of absurdity? Is it even futile to attempt such an endeavor . . . maybe, it is advisable, perhaps not."[6] For Sedira, the veil is "unrepresentable" because it has been both overexposed and underexposed. Its overexposure comes from Muslim veiling having been one of the central themes repeatedly explored by European and American artists since the nineteenth century. The lack of proper exposure happens because, despite the persistent weight of this Euro-American artistic tradition, veiling continues to be misunderstood, confined to a simplistic signification.

The image of the oppressed, coerced, silenced Muslim woman still permeates Euro-American views today. Many assume that veiled Muslim women are asexual or hypersexual, and beyond their sexuality, even potential suicide bombers. The challenge for contemporary Muslim artists is to bypass this static visual language and to disrupt automatic readings of Muslim women. Because the Muslim veil sits at the crux of multiple contradictory questions, and is situated in a lineage of firmly entrenched art traditions, contemporary visual artists must intervene in the history of representations of Muslim women and veiling without repeating the same stereotypes. Their challenge is to resist the temptation of simply reversing existing stereotypes, because this would construct another confining view of complex subjects.

Two main questions take center stage in their artistic production: (1) How can one challenge the reductionism in Euro-American readings of the Muslim veil and initiate a new dialogue that explores its contradictions and complex meanings? (2) How is it possible to move the conversation beyond the physical veil worn by some Muslim women and redirect it toward the mental veil, what Sedira calls that "transparent and subtle mental code" that veils the mind of non-Muslims?[7]

In response to these questions, Sedira has tried to move the debate

on veiling forward by *transforming the image*, thus providing new strategies for reading the veil.[8] Her aim is also to *subvert* conventional artistic representations of veiled Muslim women, to offer a transgressive image that opens up layers of alternative meanings. She thus invites us to move away from binary ways of thinking (the veil is coercive, the veil is empowering) and to develop a new language that can articulate the complexities, subtleties, ambiguities, contradictions, generalities, and specificities of veiling.[9]

I always find myself particularly drawn to Sedira's photographic triptych titled *Self-Portrait or the Virgin Mary* (2000) because it challenges simplistic interpretations of veiling and invites us to consider new meanings. Sedira directly confronts and disrupts viewers' presuppositions about veiling and automatic associations of veiling with Islam. After all, is the figure in Sedira's photographs the artist cloaked in a white *hijab*, or is it the Virgin Mary, mother of Jesus?

The flowing, white cloth, ethereal lighting, and the very design of the work as a triptych—a traditional *Christian* art form—all suggest the purity of the Virgin Mary. At the same time, and to those acquainted with North African sartorial traditions especially, the white cloth reminds us of veiled Algerian women circulating in public. Which one is it? By photographing herself with a white background devoid of any

Ghada Amer, *Borqa*, 1995 (© Ghada Amer; courtesy Cheim and Read, New York)

detail, Sedira offers the viewer a blank canvas that highlights the commonalities in sartorial practices of Muslim and Christian women. The sisterhood established in this triptych unites Muslim women with others who wear the veil and invites us to question the notion that the veil represents an exclusively Islamic practice. Sedira's work transforms conventional views of veiling and asks us to possibly begin writing a new history of veiled (Muslim) women.

Another artwork that seeks to transform traditional representations of veiling is the 1997 sculpture *Borqa* (*sic*) by the Egyptian American artist Ghada Amer (b. 1963). At first glance, Amer's *Borqa* seems to simply represent the most conservative form of Islamic dress, the face veil that some women wear by choice, others by tradition, and many others still by force (e.g., in Saudi Arabia or Afghanistan). It is all black, austere, and, in fact, ghostlike with its wide gaping eyeholes.[10] On closer inspection, however, we begin to notice some differences between this *Borqa* and other *burqas* and *niqabs* we may have seen on television or in magazines. Amer's garment has a piece of lace at the level of the mouth, not at that of the eyes like traditional Afghan *burqas*. In various interviews,

Amer has explained that the lace in her *Borqa* gives in Arabic calligraphy the dictionary definition of the word "fear." It thus becomes evident that Amer's *Borqa* does not just represent a *burqa* but comments on it as well.

Amer's transformation of the traditional *burqa*, which does not have a mouthpiece, reflects the artist's anxiety in the late 1990s at witnessing the mounting social and religious conservatism in her country of birth, Egypt. It reflects her fear of being, one day, forced to wear a *burqa* or a *niqab* when going back for vacation.

Originally, Amer had intended her *Borqa* to be the one she would don if she were ever forced to wear one. The word "fear" reproduced in the lace makes us wonder: Who is afraid of whom? Is it the artist who fears government and religious authorities imposing the veil on her? Or is it the authorities who ought to be afraid of women like Amer who refuse to be silenced and who will always find ways to have their voices heard? In this sense, and even as it portrays the *burqa* as a symbol of female oppression and governmental imposition, Amer's *Borqa* also represents her own voice. It is a voice of rebellion and one that asserts subjectivity. Amer may be forced to wear a face veil one day, but that attire can never silence her entirely, as she will continue to speak literally through its cloth.

The lace in Amer's sculpture is interesting also because it uses century-old techniques of handmade French lace production characteristic of the city of Bayeux in Normandy. In this sense, Amer's *Borqa*, with its Arabic calligraphy and traditional French lace-making methods, stands as a symbol of the multiple cross-cultural exchanges between Muslim and non-Muslim societies. Amer knows both societies intimately, having lived in France since she was eleven years old and prior to moving to the United States as an adult.

The association of an Islamic sartorial object with traditional French lace further transforms the *burqa*. The addition of lace, a detail reminiscent of lingerie, recalls the sensuality of the veil as portrayed in some nineteenth-century Euro-American painting traditions. The addition of lace also reminds us of the decorations and embellishments typical of face veils in the Ottoman Empire, including Egypt, that continue to be in style among some Bedouin women today. At that time and in these societies, face veils were ornate and thoroughly adorned with gold and silver coins and jewels. Face veils symbolized high social status and were worn by Muslim, Christian, and Jewish women. Amer's *Borqa* points us to this time period when face veils did not mark religious differences but served as fashion, social, and economic statements. Her *Borqa* reminds us that face veils are above all a cultural practice, much more than a religious injunction.

Not least, Amer's *Borqa* shows us that Muslim dress does not have to be austere. It can also be a sexy accessory akin to lingerie, freely displayed by some Muslim women. In this way, Amer's *Borqa* recalls the luxury Yves Saint Laurent scarves that some women wear as fashionable *hijab* (see chapter 8). By combining concepts of Islamic modesty with French chic, Amer's representation of the traditional Muslim veil challenges common stereotypes about the conservativeness of veiled women. Finally, the association of lace and the *burqa* in Amer's sculpture hints at the irony of the fact that despite recent French legislation banning Muslim veils, French lace production profits economically from the persistence of conservative Muslim sartorial practices.

VEILING IN CONTEMPORARY MUSIC

In the past decade, Muslim music performers have joined other artists in actively challenging and transforming stereotypes of Muslim women and veiling. Their music and lyrics offer a welcome addition to discussions of veiling because they are more easily accessible to a larger (and generally younger) audience who may otherwise be more resistant to or disengaged from the topic. This is without any doubt my students' favorite form of artistic expression and the one they connect with most readily.

The relatively late arrival of Islamically themed popular music on the contemporary art scene may be due to the fact that music, and women's voices especially, have long been considered erotically arousing by some conservative branches of Islam and are hence severely censored in some places, if not prohibited altogether. Until today, some conservative Muslim communities associate singing (and dancing) with prostitution and believe it leads to damnation.

Considering this way of thinking, it is remarkable to witness some Muslim musicians' courage when they produce music under criticism and condemnation. This is testimony to their strong belief in the power of music to communicate a message and produce change.

Most of the performers who sing about veiling and who seek to challenge conventional perceptions of Muslim women's oppression live and perform in Muslim-minority societies. Their artistic productions span multiple musical traditions: hip hop, spoken word, reggae, pop, and country. My favorite style is hip hop. It is also the type of music (with spoken word) that my students prefer.

Diam's, a French hip-hop artist, began rapping about God, veiling, and freedom in 2009, after an extremely successful music career and following her conversion to Islam, which came after a bout of depression and hospitalization. She stated that religion had helped her cope better with stresses than medications.

In her song titled "Lili," Diam's raps about a sixteen-year-old veiled Muslim girl (Lili) who is forced to leave her French high school because she wears *hijab*. Despite her loyalty to French values, her blue eyes, white skin, and red blood (the colors of the French flag), Lili is rejected, feared, shunned, and viewed as an enemy simply "because I am a woman who covers, and that I wear the veil." The lyrics of the song as a whole are extremely moving, as is the singer's voice, which alternates between pleading and aggression.

The story of Lili is of course that of all school-age Muslim girls living in France today who want to wear *hijab* but who are barred from doing so by French legislation introduced in 2004. Yet hers is also a universal story, that of Muslim women anywhere who veil and who encounter discrimination, misunderstanding, and fear. It is the story of those women who want to share with the world their love, their skills, and their dreams, but who are cast aside as victims of false assumptions and unfair laws.

Lili's story is perhaps also that of Diam's herself, of how she faced criticism and rejection from the French media and many leading French feminist organizations because of what they considered her incomprehensible conversion to Islam, and especially her decision to take up veiling and to perform onstage wearing a cap that covered her hair. This was not the Diam's they thought they knew, the Diam's they wanted to herald as a leading French rapper and the protector of the equality of the sexes.

Despite the various dimensions of "Lili," and despite the multiple interviews Diam's granted about it and her own religious conversion, the song did not succeed in producing a change in her audience. The majority of her French fans could not hear her voice in this song, her experiences, nor were they open to new perspectives on veiling. For them, veiling could only mean the oppression and subordination of women, regardless of what the woman herself declared. This is probably not an entirely surprising reaction from French audiences and contrasts greatly with the reception of Islamic hip hop in the United States.

In the United States, and despite cases of discrimination against veiled Muslim girls and women in schools, the workplace, and in governmental agencies, veiling remains a right ultimately guaranteed by the Constitution and upheld in court cases (see chapter 6). Singing about the right to veil, the right to practice one's religion, and asserting one's civil rights are more accepted and acceptable in America.

The majority of Muslim hip-hop artists in the United States are African Americans. They include Miss Latifah and Tavasha Shannon, who performs as Miss Undastood. Both are Muslim converts who wear the veil. Both are excellent examples of the role that hip hop is playing in communicating new messages about Muslim veiling in the United States.[11]

In her "Hijab Is the One Thing," Miss Undastood raps that she is "liberated, educated, making a statement." She insists on her profound belief in free will and on the fact that veiling can only be a freely embraced choice. Veiling, according to her, is an individual decision whose meaning cannot be reduced to a simplistic value system: "No, I'm not married, so I ain't wearing this for no man"; and, "Just because I cover, don't mean I am more righteous. Just because you don't, it doesn't mean you're less pious." Even though Shannon chose the stage name Miss Undastood because she felt misunderstood when she first turned to Islamic music at the age of eighteen, she feels that she is now far better understood and appreciated by Muslims and non-Muslims in America and increasingly in Great Britain. She has been featured on multiple TV and radio programs, was interviewed for national and international media sources, and is today recognized as one of the leading American Muslim hip-hop artists.

This does not mean that Miss Undastood does not face criticism for her music and lyrics. She does, from both Muslims and non-Muslims. Neither can fully understand how she can be at once a Muslim, a woman, a *veiled* woman, a rapper, and an American. But Miss Undastood does not let such criticism detract her from her goal of telling the truth, no matter how hard it is for others to hear it. Contemporary music artists enlist hip hop, true to its original intent, to communicate the deep feelings of the oppressed and to challenge biases held by the majority population.

By giving hip hop an Islamic flavor, Muslim artists living in Muslim-minority societies are creating a new hybrid form that blends a profoundly American popular cultural genre with Islamic sensibilities. They are thus demonstrating their ability to successfully bridge American (and Western) culture and an Islamic value system. The genre's popularity ensures that it reaches a younger audience of both Muslims and non-Muslims and invites them to see new aspects of veiling that they may not have thought about. Judging by my students' response to this type of music, these artists are successful.

■ Artistic productions on the subject of veiling can be considered forms of resistance—resistance against established norms, against the status quo, and against oppression. All the artists discussed here question commonly held stereotypes about veiled Muslim women and attempt to establish new associations that go against the grain of many alleged "truths" about the veil, Islam, or Muslim women.

Seen from these artistic perspectives, Muslim veiling clearly never refers to one singular type of practice, nor does it have one universal meaning or a unique form of expression. Rather, veiling describes a multiplicity of experiences. It is controversial only because it is a visible marker whose meaning cannot be contained in or grasped with a single or simple explanation. The meaning of the veil can only be revealed through the exploration of its shading, its range of expressions, its contradictory practices.

The artists discussed here are not always sufficiently known or heard in either Muslim-majority or Muslim-minority societies. They are still too often overlooked, and some remain powerless to effect social or political change. Yet if past artistic movements can serve as a lesson, the art produced today by Muslim artists—be they poets, comedians, performers, visual artists, or singers—stands to play an important role in challenging prevalent stereotypical views of Muslim women and their veiling.

All we need to do is open our eyes and ears and listen with an open heart.

They think it's all about the *burqa* . . . I'm ready to wear two *burqas* if
my government can provide security and a rule of law. That's O.K. with me.
If that's the only freedom I have to give up, I'm ready.
—Mrs. Rafaat, Afghan woman and politician (2010)

Epilogue

This book has provided a complex understanding of veiling and of the
practices of 1.5 billion people around the world. It has reminded us that
veiling is not a practice that began with the advent of Islam, nor is it one
taken up solely by Muslims. Many other women around the world cover
for various spiritual, cultural, personal, and political reasons. Moreover, the history of veiling among Muslims is one intimately linked to
European colonial incursions in Muslim-majority societies from the late
eighteenth to the early twentieth century. It is only since then that Muslim veiling has been associated with the oppression of women and the
backwardness of Islam.

By bringing out the heterogeneous voices of Muslim women who veil,
as well as of those who choose not to veil, my goal has been to challenge
common perceptions of veiling practices and many stereotypes of Muslim women. These are voices we do not hear often enough, or loudly
enough. Yet it is these women's personal experiences that we must be
attuned to if we wish to discuss Muslim veiling in an informed way. In
this regard, Mrs. Rafaat's comment in the epigraph gets underneath conventional and biased views of Muslim women and highlights the point

that veiling is not experienced as oppression by the majority of Muslim women.[1]

In contrast to what many believe, and as we have seen throughout *What Is Veiling?*, the reasons that go into a woman's decision to veil are complex and numerous; they cannot be limited to religious prescription or political imposition. While these factors are certainly important in understanding Muslim veiling, they are only one part of the story, and, by themselves, they do not account for the range of meanings that the veil continues to have for Muslim women around the world. A number of historical, geographic, social, economic, feminist, personal, and cultural reasons also help explain a woman's adoption of *hijab*. Further contingencies might be age, personal preference, occasion, family background, social class, fashion, and social pressure, all of which are equally significant in any Muslim woman's decision to veil. Veiling is a complex human rights issue whose meaning cannot be reduced to a simplistic binary of emancipation versus repression.

I sincerely hope that each time you see a veiled woman, whether she is dressed in *hijab, niqab,* or in the most glamorous fashionable attire, you will be less likely to rush to a conclusion about her religious beliefs, her relationship to her family, her desire to be liberated, or her commitment to either feminism or radical forms of Islam. Simply remember that Muslim women's voices are diverse, their veiling practices numerous, and their reasons for covering—or not covering—varied. Let us all be attuned to their voices and recognize that Muslim women are, like other women of any faith, individuals with struggles and successes, weaknesses and strengths, who are seeking to lead productive, happy, and peaceful lives in the midst of their community and in the world.

Glossary

Terms Referring to Veiling

In this glossary, which makes no claim to being exhaustive, I present an alphabetically organized set of terms used to refer to the Muslim veil and to dress worn by Muslims in different Muslim societies. I also provide some indication of the society with which they are most commonly associated. The variety of words reflects not just different linguistic cultures but also the real differences in veiling practices among Muslims.

Each piece of clothing listed below can vary from cheap, plain, and mass-produced to tailored, expensive, and high-quality material. It can have no decoration or a lot of decoration (velvet or lace trims, designs in the material, etc.), lending more distinction and sophistication to each piece.

The reader should keep in mind that the same word can at times refer to different styles of dress depending on the setting, the historical period, and the country in which it is used. In addition, some of the words listed here are known across all Muslim-majority nations; others are more local and may be unknown outside a particular geographic area or ethnic group.

Abaya   Saudi Arabia, Gulf States, Iraq (in the latter, the term is used for both male and female clothing). With globalization and labor migration, this style of dress has spread across all Muslim-majority and Muslim-minority societies.

This is the traditional dark, long, and loose cloak, black being the most common color. It is at times embroidered around the edges and has tussled tie cords. Since the *abaya* is just the body garment, it requires separate headgear to go along with it.

When it was adopted in Yemen in the early 2000s, the *abaya* was made from thinner material than the *balto*, though in double layers to ensure opaqueness. There, it is considered elegant, fashionable attire, favored by university students and young educated professionals to signal their individuality and sophistication, in contrast to its role as a state-imposed dress in Saudi Arabia.

The *abaya* is considered convenient because it can easily be worn over regular home or street clothes, instantly transforming any woman into a modestly dressed Muslim. For this reason, it has become the *hijab* of choice for a wide range of women and is now frequently sold and worn throughout many countries. It is likely to be seen in geographically and culturally diverse regions such as Saudi Arabia, Iraq, Egypt, the suburbs of Paris, or upscale malls in Raleigh, North Carolina.

Balto   Yemen

This is the Arabic pronunciation of the originally Russian *palto*, or long overcoat. This one-piece, loose-fitting, full-length overcoat, at times with cuffs and a belt, became the fashionable alternative to the traditional Yemeni *sitara* and *sharshaf* in the early 1970s. It was introduced by upper-class women who had traveled abroad, and by the 1990s, it had become the most commonly worn style of outdoor dress, adopted by younger, educated, and professional Yemeni women.

Because the *balto* defined the shoulders of the wearer and had set-in sleeves, it was initially considered inappropriate by conservative Muslims for whom it evoked a male style of dress. Traditional Yemenis quickly adopted the *balto*, however, when they learned that it was worn by conservative women in Egypt and Syria. Syrian women who migrated to Yemen after the 1982 Hama massacre played an important role in spreading the fashion of the *balto* in Sanaa. Many Yemeni women now consider the *balto* a better type of *hijab* because it conceals the woman's body more effectively than the *sharshaf*, whose upper part may reveal the garments worn underneath.

The traditional color of *baltos* was black until the 1990s. Since then, other colors have appeared, though oftentimes a woman seen wearing a more colorful *balto* is assumed to be a foreigner (from the Syrian, Jordanian, or Palestinian migrant communities), rather than a Yemeni.

Bandana   French Muslims of North African descent

This colorful scarf of Hindu origins and traditionally worn by pirates, gang members, and railroad workers has recently been adopted by Muslim girls living in France in lieu of a *hijab*. The bandana allows these girls to circumvent the 2004 law against ostentatious religious signs in public schools. It was adopted as a substitute for the veil because of its lack of religious connotation.

Bisha or Bitcha   Egypt

Black muslin face veil worn by aristocratic women in the nineteenth and early twentieth century in periods of mourning, in lieu of the traditional white *burquʿ*.

Buibui   East Africa

This is a full black cloak worn over one's clothes that is commonly seen only in Muslim-majority areas of East Africa along the coast. It confers respectability to the person wearing it.

Burqa   Afghanistan and increasingly the Sudan

This is both a face and body garment with crocheted eyeholes. The traditional color in Afghanistan is blue or white. In most other places, it is made of black cloth.

Burquʿ (multiple spellings), Burgu, or Batula   Egypt, United Arab Emirates, Oman, Saudi Arabia, Yemen

These terms refer to slightly different forms of face veiling in different social groups and communities.

In Egypt, the *burquʿ* referred to a white muslin face veil worn by aristocratic women in the nineteenth century and the early twentieth when going out in public or appearing in mixed-gender groups. In contemporary Egyptian society, a face veil is referred to as *niqab*, rather than as *burquʿ*.

In the Emirates and Oman, it refers to the metallic face mask worn by older women as a carryover from traditional tribal customs. The *burgu* is made of burnished indigo and can resemble ancient Greek helmets.

In Yemen, the *burqu'* was introduced by returning migrant workers from Saudi Arabia and has become popular since the 1990s. It consists of a one-piece face cover that ties to the back of the head with push buttons, a strap, or Velcro. The *burqu'* is made of two layers of material: a lower opaque layer with a slit for the eyes, and a top, more transparent layer that can either be thrown back over the head or pulled over the face to entirely cover the eyes. In Sanaa, the *burqu'* is worn over the *maqrama* (the large headscarf).

Busana Muslimah or Busana Islami   Indonesia

This is the generic term for *hijab* in Indonesia. It refers to any type of dress that is recognizably Islamic. Typically, this means any long-sleeved and floor-length tunic with a loose or fitted head covering. This type of clothing was a rare sight in Indonesia prior to the early 1980s.

Çarşaf   Turkey

See *chador, niqab, burqa*

Chador (or chadri; also spelled cadar)   Iran, Pakistan, Afghanistan, Indonesia

This is a head, face, and body garment worn over regular street clothes. It covers a woman's body from head to toe, leaving only the eyes visible. It is typically black, brown, or dark gray in cities, but light-colored with tiny print patterns in rural areas.

Ciput (visor ciput, ninja ciput, bin ciput)   Indonesia

These are fashionable headscarves with a bun on the top or back of the head that seek to make believe that the women wearing them have long hair tied in a bun underneath their *hijab*.

Dishdasha   Gulf states

This is the traditional dress of Bedouin men in the Gulf region. It consists of a white, ankle-length tunic with a headdress, and it continues to be worn across all social classes both by Bedouins in the desert and by members of the royal families.

Dupatta   Indian subcontinent, Pakistan

This is a long scarf, often sheer, matching a woman's garments and draped over the head and bosom. It serves as a head cover during prayers or in mosques but is left on the shoulders the rest of the time.

Echarpe   Syria

This is a synonym for *foulard*, both generic French words for "scarf."

Ferege   Western Thrace, Turkey

See *yashamk*

Foulard   Syria, France

This is the French word for "scarf," which continues to be used in Syria today (a legacy of French colonialism). It refers to a narrow scarf typically worn by Muslim women there. It covers the hair and head, including ears and throat.

Ghatweh   Syria, Palestine

This is a big, white, cotton head cover worn by Arab women from rural areas.

The *ghatweh* is wider than either *shaylas* or *dupattas* and has a history similar to that of the *kefiyyeh*.

Habara   Egypt

This was the national Egyptian dress for aristocratic women in the nineteenth and early twentieth century. It consisted of a long skirt, a head cover, and a face veil (*burquᶜ*) made of white muslin. In periods of mourning, women substituted a black muslin veil, known locally as *bisha* (or *bitcha*).

Haïk   Algeria, Morocco

This is a long, loose, traditionally white scarf worn over street clothing, covering part of the body and face and held in place with one hand. It used to be worn only by middle-class, urban women, but today it is associated with women from lower socioeconomic classes.

See *milaya* and *shoqqa*

Hijab   This is the generic word for veiling used by all Muslims regardless of background. It requires the adoption of a body garment and headgear, which are intended to conceal a woman's body, hair, ears, and neck. Women who wear *hijab* are called *hijabis*, and they do not cover their faces (in contrast to *niqabis*, who do), hands, or feet. *Hijab* is achieved through various means, as this glossary demonstrates. At times, *hijab* denotes Western-style attire with longer hemlines and sleeves. At other times, it refers to the ready-made overcoats worn over regular home or street clothes.

Hijab Islami   Yemen, Egypt

This term was coined in the 1970s and translates as "Muslim *hijab*." It refers to the growing adoption of more conservative dress as a reaction against secularism, consumerism, and materialism in Egypt, as well as against the national governments perceived to be puppets of Western powers. In the 1970s, Muslim *hijab* was often associated with the rise of political Islam and meant adopting long-sleeved blouses, mid-calf skirts, and a headscarf.

When this style of dress took root in Yemen in the 1980s, it was considered quite daring and revealing (in contrast to how it was perceived in Egypt, where it was seen as conservative). This is because Yemeni women traditionally covered their faces in public, while the new style meant uncovering them. Today, *hijab islami* remains the dress of choice among Yemeni women of either secular or *Salafi* convictions, many of whom choose not to cover their faces in some settings (university or cultural clubs), but to do so in others (market or neighborhood). It is usually considered a sign of modernity and fashion.

Jellaba   Morocco, Algeria, Tunisia, North African immigrants in Europe (in France and the United Kingdom especially)

This is a long, loose overcoat traditionally worn by both men and women in North Africa, regardless of religious background, social class, or level of devotion. This long robe can be made of any material and color and can be either simple or quite elaborate. It covers the entire body and often has a hood to cover the head. Women prefer, nevertheless, to add a separate head cover.

Jilbab   Egypt, Syria, Indonesia, North African immigrants in Europe

This is the Qurʾanic term that refers to women's clothing. Today, the *jilbab* is tailored and made to be fashionable with matching headgear, so that women can appear both pious and modern. It is frequently associated with Western-style business suits to which a headscarf is added.

It is interesting to note that nuns in Indonesia also refer to their habit as a *jilbab*. This could be an indication that the term, in this country, does not specifically refer to Islam, but is associated with body covering in general.

Kanga   East Africa

This is a rectangular piece of brightly colored, printed cotton fabric about 1 meter by 1.5 meters, often with a Swahili proverb printed along one side, that is worn as *hijab* by East African women, especially in the countryside. Women usually wear several kangas at once, each for a different function. A woman can wear a kanga to cover her head and shoulders, another one as a skirt, a different one as an apron or a sling for carrying a baby. In everyday life, matching the various kangas is not important. Girls have a standard way of tying a kanga around their necks, as a sort of halter dress.

Kefiyyeh   Palestine, Jordan, Yemen

Originally, this was a piece of male headgear worn by Bedouin Palestinian and Kurdish men as a symbol of honor and tribal affiliation, and it was wrapped in various styles according to region and family. Today, this piece of cloth is known to Euro-American audiences as the black-and-white checkered cotton scarf worn by the late Yasser Arafat. This scarf was a trademark of Palestinian nationalism in the 1930s and of the Palestinian resistance movement against Israel in the 1960s. While the Palestinian *kefiyyeh* is typically black and white, the Jordanian and Yemeni one is red and white.

In the 1970s, this male head cover was adopted by Palestinian Muslim *women* who began to wrap it around their head and shoulders in lieu of a veil to demonstrate their support of the armed struggle against Israel. This kind of scarf is worn today by youth across the globe both as a political statement and as a fashion accessory. It is now readily available in all colors and sold in many international markets.

Kerudung   Indonesia

This is a gauzy, loose headscarf worn by older women who have completed the pilgrimage to Mecca (*hajj*). It was typical in Indonesia prior to the 1980s, before the *jilbab* and the *busana islami* became popular.

Khimar   Yemen, Egypt, and elsewhere

This is a generic term used in the Qur'an to refer to women's clothing. Today, the *khimar* refers to the most common style of head covering that Muslim women wear. It consists usually of two pieces: a small, narrow underscarf that covers the forehead, and a larger, thicker black scarf that is tied at the back of the neck. At times, the *khimar* is long, extending to the waist, thus covering not just the hair, ears, and neck but also the shoulders and the arms to the wrists.

Many Yemeni women consider the *khimar* more practical than the traditional *maqrama*, which tends to slip and must be continuously readjusted. Because the *khimar* is tied in the back and easily stays in place, it is the preferred form of veiling for women who play a more public role.

Lithma   Yemen

This is a face cover consisting of a long piece of black cloth that is tightly wrapped around the upper and lower part of the face. When going outdoors, women also add another thin face veil over the *lithma* to cover the eyes. Today, new styles of *lithma* have appeared, consisting of two pieces of round-knitted stretch material that are easier to put on and take off.

Maghnaé   Iran

This is a short, shape-revealing *chador* that some women wear as a form of resistance to the imposed and traditional *chador*. It is associated with the concept of "bad *hijab*."

Manteau (also spelled manto; pl. mantoha)   Syria, Iran, Lebanon, Turkey

This is a French word meaning "coat," and it refers to the full-length, form-concealing overcoat (or outer garments in general) worn by some Muslim women when going out in public. It comes in different styles and colors. It is synonym to the fashionable *jilbab*.

Mantila   Greece

This is the generic Greek term for "headscarf" or "veil." It is used to refer both to the traditional female Christian head covering and to the Muslim scarf.

Maqrama   Yemen

This refers to either a long, thin, rectangular scarf that is draped over the hair, or a large, usually colored, square scarf that covers the hair. It is worn by women who are fashion conscious and who have adopted the *balto*.

Marmuq   Yemen

This is a full face veil made of black material with white and red circles that women in Yemen wear with the *sitara*.

Milaya (also milaʾ and milfafa)   Egypt, Syria

This is a long, loose scarf or large cloth worn over home or street garments that was especially popular until the middle of the twentieth century. It covers parts of the body, head, and face and is held in place with one hand. It is usually black and requires separate headgear.

See *haïk* and *shoqqa*

Moussor   Senegal (Pulaar, Bambara, and Serere ethnic groups in particular)

This is the traditional headscarf worn by Senegalese women especially after marriage to protect themselves from evil spirits. This garment has been an integral part of Senegalese sartorial traditions since well before the introduction of Islam, and it is today worn indiscriminately by Muslims, Christians, and adherents of local African religions.

Niqab   This is a generic term that refers to the face veil. It is a free-flowing piece of black (at times, white) cloth that can be of different lengths and that is tied around the head and over the head veil, covering the lower part of the face. It is meant to hide a woman's entire face except for her eyes. Women who wear *niqab* are referred to as *niqabis* to distinguish them from the *hijabis*, those who wear *hijab* but not a face veil.

Even though it is increasingly adopted by Yemeni women, the *niqab* is not considered a local tradition, but rather evocative of a cosmopolitan Muslim identity. Many Yemeni women prefer it to the *lithma* because it is more convenient, allowing women to eat and drink in public simply by lifting the lower part of the face veil without showing the face.

Many Muslims consider the *niqab* a very conservative kind of veiling, and one not mandated by the Qur'an. Most women who wear a *niqab* also adopt dark overcoats, *baltos, jilbabs,* or *abayas,* as well as thick dark socks and gloves. They are typically assumed to have Islamist or Salafi sympathies.

Peçe   Turkey

This is a thick black face veil, equivalent to the *burqa*.

Purdah   South Asia

This term refers to the traditional spatial division between men and women, as well as the segregation of women as a mark of virtue and respectability. This term refers also to the South Asian concept of *chadri aur chardivari,* literally meaning "a curtain and four walls," which is viewed as the ideal space for women. It has become a general term used for modest clothing and *hijab*.

Qina'   Arabia

This is a generic term for both male and female head and face covers.

Rida'   Arabia

This is a generic term for outer garments covering the body from head to toe.

Russari (also spelled rosari)   Iran

This is the Persian word for "headscarf." It is traditionally worn tied under the chin.

Safsari   Tunisia

This is an outer garment worn by Tunisian women from the lower classes.

Sari   India

This is a wrap-around garment, part of which is draped around the waist and the rest hanging over the right shoulder. The cloth that hangs from the shoulder is used to cover the hair, but only during prayer times.

See *tobe*

Shalwar Qamis   Pakistan, South Asian Muslims around the world

This is the traditional clothing worn in South Asia by Muslims, Christians, and Parsis (South Asian Zoroastrians) women as well as by men. Its connotations go beyond religion and extend to culture, respectability, and etiquette. The *shalwar* (baggy pants) *qamis* (tunic) is thus not specific to Muslims or to women. This garment can be brightly colored, and in the case of women, it is usually accompanied by a *dupatta,* rarely a face veil.

Sharshaf (also spelled çarşaf)   Yemen

This is a traditional style of dress worn by Yemeni women on formal occasions (in contrast to the *sitara,* which is worn on a daily basis). It is a voluminous, loose cloak gathered at the waist and usually accompanied by a thick face veil (*lithma*). While this outfit is typically black in Sanaa, it tended until recently to be more colorful in rural areas.

The *sharshaf* was introduced to Yemen by the Ottoman Turks and, until the 1962 revolution that transformed the imamate into a republic, was worn only by a small number of elite women closely related to the *imam*. Since then, it has become popular among the middle class and is now increasingly adopted by women in rural areas and by the urban poor.

The *sharshaf* is associated with fashion, urbanism, and sophistication because it had been adopted by the first generation of women who sought an education in the early 1970s. These women began to experiment with the length of the skirt, adopting a shorter *sharshaf* worn over stockings or wide-legged trousers (instead of the traditional Yemeni *sirwal*, or pants). Some also introduced the *sharshaf maxi*, with a skirt resembling the maxi skirt of the 1970s worn by European non-Muslim women. Some Yemeni women also experimented with the material and color of the *sharshaf*. Shiny satins and velvet became especially fashionable and were, at times, an expression of rebellion against social and familial pressures. All innovations to the traditional *sharshaf* came under heavy attack by conservative Islamist factions.

Today most women in Sanaa are adopting more fashionable dress (the *abayas* especially). Those who continue to wear the *sharshaf* assert they are doing so to express authenticity and faithfulness to traditional Sanai traditions.

Shaylah (also spelled chale)   Iran, Gulf states

This is a misspelling of the French term *châle* referring to a long, narrow scarf worn around the head and left unwrapped and hanging on the shoulders. It is available in all types of fabrics and designs, including designer models that may include fringed, monogrammed, and embroidered edges.

Shoqqa   Upper Egypt

This is a long scarf typically worn by rural women in upper Egypt when going out in public. It is held over the head and face with the hands, leaving only one eye visible.

See *milaya* and *haïk*

Sitara   Yemen

This is a large, rectangular cotton sheet dyed red and blue worn by Yemeni women when going out on short errands in the neighborhood. It is considered convenient because it can be quickly thrown over indoor clothes. Since the 1920s, the *sitara* has been imported from India, where it is mass produced and exported specifically for the Yemeni market.

Tegelmust   The African Tuareg tribes (Berber-speaking Muslims) from Southern Algeria, southwestern Libya, Mali, Niger

This is the *male* face veil worn by the Tuareg as a marker of maturity, status, and influence. Tuareg women, in contrast, do not wear face veils, though they may at times draw their shawls over the lower part of their faces when expressing reserve.

Tsember   Western Thrace, Turkey

This is the term for the loosely worn headscarf worn by Muslim village women in Greece. This kind of scarf is tied under the chin and is not strictly meant to cover the hair.

Tobe   Sudan

This is a loose, wrap-around garment, similar to the Indian *sari* but with different length material and a different wrapping method. It is commonly worn in the northern part of the country and covers both a woman's body and head.

Tudung   Malaysia, Indonesia

This is the Malay word that refers to any type of head covering, including peasant straw hats. It is also used for the head covering of Muslim women. In northern Sumatra (Indonesia), the term is associated with rural, lower-class, and peasant headgear.

Türban   Turkey, Western Thrace

This is the (originally French) term referring to headscarves worn by Muslim men and fashion-conscious Muslim women. The *türban* is made of expensive, colorful fabrics that match the rest of the clothes worn. It is wrapped tightly around the face, covering the hair, ears, and throat, and tied with a knot under the chin or at the back of the neck. Because this type of headscarf is meant to be a fashionable accessory, women wearing it will usually also wear Western street clothes.

Yashmak (also spelled yaşmak)   Western Thrace, Ottoman Empire

This term has two different meanings. Today, it is used in Western Thrace to refer to the long overcoat worn by Muslim women living there. When the *yashmak* is black or black and white, it is referred to as *ferege*.

The term also refers to the transparent gauze face veil worn by women in Ottoman society from the eighteenth century to the early twentieth; it revealed the eyes and only loosely covered the face. While the face veil continues to be worn by some women in Muslim-majority countries that were part of the former Ottoman Empire, the word used to refer to it is no longer *yashmak*, but any of the ones presented in this glossary.

Notes

INTRODUCTION

1. Heath, *The Veil*, 1. This collection of essays is full of useful information on the history of veiling around the world and in multiple cultural traditions.

2. While I am aware that the terms "East" and "West" are relative concepts and that each is diverse in its own right, I am using them with very specific intent and as shorthand. When discussing the nineteenth century, I am using the terms "West" and "Western" to refer specifically to European perspectives; for the twentieth century, these terms refer to Euro-American societies. My intent is not to invoke a binarism or a radical opposition.

3. The erotic meaning of the veil has not disappeared today, as evident in publications such as *Playboy* and *Hustler* or in fashion magazines such as *Vogue*. However, in popular expression, this sexual meaning has receded in favor of other images tied to contemporary political concerns.

4. See Ahmed, *A Quiet Revolution*.

5. Driver and Miles, *The Assyrian Laws*, 406–9. On pre-Islamic veiling, see also Heath, *The Veil*, and Goto, "Qurʾan and the Veil."

6. Driver and Miles, *The Assyrian Laws*, 408–11.

7. For example, Gen. 24:64–65 and Isa. 47:2.

8. On Haredi women, see Von Mittelstaedt, "The Advance of the Zealots."

9. On the Church Fathers' view of women and clothing and its impact on medieval European traditions, see Blamires, *Woman Defamed and Woman Defended*.

CHAPTER ONE

1. Stowasser, *Women in the Qurʾan*, 104.

2. Ibn Saʿd, cited in Goto, "Qurʾan and the Veil," 281.

3. Bucar, *The Islamic Veil*, 44.

4. Al-Tabari, cited in Goto, "Qurʾan and the Veil," 288–89; see also Hajjaji-Jarrah, "Women's Modesty," 186–93.

5. Al-Zamakhshari, cited in Goto, "Qurʾan and the Veil," 289.

6. This entire section on al-Razi is indebted to Hajjaji-Jarrah, "Women's Modesty," 199–203.

7. Al-Jawzi, cited ibid., 204.

8. On veiling in *hadith*, see Clarke, "*Hijab* According to *Hadith*." I am indebted to her work throughout this discussion.

9. For further information on how family law in particular becomes transformed with colonization, see Abdullahi A. An-Naʿim, "Islamic Family Law," Emory University, http://www.law.emory.edu/ifl (November 2, 2013); and Otto, *Sharia Incorporated*.

CHAPTER TWO

1. For an example of leading progressive Muslim scholars, see the publications of Amina Wadud, Mohja Kahf, Julianne Hammer, Omid Safi, Asma Barlas, and Leila Ahmed. Their work is cited in this chapter and in the bibliography of the book.

2. Even though this verse is intended to protect Muslim women, it does not protect female slaves, whether they converted to Islam or not. By dressing differently, slaves would be recognized as such, and continued harassment was presumably permitted. In fact, a *hadith* traditionally attributed to Umar forbids slave women to veil precisely in order to be recognized.

3. This *hadith* is repeated by many Islamic studies scholars, including Goto, Ahmed, and Mernissi.

4. See, for instance, Roded, *Women in Islamic Biographical Collections*; and Mernissi, *The Forgotten Queens*.

5. This renewed understanding of the role of early history does not always lead to the same conclusions. For a different perspective, see Afsarrudin, *The First Muslims*.

6. This perspective has been described by Diouf in *Servants of Allah*, 72–80 and expressed by Wadud, *Inside the Gender Jihad*, 221. It is also recalled by Kahf, "From Her Royal Body," 30–31. In fact, this is one key reason why many African Americans, whether Muslims or not, often wear clothing that cover their legs and head when going out in public.

7. Wadud, *Inside the Gender Jihad*, 223.

8. Abdul-Ghafur, *Living Islam Out Loud*, 5.

9. Saed's essay is included in Abdul-Ghafur, *Living Islam Out Loud*, 92.

10. See Zarqa Nawaz's documentary *Me and the Mosque*.

11. Azhar Usman's skit can be heard in ibid.

12. I personally led mixed-gender prayers in the early 1980s while studying at Bryn Mawr College and serving as the president of the Muslim Student Association there. At the time, I was the most knowledgeable student about Islam and the only one fluent in Arabic.

13. On Hui Muslims in China and on the practice of women-only mosques, see Jaschok and Jingjun, *Women, Religion, and Space in China*, as well as their *The History of Women's Mosques in Chinese Islam*. See also the following documentary videos about Chinese Hui Muslim *imams* and all-women mosques in China by McLaughlin and Lovell: *The Last Call to Prayer* (2012) and *Female Imams* (2012). These films explore the difference between central Henan Hui and Western Hui Muslims, the latter of whom have more Arab influence. I would like to thank Sharron Lovell for generously sharing her work with me.

CHAPTER THREE

1. Maryam's words are reported by Bowen in his *Why the French Don't Like Headscarves*, 79.

2. The *burqa* used to be required in Afghanistan under Taliban rule, but it was officially banned in 2001 after the American invasion of the country.

3. The Saudi morality police is called the *mutawa*. It is composed of both bearded

male and veiled female officers who zealously stand guard throughout the cities, at the entrances of hotels, malls, or coffee shops, and admonish women who do not conform to the Saudi dress code. They do not hesitate to intervene and rebuke any woman who shows even a few strands of hair, since it is assumed that such (immodest) behavior is associated with daring liberalism, imported from Euro-American societies. In the Sudan, women who defy the new dress code imposed by the government in 1989, namely, the Saudi-style *abaya* or the Iranian *chador*, or who are seen wearing skirts or trousers, may be flogged with hundreds of lashes.

4. A similar drop in the enrollment of female students can be observed in Tajikistan, which introduced legislation in 2005 banning the *hijab* in schools and universities.

5. Other examples of male veiling include the *warias* in Indonesia and the *hijras* in India. On male veiling, see El Guindi, *Veil*; Rasmussen, "The Slippery Sign"; and Boellstorff, "Playing Back the Nation."

6. A similar campaign advocating proper veiling practices in Indonesia is discussed by Bucar in her recent *The Islamic Veil*, 110.

CHAPTER FOUR

1. *Arabian Nights* (also known as *One Thousand and One Nights*) is the title of a collection of Arabic-framed tales that entered the European literary canon in the early eighteenth century with Antoine Galland's famed French translation in 1704 and, a century later, with Sir Richard Burton's 1850 English rendition. Today, these stories continue to be well known in their filmic and children versions, such as *Aladdin*.

2. Picasso did a series of fifteen variations on Delacroix's *Femmes d'Alger dans leur appartement* (designated as versions A to O) between December 1954 and February 1955. His goal was to create a new artistic expression, as well as to challenge conventional representations of Muslim women and their simplistic association with eroticism.

3. Montagu, *Turkish Embassy Letters*, 59.

4. On the transformation of the meaning of breasts from the Middle Ages to the eighteenth century, see Miles, *A Complex Delight*.

5. Fanon, "Algeria Unveiled," 76. The *haïk* is the traditional Algerian white veil that envelopes the woman's head, face, and body and that is held in place with one hand. Fanon was perhaps the first to recognize that the French colonial act of unveiling Algerian women "provoke[d] the native's bristling resistance" and that the Algerian cult of the veil during the country's war of independence was therefore a direct response to the colonialist's offensive against the veil.

6. The official reason given for these photographs was that they were needed for the new French identity cards issued to the Algerian population. Yet it soon became clear that the photos had been ordered by the French government to better control the movements of the Algerian population and to prevent its unification in the struggle for independence.

7. Garanger, foreword to *Femmes algériennes 1960*. Algerian women's active resistance during the Algerian war of independence has also been retold in a 1998 collection of short stories by the Franco-Algerian novelist and critic Assia Djebar titled *Women of Algiers in Their Apartment*. By using the same title for her work as that

for Delacroix's famous orientalist painting, Djebar recalls and rewrites the forgotten legacy of Algerian women's activism and places it front and center in the history of Algeria. Her goal is to substitute this political history for the longstanding orientalist violence suffered by Algerian women, a violence continued by Muslim Algerian rulers who have conveniently forgotten women's participation alongside men during the war.

8. Lord Kromer, cited in Ahmed, *Women and Gender in Islam*, 153.

9. Ahmed, *Women and Gender in Islam*, 153.

10. Kahf, *E-mails from Scheherazad*, 70.

CHAPTER FIVE

1. Blair's words were part of a news conference cited in a *New York Times* article by Alan Cowell titled "Blair Criticizes Full Islamic Veil as 'Mark of Separation,'" published on October 18, 2006. In keeping with European usage, I will use in this chapter the terms *burqa* and *niqab* interchangeably even though they are not, technically speaking, the same thing.

2. This is an estimate only, as by law, France does not include in its census questions on religious beliefs or affiliations. The number given here includes both strict followers of the religion and the majority who is secular.

3. Bowen, *Why the French Don't Like Headscarves*, 24–25.

4. Mr. Laurent Lévy, cited in *Le Monde*, September 25, 2003.

5. The commission recommended various strategies, such as the addition of classes on the history of religions to school curricula and the creation of the office of "Muslim chaplain" in hospitals and prisons. It also proposed that alternatives to pork and fish be made available in schools, prisons, and hospital cafeterias, and that a national holiday both for Jews and for Muslims be officially introduced in the school calendar.

6. The text of the law banning the wearing of religious signs (and most specifically the Islamic veil) in French public schools is translated by Bowen, *Why the French Don't Like Headscarves*, 136.

7. Scott, *The Politics of the Veil*, 167. Even though Scott addresses only the banning of the veil in her book, the arguments she makes apply also to the ban on the *burqa*.

8. Ibid., 168.

9. Fadela Amara expressed these views in an interview with the *Financial Times* that was published in the article "French Minister Calls for Full Ban on Burka" by Ben Hall on August 15, 2009.

10. This is the phrase used by Houria Bouteldja, http://lmsi.net/De-la-ceremonie-du-devoilement-a.

11. Scott, *The Politics of the Veil*, 10.

12. The views of the Stasi Commission are summarized in Bowen, *Why the French Don't Like Headscarves*, 116.

13. This is what the European deputy Alima Boumediene-Thiery noted in her plenary address, titled "Les femmes maghrébines: Issues de l'immigration dans l'Union Européenne," at the opening of the Unesco Scholarly Program on Migration and Human Rights at the University Hassan II in Casablanca, Morocco, in 2001.

14. Brouard and Tiberj, *As French As Everyone Else?*

15. Consider the example of Rachida Dati, the former justice minister under President Sarkozy, who is a French citizen of Moroccan descent and who has been heralded as showing that Arab women can be part of the French political scene. When she became a single mother in 2008, the media never presented her as an example of an integrated French citizen of Arab descent; she was simply ignored.

16. The French term *communautarisme* has been defined by Scott as follows: "The priority of the group over national identity in the lives of individuals." See her *The Politics of the Veil*, 11.

17. Steven Erlanger and Elvire Camus, "In a Ban, a Measure of European Tolerance," *New York Times*, September 1, 2012, http://www.nytimes.com/2012/09/02/world /europe/tolerance-eases-impact-of-french-ban-on-full-face-veils.

18. Mushaben, "More Than Just a Bad-Hair Day," 188.

19. Fariba, Muslim student interviewed by Bowen during his research on the debate over headscarves in France, cited in his *Why the French Don't Like Headscarves*, 78.

20. Scott, *The Politics of the Veil*, 17.

CHAPTER SIX

1. Moore, "Visible through the Veil." This entire section on discrimination against veiled women and the legal ramifications of the court cases is indebted to Moore's article.

2. Amy Joyce, "Discriminating Dress," *Washington Post*, September 25, 2005, http:// www.washingtonpost.com/wp-dyn/content/article/2005/09/23/AR2005092300824 .html.

3. http://www.theamericanmuslim.org/tam.php/features/articles/whitehall_jewel ers_sued_for_refusing_to_hire_muslim_woman_wearing_headscarf.

4. http://today.msnbc.msn.com/id/23556551/ns/today-today_people/t/harvard -gym-restriction-stirs-controversy.

5. An example of the new type of safe head cover is "Capsters," created by Cindy van den Bremen at the Design Academy Eindhoven in 1999. The company's website explains that these coverings were designed to give Muslim girls and their teachers in the Netherlands an alternative to the traditional *hijab*, thus allowing girls to participate in sports classes. The designs were realized in close cooperation with Muslim girls and an *imam*. They became very popular not only with Muslims but also with other women and even with men, and they sell globally. See the company's website, https://www .capsters.com/background.jsp.

6. Leila Ahmed has studied the resurgence of veiling in America (and in the Middle East) in her recent *A Quiet Revolution*.

7. Hoodfar, "More Than Clothing," 30.

8. Haddad, "The Post-9/11 *Hijab* as Icon," 254.

9. Williams and Vashi, "*Hijab* and American Muslim Women," 281.

10. Al-Sarraf, "Hijab and All," 239.

11. For a powerful expression of one Muslim woman's surprise at how she was perceived by American feminists, see Leila Ahmed's autobiography, *A Border Passage*.

12. Al-Hibri, "Tear Off Your Western Veil," 161.

13. Fayad, "The Arab Woman and I," 170.

14. The NPR interviews can be heard at "Lifting the Veil: Muslim Women Explain Their Choice," *Hidden World of Girls*, NPR, April 21, 2011, http://www.npr.org/2011/04/21/135523680/lifting-the-veil-muslim-women-explain-their-choice.

CHAPTER SEVEN

1. This view has recently been challenged by a new group of feminists (Femen) that started in Ukraine in 2008 and that has since spread to metropolitan cities around the world. Femen calls for the right for women to wear anything they like, from topless attire to more conservative dress. On the activism of this group, see "Breast Beating," *Economist*, May 25, 2013.

2. Wadud, *Inside the Gender Jihad*, 219–20.

3. For concise views of the dual nature of feminism among Arabs and Muslims, see Ahmed, *Women and Gender in Islam*, cooke, *Women Claim Islam*, and Badran, *Feminism in Islam*. I should point out that the label "Islamic feminism" does not have a monolithic meaning and is highly contested among scholars and Muslim practitioners alike. Some view the label as redundant; others assert that Islamic feminism is more radical than secular feminism; and others still reject the category because of what they view as its imperialist and Western overtones. For a useful discussion of the ethics of naming, see cooke, *Women Claim Islam*; Barlas, "Engaging Islamic Feminism"; and Badran, *Feminism beyond East and West*. For an overview of the rise of Islamic feminism throughout the Middle East today, see Coleman, *Paradise underneath Her Feet*.

4. On the history of the early feminist movement, see Ahmed, *Women and Gender in Islam*.

5. Qasim Amin, cited in Ahmed, *Women and Gender in Islam*, 160.

6. Atatürk, cited in Bernard Lewis, *The Emergence of Modern Turkey*, 165.

7. Ahmed, *Women and Gender in Islam*, 181.

8. Ibid., 180.

9. El Guindi, "Veiling *Infitah* with Muslim Ethic," 470.

10. A number of studies have focused on the resurgence of veiling since the late 1970s. See, for instance, Mahmoud, *Politics of Piety*; Karam, *Women, Islamisms, and the State*; MacLeod, *Accommodating Protest*; and Badran, *Feminism, Islam, and Nation*.

11. The case of Palestinian women is especially interesting in this regard. Since the *intifada*, they have worn *hijab* as an assertion of nationalism and anti-Zionism. In this logic, unveiled Palestinian women are perceived as anti-nationalist, pro-Israeli, and even as collaborators. They have consequently suffered harassment especially in Gaza. See Hammami, "Women, the *Hijab*, and the *Intifada*."

12. I am leaving aside the mixed-gender spaces characteristic of premodern farms and markets, as well as rural areas, where men and women have worked side by side for centuries. Graveyards, shrines, and even mosques have of course also always been mixed-gender public spaces, and as a result, they have always drawn much criticism from conservative clerics, market supervisors, and morality police. I am speaking here mostly about the *new* mixed-gender spaces that have appeared due to shifts in education, employment, and transit patterns.

13. The notion that *hijab* protects women from unwanted sexual advances or even sexual harassment has recently been challenged by the multiple reports of sexual assault on the streets of major urban cities throughout North Africa. See, for instance, the excellent film *Cairo 678* (dir. Mohamed Diab, 2010), which is based on the recent events that led to a law criminalizing sexual harassment in Egypt. In this film, the women who experienced sexual assault and who filed a lawsuit against their aggressors came from different social classes and one of them was veiled.

CHAPTER EIGHT

1. This website is cited in Asra Nomani, "How Retailers Are Marketing to Fashion-Conscious Muslim Women," http://www.allied-media.com/AM/Hijab_Chic.html (November 2, 2013).

2. Gökarıksel and Secor, "Between Fashion and *Tesettür*," 135.

3. McKee, cited in Sara Buys, "Muslim Women: Beneath the Veil," *Independent*, October 29, 2006.

4. Jamesa Fileds Nikiema, cited in "Wrapped Up in Style," *Los Angeles Times*, June 6, 2010.

5. See the Ahiida website, http://www.ahiida.com/About-Ahiida.html.

6. Reported in Jones, "Images of Desire," 97–100.

7. Ibid., 107.

8. The question of human representation in Islam is subject to much controversy. Most conservative Muslims believe that human representation is prohibited in Islam. This stance could be discerned during the 2006 outrage surrounding the Danish cartoons portraying the Prophet Muhammad. Yet scholars have shown the extent to which such a view contradicts the rich Muslim tradition of representing human bodies in erotic literature as early as the eighth century on Umayyad frescoes in Syria and in sixteenth-century miniatures in Tabriz (Iran). There is also a long tradition of representing the Prophet Muhammad in miniatures since at least the fourteenth century. See Schimmel, *And Muhammad Is His Messenger*, and Christiane J. Gruber, "Meʿrāj: Illustrations," in the *Encyclopaedia Iranica*, http://www.iranicaonline.org/articles/me raj-ii-illustrations. See also Gruber's forthcoming "The Praiseworthy One: The Prophet Muhammad in Islamic Texts and Images."

9. Robert, cited in Lewis, "Marketing Muslim Lifestyle," 83.

10. For relevant illustrations of these types of images, see figure 4 in Gökarıksel and Secor, "Between Fashion and *Tesettür*," 131. See also figures 2 and 3 in Sandikci and Ger, "Constructing and Representing the Islamic Consumer," 198, 199.

11. Taylor, cited in Lewis, "Marketing Muslim Lifestyle," 83.

12. Joseph, cited in ibid., 76.

13. See the interview with al-Mubarak in "'Miss Beautiful Morals' Saudi Arabia: Winner Shows Most Respect for her Parents" by Donna Abu-Nasr in the *World Post*, May 6, 2009.

14. Beauty pageants have been under scrutiny among American feminists at least since 1968, when a dozen of them protested the Miss America pageant in Atlantic City. At that time, they dumped some high-heeled shoes and makeup into a "freedom trash

can." Similarly in 2012, Femen's "sextremists" demonstrated against Milan's fashion week to contest the use of stick-thin models allegedly promoting anorexia. See "Breast Beating," *The Economist*, May 25, 2013.

15. Barbie has also come under scrutiny from Euro-American feminists who contest the doll's appropriateness as a role model for women. In May 2013, a Berlin-based activist brandished a burning cross with a crucified Barbie at the opening of a life-size replica of the doll's house. See "Breast Beating."

16. On the history and meaning of Fulla, see Yaqin, "Islamic Barbie."

CHAPTER NINE

1. Abdul-Khabeer's poem appears in Abdul-Ghafur, *Living Islam Out Loud*, 97–115.

2. Examples of Shazia Mirza's comedy shows are available on the Internet and on her own website, http://www.shazia-mirza.com and http://www.youtube.com /watch?v=TGEY8cZuGF4 (November 2, 2013).

3. *The Hijabi Monologues* have at times been described as a Muslim version of Eve Ensler's *Vagina Monologues*. See Sahar Ullah's interview as part of a press release by the British Council at http://www.britishcouncil.org/tn2020-about-us-press-room-press -release-01.pdf (November 2, 2013).

4. Linda Sarsour, "I'm Tired," YouTube, http://www.youtube.com/watch?v=1I2_kP 523SM (November 2, 2013).

5. A few European artists sought to present alternative views of Muslim women before the 1980s, but they were isolated cases, not a movement like the one we are witnessing now. On these earlier artists, see Antle, *Cultures du surréalisme*.

6. Zineb Sedira, "Mapping the Elusive," in Bailey and Tawadros, *Veil*, 58.

7. Ibid.

8. There are other artists from different diasporas who have also actively dedicated part of their artistic production to transforming traditional artistic representations of veiling and thus challenged common stereotypes of veiled Muslim women. See, for instance, the Algerian Houria Niati's *No to Torture* (1982); the Pakistani Rashid Rana's *Veil Series* (2004); the Turkish Burcu Yacğioğlu's *Seni Yutardim* (2009); or even the American Irving Penn's *Two Guedras* (1972).

9. Bailey and Tawadros, *Veil*, 64.

10. Amer's *Borqa* is technically speaking a *niqab*, since it is a face veil that does not conceal the eyes. The reason why Amer calls her sculpture *Borqa*, and not *Niqab*, is because this is how the face veil is commonly referred to in her native Egyptian dialect, and also in France where the sculpture was commissioned.

11. There are more male singers who have taken up the subject of veiling than women. For some examples, see Native Deen and Yusuf Islam (formerly Cat Stevens).

EPILOGUE

1. Mrs. Rafaat, cited in "Afghan Boys Are Prized, So Girls Live the Part," *New York Times*, September 20, 2010.

Bibliography

BOOKS, CHAPTERS, AND ARTICLES

Abdul-Ghafur, Saleemah, ed. *Living Islam Out Loud: American Muslim Women Speak.* Boston, Mass.: Beacon Press, 2005.

Abu-Lughod, Lila. "Do Muslim Women Really Need Saving? Anthropological Reflections on Cultural Relativism and Its Others." *American Anthropologist* 104.3 (2002): 783–90.

Afsarrudin, Asma. *The First Muslims: History and Memory.* Oxford: Oneworld, 2007.

Ahmed, Leila. *A Border Passage: From Cairo to America—A Woman's Journey.* New York: Farrar, Straus and Giroux, 1999.

———. *A Quiet Revolution: The Veil's Resurgence, from the Middle East to America.* New Haven: Yale University Press, 2011.

———. *Women and Gender in Islam.* New Haven: Yale University Press, 1992.

Al-Hibri, Azizah. "Tear Off Your Western Veil." In *Food for Our Grandmothers: Writings by Arab-American and Arab-Canadian Feminists*, edited by Joanne Kadi, 160–64. Boston: South End Press, 1994.

Ali, Kecia. *Sexual Ethics and Islam: Feminist Reflections on Qur'an, Hadith, and Jurisprudence.* Oxford: Oneworld, 2006.

Alloula, Malek. *The Colonial Harem.* Minneapolis: University of Minnesota Press, 1986.

Al-Majid, Ahmad. "How a Twenty-Five-Year-Old Saudi Entrepreneur Is Rethinking the *Hijab.*" *Wamda*, November 20, 2012.

Antle, Martine. *Cultures du surréalisme: Les représentations de l'autre.* Paris: Acora, 2001.

Al-Sarraf, Amira. "Hijab and All: She Lives the Good Life in Pasadena." In *Voices of American Muslims: Twenty-Three Profiles*, edited by Linda Brandi Cateura, 235–45. New York: Hippocrene Books, 2005.

Badran, Margot. *Feminism beyond East and West: New Gender Talk and Practice in Global Islam.* New Delhi: Global Media Publications, 2007.

———. *Feminism in Islam: Secular and Religious Convergences.* Oxford: Oneworld, 2008.

———. *Feminism, Islam, and Nation: Gender and the Making of Modern Egypt.* Princeton: Princeton University Press, 1995.

Bailey, David A., and Gilane Tawadros, eds. *The Veil: Veiling, Representation, and Contemporary Art.* Cambridge: MIT Press, 2003.

Balasescu, Alexandru. "Haute Couture in Tehran: Two Faces of an Emerging Fashion Scene." *Fashion Theory* 11.2–3 (2007): 299–317.

Barlas, Asma. "Engaging Islamic Feminism: Provincializing Feminism as a Master

Narrative." In *Islamic Feminism: Current Perspectives*, edited by Anitta Kynsilehto. Tampere, Finland: Tampere Peace Research Institute, 2008.

Blamires, Alcuin. *Woman Defamed and Woman Defended: An Anthology of Medieval Texts*. Oxford: Clarendon Press, 1992.

Boellstorff, T. "Playing Back the Nation: *Waria*, Indonesian Transvestites." *Cultural Anthropology* 19.2 (2004): 159–95.

Bowen, John. *Why the French Don't Like Headscarves: Islam, the State, and Public Space*. Princeton: Princeton University Press, 2007.

Brouard, Sylvain, and Vincent Tiberj. *As French As Everyone Else?* Philadelphia: Temple University Press, 2011.

Bucar, Elizabeth. *The Islamic Veil: A Beginner's Guide*. Oxford: Oneworld, 2012.

Cateura, Linda Brandi, ed. *Voices of American Muslims: Twenty-Three Profiles*. New York: Hippocrene Books, 2005.

Clarke, Linda. "*Hijab* According to *Hadith*: Text and Interpretation." In *The Muslim Veil in North America: Issues and Debates*, edited by Sajida Sultana Alvi, Homa Hoodfar, and Sheila McDonough, 214–86. Toronto: Women's Press, 2003.

Coleman, Isobel. *Paradise underneath Her Feet: How Women Are Transforming the Middle East*. New York: Random House, 2010.

cooke, miriam. *Women Claim Islam: Creating Islamic Feminism through Literature*. New York: Routledge, 2001.

Diouf, Sylviane. *Servants of Allah: African Muslims Enslaved in the Americas*. New York: New York University Press, 1998.

Driver, Godfrey R., and John C. Miles, eds. *The Assyrian Laws*. Oxford: Clarendon Press, 1935.

El Guindi, Fadwa. "Veiling *Infitah* with Muslim Ethic: Egypt's Contemporary Islamic Movement." *Social Problems* 28.4 (1981): 465–85.

———. *Veil: Modesty, Privacy, and Resistance*. Oxford: Berg, 1999.

Elver, Hilal. *The Headscarf Controversy: Secularism and Freedom of Religion*. Oxford: Oxford University Press, 2012.

Fanon, Franz. "Algeria Unveiled." In *The Veil: Veiling, Representation, and Contemporary Art*, edited by David A. Bailey and Gilane Tawadros, 72–87. Cambridge: MIT Press, 2003.

Fayad, Mona. "The Arab Woman and I." In *Food for Our Grandmothers: Writings by Arab-American and Arab-Canadian Feminists*, edited by Joanne Kadi, 170–72. Boston: South End Press, 1994.

Garanger, Marc. *Femmes algériennes 1960*. Paris: Contrejour, 1989.

Gökarıksel, Banu, and Anna Secor. "Between Fashion and *Tesettür*: Marketing and Consuming Women's Islamic Dress." *JMEWS* 6.3 (2010): 118–48.

Goto, Emi. "Qur'an and the Veil: Contexts and Interpretations of the Revelation." *International Journal of Asian Studies* 1.2 (2004): 277–95.

Haddad, Yvonne Yazbeck. *Not Quite American? The Shaping of Arab and Muslim Identity in the United States*. Waco, Tex.: Baylor University Press, 2004.

———. "The Post-9/11 *Hijab* as Icon." *Sociology of Religion* 68.2 (2007): 253–67.

Hajjaji-Jarrah, Soraya. "Women's Modesty in Quranic Commentaries: The Founding Discourse." In *The Muslim Veil in North America: Issues and Debates*, edited by

Sajida Sultana Alvi, Homa Hoodfar, and Sheila McDonough, 181–213. Toronto: Women's Press, 2003.

Hammami, R. "Women, the *Hijab*, and the *Intifada*." *Middle East Report*, nos. 164–165 (1990): 24–28, 71, 78.

Hammer, Juliane. *American Muslim Women, Religious Authority, and Activism: More Than a Prayer*. Austin: University of Texas Press, 2012.

Heath, Jennifer, ed. *The Veil: Women Writers on Its History, Lore, and Politics*. Berkeley: University of California Press, 2008.

Hoffman, Valerie J. "Qurʾanic Interpretation and Modesty Norms for Women." In *The Shaping of an American Islamic Discourse: A Memorial to Fazlur Rahman*, edited by Earle H. Waugh and Frederick M. Denny, 89–122. Atlanta: Scholars Press, 1998.

Hoodfar, Homa. "More Than Clothing: Veiling as an Adaptive Strategy." In *The Muslim Veil in North America: Issues and Debates*, edited by Sajida Sultana Alvi, Homa Hoodfar, and Sheila McDonough. Toronto: Women's Press, 2003.

hooks, bell. *Feminism Is for Everybody: Passionate Politics*. Cambridge, Mass.: South End Press, 2000.

Jaschok, Maria, and Shui Jingjun. *The History of Women's Mosques in Chinese Islam: A Mosque of Their Own*. Richmond, Va.: Curzon, 2000.

———. *Women, Religion, and Space in China: Islamic Mosques and Daoist Temples, Catholic Convents and Chinese Virgins*. New York: Routledge, 2011.

Jones, Carla. "Fashion and Faith in Urban Indonesia." *Fashion Theory* 11.2–3 (2007): 211–32.

———." Images of Desire: Creating Virtue and Value in an Indonesian Islamic Lifestyle Magazine." *JMEWS* 6.3 (2010): 91–117.

Kadi, Joanna, ed. *Food for Our Grandmothers: Writings by Arab American and Arab Canadian Feminists*. Cambridge, Mass.: South End Press, 1994.

Kahf, Mohja. *E-mails from Scheherazad*. Gainesville: University Press of Florida, 2003.

———. "From Her Royal Body the Robe Was Removed: The Blessings of the Veil and the Trauma of Forced Unveilings in the Middle East." In *The Veil: Women Writers on Its History, Lore, and Politics*, edited by Jennifer Heath, 27–43. Berkeley: University of California Press, 2008.

Karam, Azza. *Women, Islamisms, and the State: Contemporary Feminisms in Egypt*. Basingstoke, UK: Macmillan, 1998.

Lanfranchi, Sania Sharawi. *Casting off the Veil: The Life of Huda Shaarawi, Egypt's First Feminist*. London: I. B. Tauris, 2012.

Lewis, Bernard. *The Emergence of Modern Turkey*. London: Oxford University Press, 1961.

Lewis, Reina. "Marketing Muslim Lifestyle: A New Media Genre." *JMEWS* 6.3 (2010): 58–90.

MacLeod, A. E. *Accommodating Protest: Working Women, the New Veiling, and Change in Cairo*. New York: Columbia University Press, 1991.

Mahmoud, Saba. *Politics of Piety: The Islamic Revival and the Feminist Subject*. Princeton: Princeton University Press, 2005.

Mernissi, Fatima. *The Forgotten Queens of Islam*. Minneapolis: University of Minnesota Press, 1993.

————. *The Veil and the Male Elite: A Feminist Interpretation of Women's Rights in Islam*. Reading, Mass.: Perseus Books, 1991.

Miles, Margaret R. *A Complex Delight: The Secularization of the Breast, 1350–1750*. Berkeley: University of California Press, 2008.

Montagu, Mary Wortley. *Turkish Embassy Letters*. New York: Penguin, 1997.

Moore, Kathleen M. "Visible through the Veil: The Regulation of Islam in American Law." *Sociology of Religion* 68.2 (2007): 237–51.

Morey, Peter, and Amina Yaqin. *Framing Muslims: Stereotyping and Representation after 9/11*. Cambridge: Harvard University Press, 2011.

Mujahed, Jamila, and Bassano di Tuffilo. *Burqa!* Rome: Donzelli editore, 2007.

Mushaben, Joyce Marie. "More Than Just a Bad-Hair Day: The Head-Scarf Debate as a Challenge to Euro-National Identities." In *Crossing Over: Comparing Recent Migration in the United States and Europe*, edited by Holger Henke, 182–222. New York: Lexington Books, 2005.

Otto, Jan Michiel. *Sharia Incorporated: A Comparative Overview of the Legal Systems of Twelve Muslim Countries in Past and Present*. Leiden: Amsterdam University Press, 2011.

Papanek, Hanna. "Purdah in Pakistan: Seclusion and Modern Occupations for Women." In *Separate Worlds*, edited by Hanna Papanek and Gail Minault, 190–216. Columbus, Mo.: South Asia Books, 1982.

Rasmussen, S. J. "The Slippery Sign: Cultural Constructions of Youth and Youthful Construction of Culture in Tuareg Men's Face Veiling." *Journal of Anthropological Research*, no. 66 (2010): 463–84.

Roded, Ruth. *Women in Islamic Biographical Collections: From Ibn Saʿd to Who's Who*. Boulder, Colo.: L. Rienner Publishers 1994.

Safi, Omid, ed. *Progressive Muslims: On Justice, Gender, and Pluralism*. Oxford: Oneworld, 2003.

Sandikci, Özlem, and Güliz Ger. "Constructing and Representing the Islamic Consumer in Turkey." *Fashion Theory* 11.2–3 (2007): 189–210.

Schimmel, Annemarie. *And Muhammad Is His Messenger: The Veneration of the Prophet in Islamic Piety*. Chapel Hill: University of North Carolina Press, 1985.

Scott, Joan. *The Politics of the Veil*. Princeton: Princeton University Press, 2007.

Shaheen, Jack G. *Guilty: Hollywood's Verdict on Arabs after 9/11*. Northampton, Mass.: Olive Branch Press, 2008.

————. *Reel Bad Arabs: How Hollywood Vilifies a People*. Northampton, Mass.: Olive Branch Press, 2001.

Stowasser, Barbara Freyer. *Women in the Qur'an: Traditions and Interpretation*. New York: Oxford University Press, 1994.

Von Mittelstaedt, Julianne. "The Advance of the Zealots: The Growing Influence of the Ultra-Orthodox in Israel." *Spiegel*, January 13, 2012.

Wadud, Amina. *Inside the Gender Jihad: Women's Reform in Islam*. Oxford: Oneworld, 2006.

————. *Qur'an and Woman: Rereading the Sacred Text from a Woman's Perspective*. New York: Oxford University Press, 1999.

Williams, Rhys H., and Gira Vashi, "*Hijab* and American Muslim Women: Creating the Space for Autonomous Selves." *Sociology of Religion* 68.3 (2007): 269–87.

Wolfe, Michael, ed. *Taking Back Islam: American Muslims Reclaim Their Faith.* Emmaus, Penn: Rodale Press, 2002.

Yaqin, Amina. "Islamic Barbie: The Politics of Gender and Performativity." *Fashion Theory* 11.2–3 (2007): 173–86.

Zahedi, Ashraf. "Concealing and Revealing Female Hair: Veiling Dynamics in Contemporary Iran." In *The Veil: Women Writers on Its History, Lore, and Politics*, edited by Jennifer Heath, 250–65. Berkeley: University of California Press, 2008.

SCHOLARLY AND PEDAGOGICAL WEBSITES

http://veil.unc.edu: This pedagogical website (codeveloped by the author) offers an overview of the meaning of the veil from an interdisciplinary and global perspective. It lists useful documentaries on veiling, a selection of music that treats the subject of Muslim women and veiling, a number of artworks on the same topic, and it provides a resources section with suggested lesson plans for instructors.

http://veilingfashion.unc.edu: This site, developed by Dr. Banu Gökarıksel, focuses on the Islamic fashion industry in Turkey today.

DOCUMENTARY FILMS

Beneath the Veil, directed by Cassian Harrison for Channel 4, UK (2001): documentary on aspects of Afghan women's daily life and veiling practices.

Covered: The Hejab in Cairo, Egypt, directed by Tania Kamal-Eldin (1995): documentary on the new veiling in Egypt in the 1980s.

Female Imams, directed by Kathleen McLaughlin and Sharron Lovell (2012): documentary on the difference between central Henan Hui and Western Hui Muslims who have more Arab influence (http://vimeo.com/38009714).

Hollywood Harems, directed by Tania Kamal-Eldin (1999): video montage taken from the golden age of Hollywood films featuring Hollywood's orientalist fascination with Middle Eastern culture, harems, and veiled women.

Je porte le voile [*I Wear the Veil*], by Natasha Ivisic and Yannick Letourneau (2009): documentary about Muslim women's veiling in Quebec (Canada).

Last Call to Prayer, directed by Kathleen McLaughlin and Sharron Lovell (2012): documentary about China's Hui Muslims and the tradition of all-women mosques led by female *imams* (http://www.chinafile.com/last-call-prayer).

Me and the Mosque, directed by Zarqa Nawaz (2005): full-length documentary on the physical and social space that Muslim women are given in mosques in Canada (http://www.nfb.ca/film/me_and_mosque).

Reel Bad Arabs: How Hollywood Vilifies a People, directed by Sut Jhally (2006): This video is based on Jack Shaheen's book of the same title and documents the degrading and stereotypical cinematic representations of Muslim, Arab, and Middle Eastern characters from the early silent films till the more recent Hollywood blockbusters.

They Call Me Muslim, directed by Diana Ferrero (2006): Two veiled Muslim women from different countries (one from France, the other from Iran) speak about their challenges when wearing the *hijab* because one country does not allow it, while the other requires women to wear it.

Turkey's Tigers, directed by Jon Alpert and Matthew O'Neill (2006): a PBS *Wide Angle* documentary about the Muslim fashion industry in Turkey.

Wearing Hijab: Uncovering the Myths of Islam in the United States, directed by Mary Ann Watson (2003): Interviews with six Muslim American women from six different ethnic backgrounds about the spiritual and cultural meanings of their veiling practices.

Index

Bowen, John, 56, 106

Brandet, Pierre-Henry, 109

Breaking the Veils: Women Artists from the Islamic World (art exhibition), 187

Breasts, 28, 43, 85, 86

Brouard, Sylvain, 107, 108

Bryn Mawr College, 13, 38, 212 (n. 12)

Bucar, Liz, 28

Buibui, 202

Al-Bukhari, 24, 32, 45

Burgu, 63, 202–3

Burkini, 163

Burqa, 7, 56, 202; art and, 188–89, 193; comedy and, 70, 71, 184; Taliban and, 11, 12, 61–62, 69–70, 113, 213 (n. 2, chap. 3)

—mandatory bans on: and colonialism, 88; in Europe, 92–93, 214 (nn. 1, 7, chap. 5); in France, 94–96, 104–5, 106, 178; in United States, 117–18

Burqa! (Bassano di Tuffilo), 69

Busana islami, 144, 203

Bush, George W., 4

Bush, Laura, 4

Canada, 121–22, 171

Cartoons, 69–72

Catholicism, 9

Chador, 10–11, 12, 57, 58, 64, 203, 213 (n. 3, chap. 3)

Chénière, Ernest, 97

Chérifi, Hanifa, 99, 101

China, 54–55

Chirac, Jacques, 101, 102

Christianity, and veiling, 7–9

Ciput, 203

Civil Rights Act, 117

Clarke, Linda, 32, 33, 48

Colonialism: feminism and, 136–37; "saving" veiled Muslim women and, 3, 4, 81, 87, 92; unveiling and, 5, 87, 88, 100, 136–37, 138, 140–41, 213 (nn. 5–6, chap. 4), 214 (n. 7, chap. 4); veiling and, 91–92

Comedy, 52, 69, 70, 71, 183–85

Communautarisme, 108, 215 (n. 16)

cooke, miriam, 133

Coptic Christians, 135, 136

Council for Arab-Islamic Relations (CAIR), 115, 116

Cromer, Lord, 91–92, 137

Crosby, Bing, 89

"Day in the Life, A" (poem, Abdul-Khabeer), 177

Delacroix, Eugène, 79–81, 82, 112, 213 (n. 2, chap. 4)

Democracy, and veiling, 4, 110, 122

De-veiling, 126–30. See also *Hijab*

Diam's, 195

Discrimination Research Center, 117

Dishdasha, 203

Dolce and Gabana (D&G), 158, 159

Dupattas, 11, 13, 60, 203

Ebrahim, Mona, 148

Echarpe, 203

Education, 58, 68, 138, 145, 213 (n. 4, chap. 3)

Egypt: beauty pageants and, 172; fashion and, 159, 160–61, 164; feminism and, 135–39, 141–42; re-veiling and, 143, 144, 146; unveiling and, 135–39, 141–42; veiling and, 64, 69, 91–92, 193, 218 (n. 10)

Egyptian Feminist Union (EFU), 136

El Guindi, Fadwa, 143, 144

E-mails from Scheherazad (poems, Kahf), 180–83

Emel, 166, 168, 170

Equal Employment Opportunity Commission (EEOC), 117

Eroticism of veiling, 3–4, 77–78, 79, 80–81, 83–84, 85, 211 (n. 3), 213 (n. 2, chap. 4)

Etiquette, 35, 36

Europe: Islamic luxury fashions and, 155–57, 194; mandatory bans on

Lévy, Lila, 100, 101

Lewis, Reina, 169, 170

Liberation of Woman, The (Tahrir al-Mar'a, Amin), 137, 138

"Lili" (song, Diam's), 195

Lithma, 63, 206

Living Islam Out Loud: American Muslim Women Speak (Abdul-Ghafur), 50

Lotous, 166, 169

Maghnaé, 206

Mahla, 169

Malaki jurisprudence, 36, 37

Manteau, 206

Mantila, 206

Maqrama, 206

Marmuq, 206

Marriage, 6, 62–63

Mattu, Ayesha, 1

Maznavi, Nura, 1

McKee, Marigay, 155–56

Me and the Mosque (documentary, 2005), 51–52

Mernissi, Fatima, 45, 47

Milaya, 206

Mirza, Shazia, 183–84

Miss Arab World Beauty Contest, 172

Miss Latifah, 196

Miss Undastood, 176, 196

Modesty, 27–28, 29–30, 32–33, 43, 49–50, 59, 124, 134, 163, 164

Mohanty, Chandra, 92

Montagu, Lady Mary Wortley, 83

Moore, Kathleen, 116

Mornay, Comte de, 80

Morsi, Mohamed, 69

Moschis-Gauguet, Aliki, 187

Mosques: gender equality and, 46, 50–55, 212 (n. 12); gender segregation and, 25

Moussor, 60, 64, 206

Mubarak, Hosni, 160

Al-Mubarak, Khadra, 172

Muhajjaba, 153–54

Muhajjabat, 146

Muhammad, Prophet: equality of men and women and, 39–40, 46–47; *hadith* and, 22, 32, 33, 34; Qur'an and, 22, 24–26, 38–39, 44, 51; veiling and, 23–25, 48; wives of, 45, 47; women's clothing and, 26, 34–35, 45

Mujahed, Jamila, 69

Multiculturalism, 97–98

Musa, Nabawiyya, 135

Music, and veiling, 194–97, 219 (n. 11)

Muslim Brotherhood, 69

Muslim dolls, 173–75

Muslim Girls, 171

Muslim men: clothing and, 128; enforcing veiling in Europe and, 94, 95, 105, 109; gender equality and, 39–40, 46–47, 55; gender segregation and, 23–25; Hat Law in Turkey and, 139–40; rules of modesty and, 27–28, 32–33; veiling and, 59–60, 213 (n. 5, chap. 3)

Muslim women: adornments and, 29, 30, 31, 34; in Africa, 49, 60; artistic depictions of, 3–4, 79–84, 213 (n. 2, chap. 4); clothing rules and, 30–31, 32–34, 37, 42–43; de-veiling and, 126–30; education and, 58, 68, 138, 145, 213 (n. 4, chap. 3); gender equality and, 39–40, 46–47, 55; gender segregation and, 23–25, 51–55, 92, 138, 164; Hollywood films and, 88–91, 112–13; middle classes and, 151–54, 157, 171; mosques and, 25, 46, 50–55, 212 (n. 12); Muslim dolls and, 175; in Muslim-majority countries, 49, 59, 140, 148–49; in Muslim-minority countries, 50, 121–23, 127, 129, 178, 197; as in need of liberation, 4, 5, 85, 89; photography and, 84–88, 100, 117–18, 213 (n. 6, chap. 4); Qur'an on clothing and, 25–27, 42, 43–46, 212 (n. 2); rules of modesty and, 27–28, 29–30, 43, 49–50, 59, 124, 134, 163,

Sahar Amer, *What Is Veiling?* (2014).

Rudolph T. Ware III, *The Walking Qurʾan: Islamic Education, Embodied Knowledge, and History in West Africa* (2014).

Saʿdiyya Shaikh, *Sufi Narratives of Intimacy: Ibn ʿArabī, Gender, and Sexuality* (2012).

Karen G. Ruffle, *Gender, Sainthood, and Everyday Practice in South Asian Shiʾism* (2011).

Jonah Steinberg, *Ismaʾili Modern: Globalization and Identity in a Muslim Community* (2011).

Iftikhar Dadi, *Modernism and the Art of Muslim South Asia* (2010).

Gary R. Bunt, *iMuslims: Rewiring the House of Islam* (2009).

Fatemeh Keshavarz, *Jasmine and Stars: Reading More than "Lolita" in Tehran* (2007).

Scott A. Kugle, *Sufis and Saints' Bodies: Mysticism, Corporeality, and Sacred Power in Islam* (2007).

Roxani Eleni Margariti, *Aden and the Indian Ocean Trade: 150 Years in the Life of a Medieval Arabian Port* (2007).

Sufia M. Uddin, *Constructing Bangladesh: Religion, Ethnicity, and Language in an Islamic Nation* (2006).

Omid Safi, *The Politics of Knowledge in Premodern Islam: Negotiating Ideology and Religious Inquiry* (2006).

Ebrahim Moosa, *Ghazālī and the Poetics of Imagination* (2005).

miriam cooke and Bruce B. Lawrence, eds., *Muslim Networks from Hajj to Hip Hop* (2005).

Carl W. Ernst, *Following Muhammad: Rethinking Islam in the Contemporary World* (2003).